Doing Educational Research
A Practitioner's Guide to Getting Started
SECOND EDITION

Carol Mutch

NZCER PRESS

Wellington 2013

NZCER PRESS
New Zealand Council for Educational Research
PO Box 3237
Wellington

© Carol Mutch, 2013

First edition 2005

National Library of New Zealand Cataloguing-in-Publication Data
Mutch, Carol.
Doing educational research / Carol Mutch.
Includes index.
ISBN 978-1-927151-92-1
1. Education—Research. 2. Action research in education. I. Title.
370.7—dc 23

All rights reserved

Designed by Cluster Creative

Distributed by NZCER
PO Box 3237
Wellington
New Zealand
www.nzcer.org.nz

Dedication

To Michael, Blair, Adam and Isaac, and all the others who lost their lives in the Pike River Mine disaster and the Canterbury earthquakes; and to your families and friends who think of you every day.

Contents

Acknowledgements	vii
Preface to the second edition	ix
Glossary	1
Introduction	13
1. Understanding the nature of educational research	19
What is research?	20
What are research's historical roots?	21
Why conduct research?	22
What is educational research?	23
What are the main approaches to research?	24
How do you make sense of the research literature available?	26
How does research relate to your everyday work?	28
2. Selecting a research design	33
What does it mean to be a researcher?	34
What are the decisions that all researchers make?	38
How do you choose a topic?	39
How do you develop a research question?	42
What kind of research design will best suit your purposes?	47
How do you choose who or what to study?	47
3. Considering the place of theory	57
What is theory?	58
What are the different types of theory?	58
Why do theories that explain the same phenomena vary so widely?	61
How does theory relate to research?	63
How do you begin to define your theoretical stance?	64
How do you prepare for working with people with different theoretical frameworks or in settings with different world views?	66
4. Examining the ethical issues	75
Why are ethics important in research?	76
What are some key ethical concepts?	77
How do you prepare for ethical approval?	80
How do you approach your participants?	81
What do you need to consider when researching in your own workplace?	84
How do you act ethically in cultural settings other your own?	85
5. Reviewing the literature	89
Why conduct a literature review?	90
Where do you start?	90
How do you keep track of everything?	93
How do you write up a literature review?	95
Why are referencing conventions important?	96

6. Choosing methods, strategies, and tools — 103
What is the link between theory, methodology, and method? — 104
How does your research question link to your research design? — 104
What are common methodologies used in educational research? — 106
How do you ensure your research can be trusted? — 109
What are common methods, strategies, and tools used in educational research? — 110
What is mixed methodology? — 125

7. Writing research proposals — 131
What is the purpose of a research proposal? — 132
What is a common format for a research proposal? — 133
At what stage do you write a research proposal? — 134
How much do those who approve your proposal influence its content and format? — 135
How do you set a budget? — 136

8. Conducting the research — 141
What factors make for successful implementation? — 142
What equipment do you need and how do you manage it? — 142
What are field notes and why do you take them? — 144
How do you manage all that data? — 145
What is a research journal and why is it helpful? — 146
What do you need to be aware of when conducting research with children? — 147

9. Analysing the data — 151
How do you analyse quantitative data? — 152
How do you display quantitative data? — 157
How do you analyse qualitative data? — 163
How do you display qualitative data? — 166
How do you interpret your findings? — 169
What is the place of tentative theorising? — 171

10. Writing up, reaching out, and moving on — 175
How do you write a research report? — 176
How do you tailor your report to reach different audiences? — 180
How do you prepare a conference presentation? — 180
How do you get published? — 184
How do you stay motivated? — 187
Is research worth it? — 189
Where to next? — 192

11. Current trends and future possibilities — 197
How have changes in technology influenced research? — 198
What are some recent developments in quantitative research? — 204
What are some recent developments in qualitative research? — 208
Is mixed methods research a 'third paradigm'? — 211
How similar or different are research and evaluation? — 215
Are there new developments in cultural and ethical frameworks? — 216
How have textual, visual and arts-based approaches developed? — 220
What can reflective approaches contribute to research? — 225
What can be gained from collaborative research? — 228
Where might research go in the future? — 230

Index — 241

Acknowledgements

The first edition of this book was a tribute to all the educational practitioners I had worked with over the years, in particular, those enrolled in
- Advanced Studies for Teachers courses,
- the Bachelor of Teaching and Learning upgrades,
- the Master of Teaching and Learning, both in New Zealand and Samoa, and
- the Resource Teacher of Literacy Training Programme,

who taught me so much as we have struggled, laughed, cried, shared, and celebrated on our research journeys.

Thanks are due to those researchers who agreed to allow me to cite their research projects in this book—you give heart to practitioner-researchers everywhere. Particular thanks to Vikki, whose insightful comments appear in the last chapter. Thanks also to my colleagues, whose ideas I have borrowed, used, and adapted over the years.

Thanks to NZCER, Bev Webber, in particular, for seeing the potential in my idea and providing ongoing encouragement, to the reviewers for their detailed critiques and thoughtful insights, and to Paula Wagemaker for her precise editing.

Thanks to Bridget, Ruth, and Marge, who were only ever a phone call away and followed up my requests promptly, listened to my anxieties calmly and laughed at my funny stories. Thanks to Dave—the world's most helpful librarian.

Finally, this book would not have been possible without the support of the Centre for the Studies of Higher Education, Nagoya University, Japan, who provided me with the time and space to write undisturbed for several months—domo arigato gozaimashita.

> Ehara taku toa i te toa taki tahi, engari he toa taki tini
> This work is not mine alone but the contributions of many

The second edition allows me to acknowledge and thank all the researchers, teachers and students of research methods who used the book to support their researching, teaching and learning. I have appreciated the positive feedback from you over the years.

Since the first edition I have extended my research networks and experiences and would like to add my thanks to my colleagues at the University of Canterbury, the Education Review Office and the University of Auckland. I would also like to acknowledge all those I have collaborated with on research and writing projects, especially those helping bring research on disaster situations to a wider audience.

Particular thanks go to my students and colleagues in the School of Critical Studies in Education who have contributed their ideas or research examples to the new chapter in this edition.

Again my appreciation goes to David Ellis and everyone at NZCER for encouraging me to produce a second edition.

Carol Mutch, June 2013

Preface to the second edition

When I wrote the first edition of *Doing educational research*, I hoped that it would fill a niche. I had visions of a teacher–researcher or research student pulling the book off the shelf and breathing a sigh of relief that at last they had an easy but comprehensive explanation of how to undertake a small research project in the Aotearoa New Zealand context. To my delight, it filled that niche and more. It went on to become an NZCER Press best-seller and a course text in many institutions in New Zealand and overseas.

When the invitation came to prepare a new edition, I re-read the book to find the places that needed revising. The first thing that struck me was that apart from updating reading lists, there were no major changes I wanted to make to the text. As an introduction to big ideas for a novice researcher or a refresher for a more experienced researcher it remained sound. However, I needed to acknowledge that research approaches and issues had not remained static and that there were changes that had occurred. In order to be sure that the changes I had observed were significant and of interest to readers of this book, I needed a broader picture. First, I went back over feedback I had received which noted that mixed method research, collaborative approaches and reflective approaches were not well covered. I then visited the university library and read new research methods texts or new editions of popular texts, such as Cohen, Manion and Morrison. I noted what they had included that I did not or that I had brushed over lightly. I went through several years of recent issues of educational research journals, such as *Educational Researcher*. I informally surveyed students and colleagues who knew the book, asking, "What would you change; what would you keep; and what would you add?" From that mass of data I distilled several common themes. Things I needed to keep were the conversational tone, the easy-to-understand explanations and the concrete examples that covered the range of New Zealand contexts. Things I could change were mostly around discussing the impact of technology on research and updating references and websites. Things I could add often related to people's own interests and preferences but were also borne out in the trends in books and journals. These included developments in traditional methodologies and experimentation with new ones; a rise in ethical and cultural considerations; new theoretical frameworks; and the politics of research.

In the end, the decision was made to leave the bulk of the book as it was and add a new final chapter rather than try to integrate the changes into the existing chapters. A further decision was made to leave the references as they were because given the speed of technological change, no sooner would these be updated in this chapter than they would be out of date. A quick Google search and a reader could find the latest version.

A comprehensive literature review and many months of draft writing later led to something approaching a book on its own. In order to keep the chapter manageable and coherent, some aspects were dropped and others retained. Some of the suggestions, such as the politics of research, will lend themselves to articles in the near future. Several colleagues critiqued the trimmed draft chapter before it went out for peer review.

This new edition, therefore, retains what has worked in the past while providing a snapshot of current trends that will interest the target audience for this book. It cannot comprehensively cover every new and innovative idea but it might encourage readers to think beyond the standard approaches and re-engage in the excitement of finding answers to their questions and building our knowledge base one step at a time.

Carol Mutch, June 2013.

Glossary

Action research: an approach to research in which the focus is on the practitioner-researcher investigating his/her own practice in order to make changes or improvements.

Analytic field notes: notes in which tentative codes, categories, or themes are determined during or after conducting research in the field.

Analytic memo: a formal draft of important codes, categories, and themes arising from qualitative research.

Analytic tools: modes of analysis using technical, theoretical, statistical, and methodological approaches to interpreting data.

Annotated bibliography: a collection of readings on a particular topic, in which each reading is briefly summarised and critiqued.

Anonymity: an ethical consideration that ensures other people cannot identify a research participant or setting.

Applied research: research that focuses on questions of a practical nature.

Archival sources: older original or secondary sources used in historical research.

Artefacts: everyday historical or cultural objects that can be analysed as data.

Arts-based research: an approach that uses the visual and/or performing arts at some point in the study to generate, collect, analyse or present data.

Attributes: the categories into which particular variables can be divided.

Autoethnography: a study in which the researcher's personal experiences are described and included as key data in order to illuminate the research problem.

Bar graphs: graphs that display numerical data comparatively as solid bars.

Behaviourism: a theoretical approach to education that isolates behaviours: their antecedents and consequences in order to manage them.

Bibliography: a list of all material used in compiling a report or article, whether cited or not in the text, or a list of useful readings on a topic.

Case(s): a term used in qualitative research to describe the bounded object of study.

Case study: a study that focuses on a bounded object, usually a person, group, setting, or concept.

Closed questions: questions that have a yes/no or single answer.

Codes: the tentative ideas and themes that come through in initial qualitative analysis.

Coercion: when a research participant is forced—or feels forced—to participate.

Consent forms: signed forms completed by research participants giving their informed consent.

Collaborative research: when researchers collaborate across disciplines, institutions, sites or countries to undertake research of mutual benefit.

Compatibility thesis: the idea that different research paradigms and methods can be mixed in order to achieve enhanced research results.

Constant comparative analysis: a form of iterative qualitative analysis.

Constructivism: a theoretical approach to learning that focuses on the learner building new understandings through cognitive processing or social interaction.

Content analysis: a quantitative form of document analysis.

Control group: the group in an experiment that does not receive the treatment.

Convenience sampling: a form of non-probability sampling that uses convenient participants.

Conversational analysis: a research approach where all the nuances of a conversation or interview are analysed along with the content.

Correlational research: research that aims to show relationships between variables.

Credibility: where qualitative research aims for rigour and believability as an alternative to validity or reliability.

Critical approach to research: research that has a social justice, action-oriented focus.

Critical pedagogy: an approach to teaching with a social justice focus.

Critical theory: a theoretical approach that aims to uncover and seek redress for disadvantaged or silenced groups.

Cultural protocols: particular processes or ways of acting in cultural settings.

Census: a research approach in which the entire population is surveyed.

Data: information gathered during the research process that can be analysed and presented in order to answer a research question.

Data mining: when researchers dig deeper into large data sets to extract new patterns or interesting findings.

Database: a site where large amounts of data are stored electronically.

Data sources: the range of people, places, or things that can provide data for analysis.

Deception: where the researcher does not share all or part of the research intent or process with the participants.

Deductive: a type of logic that moves from hypothesis or theory to data collection.

Delphi technique: when experts are surveyed in iterative rounds until their responses converge and collective predictions or scenarios can be created.

Dependent variable: a variable that is dependent on or influenced by another variable.

Descriptive field notes: notes made in the field during a qualitative study that focus on a description of the setting, the participants, and/or the events.

Descriptive research: research that aims to describe a particular phenomenon.

Descriptive statistics: statistics that describe the attributes of the data without necessarily aiming for generalisation to a wider population.

Discourse analysis: analysis that focuses on text by examining language structures or by deconstructing underlying messages, particularly dominant group or political ideologies.

Document analysis: where documents or various forms of text are analysed either quantitatively or qualitatively.

Educational research: research that focuses on the range of activities or settings related to teaching and learning.

Electronic referencing system: a computer program that aids bibliographic referencing.

Emergent design: an approach to research design mostly used in qualitative research that emerges as the research proceeds.

Empirical: data that are measurable, testable, and/or observable.

Enlightenment: a time in history when scientific ideas challenged the authority of the church.

Ethical clearance: approval given for research to proceed in the light of ethical considerations having been articulated and defended.

Ethics: an underlying sense of morals or a particular code of practice.

Ethnography: the study of people and their activities in their natural settings.

Evaluation: an approach to gathering evidence in order to make a judgment about the quality, viability or efficiency of a policy, programme or practice.

Exchange theory: a theoretical approach that uses economic concepts to explain society.

Exegesis: the accompanying explanation to a non-traditional research thesis.

Existing statistics: statistics gathered for a particular purpose that can be used as further data for research.

Experiment: a research design that aims to control variables in order to examine the effects of a particular treatment.

Experimental group: the group in experimental research that receives the treatment.

Explanatory research: research that aims to provide explanations for particular phenomena or behaviours.

Exploratory research: research that sets out to provide an initial exploration of the phenomenon under scrutiny to see if it warrants further study.

Falsifiable: when a hypothesis can be disproved.

Feminism: a theoretical and methodological approach to research that is underpinned by women's views of the world and women's ways of working.

Field notes: the range of notes or jottings made before, during, and after conducting research in the field.

Focus group interview: an interview technique that brings together participants to respond to the questions in a group situation.

Formal theory: a theory that focuses on a substantial area or field of inquiry

Functionalism: a theoretical approach that views society as consisting of a set of functions.

Generalisable research: research that can be generalised to another setting or to the wider population.

Generalisation: a statement that takes the findings from a sample and extrapolates them to the population under study.

Globalisation: economic, social and political forces that influence our lives.

Graph: a pictorial way of representing data using the intersections of data pairs along a pair of axes.

Grounded theory: an approach to qualitative research in which the theory arises from or is "grounded in" the data.

Hermeneutics: a theoretical approach that highlights the questioning of assumptions.

Histogram: a graph that looks similar to a bar graph but where the x axis has regular interval data rather than nominal data.

Historical research: a style of research that focuses on past events.

Hypothesis: a researcher's "best guess" about the relationship between variables in quantitative research, which is proposed before the research begins.

Immersion in the field: when a researcher spends prolonged periods in the field, as in ethnographic research.

Incompatibility thesis: the idea that different research paradigms or methods cannot be mixed because they come from incompatible beliefs and assumptions.

Independent variable: a variable on which other variables are dependent or that influences other variables or the direction of the relationship.

Inductive: an approach to logic where the categories or theories arise out of the data.

Inferential statistics: statistical analysis that generalises to the broader population.

Informed consent: the agreement to participate in research given willingly by a participant who feels fully informed about the research purpose and process.

Instruments: the tools used to gather the data. In qualitative research, the researchers are sometimes called the "instruments" because they gather and filter the data.

Interpretive research: research that describes and interprets social situations; often a synonym for qualitative research.

Intervention: the treatment or programme put in place in experimental or quasi-experimental research.

Kaupapa Māori research: research undertaken in Māori contexts according to Māori ethics and protocols.

Line graph: a graph that joins the points of intersection of the data pairs to show a trend.

Literature review: an analysis of the relevant content, methodological, and/or theoretical literature that justifies the need for a study.

Macro-level theory: a broad theory that explains complex social interactions and structures.

Marxism: a theory derived from the writings of Karl Marx that explains social interactions in terms of economic capital and power.

Mean: A measure of central tendency (often called the "average") where the sum of the scores is divided by the number of scores.

Measures of central tendency: descriptive statistical measures that reduce scores to manageable figures representing the tendency towards the centre.

Median: the middle score when the set of scores is arranged in order.

Meta-analysis: when a large body of previously conducted research is collated and analysed against particular criteria to provide a synthesis of significant findings.

Method: a coherent strategy or set of strategies for gathering a particular type of data.

Methodology: an overarching research method that links clearly to a theoretical framework.

Micro-level theory: theories that are smaller in scope that often appear as testable propositions in quantitative research or arise from analysed qualitative data.

Mid-range theory: a theory that does not aim to explain the full workings of society but rather aspects within it.

Mixed methodology: an approach to research that uses both quantitative and qualitative methods.

Mode: a measure of central tendency that highlights the most common score(s).

Multiple realities: a view that highlights the belief that rather than a single truth there are many ways to view reality.

Narrative: an experience or event retold as a story.

Non-participant observation: an observation study where the researcher does not participate in the events being studied.

Non-probability sampling: sampling techniques used in qualitative research where participants are chosen for particular reasons.

Normal curve: the shape of the graph produced when the mean, median, and mode for a set of data are the same.

Objective stance: a view of the world in which the researcher is distanced from the activities being examined and is believed to be a neutral observer.

Observation: a research strategy that gathers data through close observation.

Observation schedule: a research tool with pre-set categories or behaviours to observe.

Open question: a type of question with a wide range of possible responses.

Paradigm: a particular view of the world, linking a theory and research style.

Participant: a person who participates in research, sometimes called a research subject.

Participant observation: an observation study where the researcher is part of the events or interactions being studied.

Participant safety: an ethical consideration where a researcher ensures that the participant will face no emotional, physical, and/or cultural risks.

Phenomenon: the object, idea or activity under scrutiny.

Phenomenology: a theoretical framework for research that focuses on the phenomenon of study.

Pie graph: a type of graph that shows scores as a percentage of the whole and looks like a pie cut into wedges.

Plagiarism: intentionally, or unintentionally, passing off the written or creative works of others as one's own.

Policy research: research that focuses on the development, implementation, or evaluation of policy.

Population: all the possible participants that meet the criteria for the study.

Position: how a researcher would describe him/herself theoretically and in relation to the research being conducted. "Declaring one's position" is important in qualitative research.

Positivist: a theoretical position that is based in a scientific approach to research.

Postmodernity: a period of time in intellectual thought arising in art and architecture in the 1960s and influencing many other fields, including research. It is underpinned by the belief that there are multiple realities rather than a single truth.

Poststructuralism: a theoretical response to structuralism which highlights the pervasiveness and complexity of structures and binaries.

Predictive research: research that aims to show trends and/or causal links that can lead to predictions.

Privacy: an ethical consideration that ensures the privacy of participants is respected. In New Zealand, this right is ensured by the Privacy Act.

Probability sampling: a sampling procedure based on the probability of any participant being selected for a particular sample.

Programme evaluation: a type of research that focuses on the effectiveness of a particular programme.

Pure research: research that is more theoretical than applied in focus or that deals with large social issues.

Purposive sampling: a sampling strategy that selects participants because they suit a particular purpose or fit a certain profile; used mainly in qualitative research.

Qualitative: a research approach that looks in depth at fewer subjects through rich description of their thoughts, feelings, stories, and/or activities.

Quantitative: a research approach that reduces numerical data to quantifiable explanations.

Quasi-experiment: a less stringent form of experimental design where there is not a matching control group.

Queer theory: a theoretical approach that challenges conventional gender constructions.

Questionnaire: a written form of a survey based around a series of pre-set questions.

Quota sampling: a form of sampling in qualitative research where participants are chosen to match particular criteria or to match the profile of the population.

Range: the difference between the highest and lowest scores in a set of numerical data.

Random sampling: a form of probability sampling where each member of the population has an equal chance of being selected.

Raw data grid: a grid or spreadsheet setting out all the raw data before they are processed.

Refereed journal: an academic journal that subjects each article to blind (author remains anonymous) peer review.

Reference list: a list of all the sources cited or referred to in a research report or article.

Referencing conventions: a way of ensuring that layout, referencing styles, and citations are consistent.

Reflective field notes: notes made during or after conducting research in the field in which the researcher reflects upon what has taken place.

Reflectivity: reflecting on one's experiences and practices.

Relexivity: considering how one's history and position influence current decisions.

Reliability: a test by which quantitative research is shown to be replicable and able to produce consistent results.

Research proposal: a detailed outline of the proposed research, often needed for approval or funding purposes.

Research synthesis: when a large body of research is collated and summarised for key overall findings.

Rich description: detailed, descriptive observations made in qualitative research.

Right to withdraw: a protection mechanism for research participants that ensures they can withdraw from the research without fear of consequences.

Sample: a sample selected to represent the whole population when the whole population cannot be researched.

Scattergram: a graph where the intersecting points of the data pairs are displayed to reveal particular patterns (also called a dot plot).

Search engine: an electronic program that searches the Internet using key words.

Self study: a research approach, similar to action research, where the researcher focuses on their own setting and practice.

Semiotic analysis: a type of document analysis that focuses on the grammatical structure of the language used in texts and/or its overt and covert messages.

Semi-structured interview: an interview where a set of guiding questions is used but where the interview is open to changes along the way.

Single-case design: where one participant is the subject of a structured intervention.

Social constructionism: a theoretical approach that views concepts as socially constructed and historically situated.

Social media: electronic communications that enhance social communication.

Stratified sample: a type of random sampling in which possible participants are first grouped according to population criteria before the random selection begins.

Structured interview: an interview that follows a pre-set interview schedule.

Survey: a quantitative approach to gathering large-scale data that are able to be generalised.

Symbolic interactionism: a theoretical approach based on one's perceptions of self and others, including how interactions are negotiated through symbolic meaning.

Systematic sampling: a random sampling technique that uses a systematic approach to select participants.

Systems theory: a theoretical approach that views society as a series of interconnecting systems.

Substantive: theory or literature focusing on a content area.

Technology: in research, technology can be a data gathering or analysis tool, a source of data in itself or a means of dissemination.

Thematic analysis: a type of qualitative analysis that focuses on drawing out themes from the data.

Theory: a statement that explains the relationship between concepts.

Unit of analysis: the phenomenon or activity that is being counted or measured.

Unstructured interviews: interviews that are more like conversations following a general theme rather than a specified set of questions.

Validity: ensuring that a study actually measures what it sets out to measure.

Variable: a describable, measurable concept that can vary according to its attributes.

Introduction

Educational research, particularly school- and centre-based research, has received a lot of press lately. Teachers at all levels are expected to undertake research to improve their teaching practices or to make use of published research to improve students' learning. However, there is little support available to help them take that first step. This book aims to fill that gap. I have designed it as an easy-to-read but informative introduction to research for busy practitioners unable to, or uncertain about, enrolling in a course of higher study in research methods. My aim is not to replace such courses or their academic texts, but to provide a basic understanding of the research process in the hope that you will be encouraged to try research for yourself and then continue to investigate the world of research in more depth, through other means, as you come to understand its importance and it rewards.

In the 1980s, I enrolled in an Advanced Studies for Teachers Course (AST) titled "Classroom-based Research". With the guidance of Dr Doreen Darnell, I surveyed students from my classroom and their parents. The results gave me an insight into classroom planning and programme decision making that I had not even considered possible. I was hooked! This gave me the skills and the courage to continue to conduct research in my classroom, to further my qualifications, to enter into tertiary-level teaching, and to become involved in major research projects. To paraphrase the song: "I've looked at research from both sides now, from in and out, but still somehow, it's research's complexities that I recall, I really don't know research at all." I admit I don't know all the answers, but I think my journey is typical of that travelled by many educational researchers in New Zealand. This book allows me to pass on my experiences, my understandings, and my passions to those of you facing the prospect of becoming involved in research for the first time or as a refresher if your skills have become a little rusty.

I have read quite a few research methods texts in my time, and the writers must have made decisions about the content, the focus, and the progression. I, too, have faced these dilemmas. The decisions I have made are threefold. First, I considered it important to outline the "big picture". Why should we conduct research? What are research's historical roots? What are the major approaches and how do you choose one that suits your purpose? Where does theory fit with research? Why are ethical considerations so important? Second, it was important to provide a step-by-step guide through the main parts of the process, with explanations where necessary and suggested references to follow up if required. Where do you start? How do you refine your research question? How do you write a funding proposal? What methods gather best data? How do you make sense of all that data? Third, I wanted to put research into an everyday context. What are the realities of conducting research when already overloaded with regular duties? How do others cope? How do you read the research literature that is already out there? How do you conduct research in bicultural or multicultural settings? How do you let others know what you have done? These three threads—the *why*, the *how* and the *so what*—are woven through the chapters, with the first thread taking more importance at the beginning of the book, the second comprising the middle to later sections, and the third thread appearing in various chapters throughout.

Some readers may be surprised to find that action research is not "up front" in this book. I decided instead to focus on a generic research overview and leave action research to specialist writers in this field. There is a brief introduction to this approach in Chapter 10.

Chapter 1 begins with the big picture. It gives definitions of what research, and educational research, in particular, actually is. It suggests reasons for conducting research in educational contexts. It categorises the main purposes of research and how these relate to education. Because research jargon often presents a stumbling block to understanding research, it introduces key terms, which also appear in a glossary at the back of the book. The first set of key terms explained in this chapter relates to the major approaches to research—quantitative and qualitative. For students of research wanting only to understand research in order to read and interpret it, this chapter ends with a guide to reading and making sense of research reports.

The next chapter is still in big picture mode and takes the main approaches to research (quantitative and qualitative) as a starting place for understanding the research process. It outlines what it means to be a researcher, what you need to know to begin conducting research, and how to select an appropriate research design for the project. It focuses on the decisions any researcher must make, and gives guidance in refining a research topic down to a researchable question.

The third chapter tackles the area that is important for beginning researchers to come to grips with, that of theory. It demystifies (without trivialising) the place of theory, introduces a few major theories that often underpin educational research, and helps researchers identify their own theoretical positions. This chapter shows, through a flow diagram, how a researcher's world view is linked to their theoretical stance, the topics they choose to research, the methods they use, and the way they analyse and write up their findings. This chapter also introduces researchers to considering the implications of researching in contexts where other world views might prevail, such as in cultural settings outside their own.

The focus of Chapter 4 is to familiarise the beginning researcher with ethical issues. Key ethical concepts are discussed before explaining that these issues are not always clear-cut and that ethical decision making is an ongoing feature of any research project. Guidance for completing ethical applications is given, and sample consent letters and information sheets are provided as templates.

Chapter 5 helps the researcher gain familiarity with the field in which they are working. It suggests the need to access and evaluate material, to link it to the proposed topic, to identify gaps in the research, and to justify the need for the research. A checklist for writing a literature review is included, and some simple guidelines to referencing conclude the chapter.

Chapter 6 continues discussing concepts already introduced, such as theory and methodology, and shows how the range of methods and strategies used in educational research relate to these and to one another. This book does not privilege any one style of research over another but tries to get the researcher to identify which methodology will gather the most relevant data to answer the research question. A summary of the common research methodologies, such as experiment, survey, and case study, is given, and particular methods, such as observations, interviews, and document analysis, are then explained in more depth.

Once researchers have an overview of research and what it can achieve, an understanding of the possibilities, and a topic to pursue, their next step is to design a research proposal. Funding bodies, academic approval committees, research sponsors, and advisory committees all expect a logical, comprehensive, and academically rigorous research proposal. Chapter 7 provides guidance on what this should include and gives advice on setting a research budget.

All researchers have tales to tell about their research experiences—some are enthusiastic and positive, others tell of emotionally draining, frustrating, and even dangerous situations. Chapter 8 therefore focuses on the need for careful planning, reviewing the technical aspects of the process, and reflecting on the researcher's role as the research proceeds. Keeping a research journal, using equipment, storing data, writing up field notes, and managing the process are all aspects discussed in this chapter.

Chapter 9 gives simple step-by-step guides to data analysis. It describes processes for analysing quantitative data using descriptive statistics and for analysing qualitative data using thematic analysis. The chapter also shows how to display the findings and suggests how to draw out tentative conclusions and theorise from the data.

Chapter 10 gives guidance on writing research reports. It has researchers consider the possible audiences for their research and how best to tailor the report to their needs. It suggests avenues for presenting and publishing for a wider audience. This chapter also helps researchers reflect on their learning and on how to keep up the motivation for researching. One approach suggested in this chapter is that of action research, an approach that is within the scope of the busy practitioner.

The new final chapter extends and updates many of the ideas introduced in the earlier chapters. It introduces some of the latest trends in quantitative and qualitative approaches as well as providing more detail on approaches to mixed method research and evaluation. The importance of researching ethically and with cultural sensitivity is also revisited in more depth. Many educators like to explore approaches that bring them closer to their participants and allow them to gain more insight into their own and their participants' experiences. To this end, there is further information on textual, visual, arts-based, reflective and collaborative approaches. The chapter ends with my current thoughts on the directions research might take in the future.

Each chapter follows a similar layout:
- *Key questions* at the beginning that focus on the expected outcomes for the chapter.
- *Useful summaries* of chapter content in the form of diagrams, illustrations, and checklists.
- *Real-life examples*, given as written materials or descriptions of people's actual experiences.
- *Summaries* in bullet point form, complemented by suggested follow-up references.
- *Key terms*, a glossary of which is given at the back of the book.
- *Notes to the text, references used in the chapter*, and *a list of other useful sources*.

My overall aim in this book is to develop an awareness of what it means to be a competent and ethical researcher. In doing this, I also want to highlight the need for cultural competence and ethical sensitivities when researchers are working outside their own frames of reference in terms of ethnicity, gender, class, and abilities.

Lastly, if, in this book, I enthuse people about research, provoke thoughtful reflection during the research process, and provide busy practitioners with the skills and confidence to embark on their own research, then I will have succeeded.

> Te manu e kai i te miro, nona te ngāhere
> Te manu e kai i te matauranga, nona te ao
>
> The bird that eats the miro berry owns the forest
> The bird that partakes of education owns the world

CHAPTER 1

Understanding the nature of educational research

What is research?

What are research's historical roots?

Why conduct research?

What is educational research?

What are the main approaches to research?

How do you make sense of the research literature available?

How does research relate to your everyday work?

What is research?

We all have ideas about research because of our prior experiences. We have filled out questionnaires, answered telephone interviews, and read the results of political polls or medical drug trials. We are familiar with phrases such as "margin of error", "response rate", "case study", and "best evidence synthesis". Coming up with a concise and accurate statement encompassing all the complexities of research might be harder for us to do. Let's look at what others have had to say.

> Research is a systematic investigation to find answers to a problem. (Burns, 2000, p. 3)

> [Research is] seeking through methodological processes to add to one's own body of knowledge and, hopefully, to that of others, by the discovery of non-trivial facts and insights. (Howard & Sharp, cited in Bell, 1999, p. 2)

> Social research is a collection of methods people use to systematically produce knowledge. (Neuman, 1997, p. 2)

> Qualitative researchers begin with a question they want to answer, a problem they want to explore, or a situation they choose to change. That question, problem or situation—which is open to modification throughout the research process—reflects the researcher, her interests and beliefs. It also drives the whole research process and determines how data is collected. (Brizuela, Stewart, Carrillo, & Berger, 2000, p. *xviii*)

We can see some common themes coming through; being systematic is one. Here is a summary based on material I've read and on discussions I've had with students and colleagues.

- Research needs to be purposeful and systematic. It gathers data in order to solve a problem, illuminate a situation, or add to our knowledge. The research question relates to the researcher's context, interests, and world view, and shapes the subsequent research decisions. Research requires a set of skills and an understanding of the process, including its strengths and limitations. It should be methodologically sound and ethically defensible. The findings should be clearly written up and made available to interested parties.

These ideas are at the very heart of this book.

Teachers often ask me what the difference is between the kinds of data gathering they do every day and "research". My answer is that there are similarities, but the purpose is often different, the process is longer, and the potential audience for the findings goes beyond the participants. The overall purpose of educational research is to enhance knowledge and understanding as opposed to planning the next learning step, while the process of research includes examining prior literature on the topic at one end and tentative theorising at the other. This book will help you build research skills and understandings and round out the full picture of the context, purposes, and processes of educational research. It will introduce you to new ideas and challenge some of your old ones. The good news is that, as teachers at all levels of education, you already bring important skills and experiences with you. You are used to gathering systematic data—from children's learning stories to examination results—and you are skilled at interpreting this data for planning and evaluation purposes. But before moving further into the research process, let us consider how research came to have such importance in our lives today.

What are research's historical roots?

Humans have always sought explanations. Whether they turned their best guess or theory into myth or religion, whether these explanations and understandings were the property of specially chosen people or available to all through some form of communication, there have always been answers to those how, what, where, when, and why questions. Some of these explanations were supported with evidence and were considered "fact"; some of them stood the test of time and became "knowledge"; some of them were so revered that they were considered "truth". In the Western world, organised religion overtook myth and traditional knowledge as the established orthodoxy, but during the Enlightenment, science began to challenge religion as the road to ultimate truth. Today, we are said to live in a postmodern world where many of these ideas co-exist and we can make sense of complexity through various means. To find a trustworthy way of making sense of and finding truth in our world, many people turn to research as a recognised and credible process for establishing fact.

One of the dilemmas that we face as consumers of research is how to take research findings at face value when research can be used to support opposing sides of an argument. In New Zealand, for example, some reading experts use research to show that teaching by phonics is the best method, while other reading experts use it to show that phonics does not work and a contextual strategy is best. The approach I take in this book is that if we understand how researchers view the world, and if we know their frames of reference, then we can understand how they might approach topics differently and come up with such different results. I believe that while researchers do their very best to be objective, research is not neutral but historically and socially situated. This statement shows that I have a particular way of viewing the world (see Chapter 3 for more discussion of these ideas), but I raise this matter here because understanding the contested nature of research gives us more confidence in accepting or rejecting research findings and being able to reconcile contradictions and see the implications for our own work.

Why conduct research?

Research is one of the key ways we can investigate phenomena (items of interest) and reduce vast amounts of data to manageable and relevant understandings—often called generalisations. We can seek out trends, establish popular interest, provide real-life examples, suggest what works in different situations, and establish cause and effect. New Zealand social researchers Carl Davidson and Martin Tolich (1999) explain that research fulfils three roles—exploring, describing, and explaining:

- *Exploratory research* aims to discover if a phenomenon actually exists. (For example, is boys' achievement really falling behind that of girls'?)
- *Descriptive research* aims to describe a phenomenon in detail. (How does boys' decreased performance manifest itself in the classroom?)
- *Explanatory research* aims to provide an explanation through cause-and-effect or contextual factors. (What factors have led to, or are apparent in, determining this lack of achievement?)

Canadian educational researcher, Gary Anderson, provides an overlapping but slightly different categorisation: "Research in education is a disciplined attempt to address questions or solve problems through the collection and analysis of primary data for the purpose of description, explanation, generalization and prediction" (Anderson, 1998, p. 6).

- *Generalisable research* allows us to take the results from one situation and generalise them to another. (If boys in this school are achieving at this level for these reasons, then we can expect that boys in a similar setting will achieve similarly.)
- *Predictive research* allows us to make predictions based on apparent trends or cause-and-effect factors. (If boys' achievement has moved downward at this rate, we can expect it to continue in this way for this number of years if the situation is unchanged.)

Davidson and Tolich (1999) describe two more general purposes of research—pure (also called theoretical or basic) and applied.
- *Pure research* tries to answer big questions of social importance. (Is achievement-based gender discrimination institutionalised in our schools?)
- *Applied research* is designed with a practical outcome in mind, and most educational research falls into this category. (What classroom programmes are successful in improving boys' achievement?)

These examples, based on the issue of boys' achievement, give you an idea of how widely or deeply you might examine an item of interest (the phenomenon). They also suggest particular ways you could gather your data. Would it be best to examine existing statistics? Would it be best to get into schools and observe in classrooms and interview students and teachers? Would it be best to trial particular programmes to evaluate their effectiveness? As you work through this book, you will start to see how your interests suggest particular questions that are best investigated in particular ways. Meanwhile, it is evident that research can be very useful to help solve some of the problems or answer some of the questions facing us in education today.

What is educational research?

Educational research falls under the broad category of social science research because it focuses on people, organisations, and interactions. It is not limited to formal educational structures, such as schools, early childhood centres, and tertiary institutions, or to recognised activities, such as teaching and learning, although the majority of research topics relate to these areas. It can cover more general topics, such as educational history or educational policy making. It can investigate a range of formal and informal learning settings from universities to kura kaupapa, from community programmes for youth at risk to working with Pacific parents in early childhood settings, and from training young farmers to home schooling. It can look at students, teachers, mentors, coaches, whānau, adult learners, community groups, babies, and toddlers—the list is endless. It can be informed by a feminist perspective or underpinned by constructivist learning theories, or it can challenge power relationships through critical theory. The focus can be at any level or within any sector. The methods can be quantitative or qualitative or a mixture of both. The research can be completed by individuals on their own, undertaken by collaborative teams, or conducted through national and international projects.

- What distinguishes educational research is its focus—people, places, and processes broadly related to teaching and learning—and its purpose—the improvement of teaching and learning systems and practices for the betterment of all concerned and society at large.

Anderson (1998) describes 10 characteristics of educational research, and I have reproduced these here because they reinforce many of the points previously made about research in general and introduce some of the concepts we will discuss later in research design (Chapter 2).

I find this a very useful summary and regularly use it to stimulate discussion with my research students. We will return to many of these ideas later in the book.

Anderson's 10 characteristics of educational research

1. Educational research attempts to solve a problem [or answer a question of interest].
2. Research involves gathering new data from primary or first-hand sources, or using existing data for new purposes.
3. Research is [mostly] based upon observable experience or empirical evidence.
4. Research demands accurate observation and description.
5. Research generally employs carefully designed procedures and rigorous analysis.
6. Research emphasizes the development of generalizations, principles or theories that will help in understanding, prediction and/or control.
7. Research requires expertise—familiarity with the field, competence in methodology, and technical skill in collecting and analysing the data.
8. Research attempts to find an unbiased solution to the problem [or answer to the question] and takes great pains to validate the procedures employed.
9. Research is a deliberate, unhurried activity which is directional but often refines the problem or question as the research progresses.
10. Research is carefully recorded and reported to other persons interested in the problem [question or issue].

(Anderson, 1998, p. 7)

What are the main approaches to research?

One common way of categorising research is by the type of data-gathering methods used.

- *Quantitative research* generally uses methods that gather numerical data in order to generalise to a broader population.
- *Qualitative research* generally uses methods that gather descriptive accounts of the unique lived experiences of the participants to enhance understanding of particular phenomena.

Each approach is based on different assumptions about the purpose of research, has arisen from different historical traditions, is often used by different disciplines, and has developed distinctly different data-gathering and interpretive strategies. Earlier in the history of educational research, we had what are known as the "paradigm wars". Because quantitative research approaches were older and had their origins in the natural sciences, their supporters argued that they were more valid and reliable. Supporters of qualitative research (which arose out of anthropological and social research) argued that scientific or positivist research did not give a full picture of what things were really like in lived situations and interactions. Qualitative research, they claimed, was more able to gather "rich" description and illuminate the phenomenon of interest in ways that educators could relate to. These days, most researchers accept that both approaches have their place and that little good is gained by arguing about which is better. These arguments sometimes resurface, however, and it is useful to know that they have had a hotly debated and somewhat acrimonious history.

Let us now look at some of the major characteristics of the two approaches.

- *Quantitative research* uses deductive logic. This means that it begins with an idea (usually called the hypothesis) and gathers evidence to prove (or disprove) it.
- *Qualitative research* uses inductive logic. This means that the key idea (or theory) arises out of the data. This is commonly called grounded theory, that is, theory that is grounded in the data.

Table 1.1 gives some of the other major differences.

Depending on their background experiences and personal preferences, most researchers feel more comfortable with one approach than with the other. Some people find dealing with statistics scary; others find the subjectivity of qualitative analysis leaves them feeling uneasy. In this book, I will try to open your minds to the possibilities of both, and aim to give you the confidence to choose based on your research interests and questions. Although I will look at each approach separately, I will be doing so for explanatory purposes only. In real-life situations, educational researchers often mix both approaches in order to gather the best data (see the example of mixed methodology in Chapter 6).

This little bit of background understanding allows us to move on to making sense of the research findings that are already out there.

Table 1.1 Major differences between quantitative and qualitative research

Quantitative research	Qualitative research
1. Has its roots in scientific traditions
2. Uses theoretical frameworks such as positivism and behaviourism
3. Focuses on many examples that are representative of a population
4. Uses random sampling
5. Uses terms such as hypothesis, reliability and validity, and variable
6. Uses methodologies such as survey or experiment
7. Uses instruments such as questionnaires or observation schedules
8. Has a research design that is structured and linear
9. Uses a researcher approach that is detached and objective
10. Gathers quantitative data—scores, frequencies, trends, measures
11. Analyses data using descriptive or inferential statistics
12. Uses deductive logic
13. Displays data as graphs, tables, and diagrams
14. Is written up in detached, third-person style	1. Has its roots in anthropology and the social sciences
2. Uses theoretical frameworks such as symbolic interactionism and phenomenology
3. Focuses on a few examples that exemplify particular cases
4. Uses purposive sampling
5. Uses terms such as lived experience, immersion in the field, and multiple realities
6. Uses methodologies such as ethnography and case study
7. Uses strategies such as semi-structured interviews and participant observation
8. Has a research design that emerges and is refined as the research proceeds
9. Involves researchers who build up relationships of trust with participants
10. Gathers qualitative data such as people's stories, descriptions, opinions, visual symbols, and graphic representations
11. Analyses data using thematic or document analysis techniques
12. Uses inductive logic
13. Displays data as quotations, schematic diagrams, and visuals
14. Is written in a first-person style, often using narrative techniques

How do you make sense of the research literature available?

It is important to take a critical approach to reading reported research. If (to give an extreme example) the tobacco companies have funded research citing the benefits of smoking, we would be wise to view the results with caution. If the results of a study drawing on a very small sample have been generalised to the population at large, we would be concerned about the study's reliability. When reading research reports, we therefore need to consider these questions:

- Who funded, sponsored, or commissioned this research?
- What was the purpose of the research?
- Who is likely to benefit from it?
- What assumptions, ideological biases, and theoretical perspectives are apparent?
- Where was the research conducted?
- When was the research conducted?

- By whom and on whom was the research conducted?
- Is the research process clearly outlined?
- Were the ethical issues addressed?
- Are the findings consistent with the data?
- Are the claims realistic given the research design and data provided?
- Are all the findings reported, or is the report selective?
- Why was the report published in this format for this audience?

Next time you read some sensational research findings in the newspaper or on the web, ask yourself some of these questions.

With academic research reports, it helps to understand the format in which they are traditionally written. This makes it easier for you when you come to write up your own research. Sometimes we're put off reading research articles because the language is very dense or the statistical tables are overwhelming. But making sense of this material is no different from helping students you might work with make sense of new and difficult text. There are cues, pointers, and signposts to help you sort out the main ideas and follow the argument. A typical framework for a report looks like this:

The format of a typical research report
- **Introduction**: has a quote, summary, statistical statement, or high-impact sentence to gain the reader's interest, followed by the purpose of the study.
- **Context or background**: explains why the study is needed at this time or how it fits within the social, educational, or political context.
- **Literature review**: establishes what else has been said or researched about this topic and how this study relates to the literature.
- **Theoretical framework**: helps the reader determine the perspective of the author or the theoretical tools that will be used to make sense of the data.
- **Methodology**: outlines the main research approach and the specific strategies used to gather the necessary data. This could also explain how the researchers dealt with ethical issues and might signal how they analysed the data.
- **Findings**: displays the data as appropriate to the research approach along with interpretations of the data and possible theory building or confirmation/disputation.
- **Discussion**: discusses the significance of the findings and the implications for this topic, the field, or practitioners.
- **Conclusion**: is usually a summary of the key points. The author(s) might round off the argument by restating the problem and how this research has contributed to its understanding or solution and might conclude with suggestions for further research.
- **List of references**: this gives full bibliographic details of all source documents cited in the text.

To evaluate the worth of the research contained in the report, you need to understand the field of study, the context, the current literature, the theoretical framework, the methodology, and so on. This will come with time as you immerse yourself in your own field, read more widely, and undertake research yourself. It does not mean that you cannot evaluate the presentation of the research. This will help you tease out the important content and will sharpen your writing skills when you write up your own research for wider dissemination. Keep the following checklist handy next time you read a research report or academic journal article.

> **Guidelines for evaluating the presentation of research reports or journal articles**
> - Did the title give a fair indication of what the report or article was about?
> - Did the opening and/or closing paragraphs summarise the key points?
> - Did you get an understanding of the purpose and the significance of this research?
> - Were there useful signposts? For example: "This research aims to . . ."; "The next section will . . ."; "The main themes are . . ."; "The key tenets of my argument are . . ."
> - Were headings used and were they helpful?
> - Were there clear links between the sections?
> - Were there tables, diagrams, graphs, or other ways of displaying or summarising data?
> - Was the argument supported by reference to the work of other writers and/or prior research?
> - Were links made between the research and the literature or between the findings and the practical realities?
> - Were you left feeling satisfied that you had read a sound, coherent, and reasoned report?

How does research relate to your everyday work?

Whether you are a consumer of, a participant in, or a producer of research, you cannot ignore research in today's educational context. Here are some ways I use research as a consumer in my everyday work:

1. To update my knowledge or understanding of something;
2. To support an idea or practice I already have;
3. To refute something that I don't feel is a good idea or practice;
4. To give me confidence in participating in a debate or discussion;
5. To make me stop and consider a different point of view;
6. To improve my practice or try new things;
7. To reconsider the way I do things or recommend how others might do things;
8. To build a case for change or to argue for something, such as increased funding or better access;
9. To try to find answers to a nagging problem; and
10. To find out how others have dealt with similar situations.

You've probably used research yourself in similar ways. If not, you might find it helps you in some of those situations. Because we all work in different contexts, we probably find that reading about research in publications such as *set: Research Information for Teachers*[1] or from reputable websites such as *Te Kete Ipurangi*[2] sparks different responses in us. Once we start reading research, we become familiar with issues, debates, projects, and researchers in our field and find that it is enjoyable, as well as professionally useful, to keep abreast of what is happening.

You are already a regular participant in research. If you fill out your census form, you provide data for the Department of Statistics. If you collate demographic and achievement information on your students, you contribute to Ministry of Education databases. You might also complete questionnaires for the local university or college of education, or have research students conduct observations in your classes or participate in interviews. Next time you are involved in one of these situations, look more carefully at the process. How were you approached? Did you agree to participate willingly? How were the data obtained? Were you informed of, or could you access, the results? Being a more informed and critical participant means you can learn from well-conducted research as well as avoid the pitfalls in shoddy work.

As a producer of research, I've found that research influences my everyday work in many ways. To date, I've been a very eclectic researcher, using whatever strategies help me answer my question or solve my problem. Here are some of my real-life examples.

When I was new to working with experienced practitioners, I wanted to know more about how they learned and how different or similar that was to how children learned. By using questionnaires, interviews, and participant observation, I came up with a set of principles that supported my work for many years.[3]

When I was teaching about curriculum development, I had a hunch that the differences between the New Zealand Curriculum Framework and Te Whāriki (the early childhood curriculum) were more than skin-deep, so I used historical research and document and discourse analysis to support my argument.[4]

When I wanted to know how young people gained their concepts of citizenship, I set about investigating curriculum documents, school policies, management practices, teaching strategies, and learning activities through a case study in a particular school.[5]

When I wanted to know who made the decisions and wielded the power in educational decision making, I conducted interviews with the policy-making élites in Wellington.[6]

When I needed to conduct research in a kura kaupapa, I worked with a Māori colleague using an action research approach to improve my knowledge, confidence, and cultural competence in such settings.[7]

These examples show that research complemented my everyday work by improving my knowledge and skill as a teacher, deepening my understanding of the content of what I taught, broadening my understanding of what happens in schools and classrooms, giving me an insight into political decision making, and enhancing my work as a researcher.

Here, now, are some examples of how practitioners in other educational settings have built research into their everyday practices.

> *Sandra was interested in multiple intelligences and ICT. She combined the two in an action research study of setting up web pages with her Years 4–6 students.*[8]
>
> *Jan worked with farmers and wanted to know how they came to construct their knowledge and practices as "farming practitioners".*[9]
>
> *Raiha wanted to collect stories from local iwi to use with her Hoaka Pounamu programme students, but at the same time ensure that any research she conducted fulfilled a reciprocal purpose.*[10]
>
> *Diane worked in an early childhood centre and wanted to know what knowledge, skills, and attitudes the early childhood curriculum (Te Whāriki) demanded from educators and whether the educators would require more specialised training.*[11]

Chapter summary

- Research is a purposeful and systematic activity designed to answer questions, solve problems, illuminate situations, and add to our knowledge.
- Research has gained credibility in today's society as a way of providing answers and establishing facts.
- The purposes of research may be to explore, describe, or explain a phenomenon, or to generalise or make predictions from a situation.
- Pure research focuses on questions of importance; applied research aims for a practical outcome.
- Educational research focuses on the context and application of teaching and learning with the aim of improving systems and practices.
- Two major approaches to research focus respectively on quantitative and qualitative data and methods.
- The research question or interest is the key factor in selecting the most appropriate research approach.
- A critical approach to reading published research is important.
- To achieve consistency, research reports follow a format that includes a statement of purpose, a literature review, descriptions of methodology and findings, a discussion, a conclusion, and bibliographic references.
- We are involved in our everyday lives as consumers, participants, and producers of research.

Notes

1. The New Zealand Council for Educational Research publishes a range of accessible research in journals such as *set: Research Information for Teachers* and *Early Childhood Folio*. See http://www.nzcer.org.nz/journals
2. *Te Kete Ipurangi:* http://www.tki.org.nz
3. Mutch, C., Scott, M., & Burt, E. (1996). Reflecting on the retraining experience: What did we learn that is of value to current and future initiatives in pre-service and in-service teacher education? In *Teacher education to standards: Proceedings of the New Zealand Council for Teacher Education Conference.* (pp. 204–214). Dunedin: Dunedin College of Education.
4. Mutch, C. (2001). Contesting forces: The political and economic context of curriculum development in New Zealand. *Asia Pacific Review,* 2(1), 74–84.
5. Mutch, C. (2003). Citizenship education in New Zealand: Inside or outside the curriculum? *Citizenship, Social and Economics Education: An International Journal,* 5(3), 164–179.
6. Mutch, C. (2004, November). *Educational policy in New Zealand: Who pays the piper?* Paper presented at the New Zealand Association for Research in Education Conference, Wellington.
7. Wong, M., & Mutch, C. (2004, July). *Developing the koru model: Using action research to reflect on our practice as cross-cultural researchers.* Paper presented at the New Zealand Action Research Network Conference, Christchurch.
8. Williamson-Leadley, S. (2001). *Setting up and implementing a class for Years 4–6 students on the design, evaluation and construction of web pages from a multiple intelligences perspective.* Unpublished Master of Teaching and Learning research project, Christchurch College of Education.
9. Allen, J. (2002). *Learning to think, thinking to learn: Dispositions, identities and communities of practice: A comparative study of six New Zealand farmers as practitioners.* Unpublished Master of Teaching and Learning thesis, Christchurch College of Education.
10. Boyes, R. (2004, November). *Nga Here Tangata: The threads of research are as numerous as those that bind us as people.* Paper presented at the New Zealand Association for Research in Education Conference, Wellington.
11. Daly, D. (2004). *What knowledge, skills and attitudes does Te Whāriki demand from educators?* Unpublished paper prepared for "TL746 Investigating Issues in Curriculum", Christchurch College of Education.

References

Anderson, G. (1998). *Fundamentals of educational research* (2nd ed.). London: Falmer.
- Provides a useful overview of educational research.

Bell, J. (1999). *Doing your research project* (2nd ed.). Buckingham: Open University Press.
- A highly readable introductory research guide.

Brizuela, B., Stewart, J., Carrillo, R., & Berger, J. (Eds.) (2000). *Acts of inquiry in qualitative research*. Cambridge, MA: Harvard Educational Review.
- The introductory section gives a good discussion of qualitative research.

Burns, R. (2000). *Introduction to research methods* (4th ed.). Melbourne: Longman.
- A good overview, particularly of quantitative methods.

Davidson, C., & Tolich, M. (Eds.) (1999). *Social science research in New Zealand: Many paths to understanding*. Auckland: Longman.
- A useful overview of research in the first part of the book. New Zealand writers.

Neuman, W. L. (1997). *Social research methods: Qualitative and quantitative approaches (3rd ed.)*. Boston: Allyn and Bacon.
- Detailed research overview, including discussion of differences between quantitative and qualitative research.

Other useful references and sources

Bogdan, R., & Biklen, S. (1992). *Qualitative research for education: An introduction to theory and methods.* (2nd ed.). Boston: Allyn and Bacon.
- Widely known qualitative text. Has a very detailed table comparing qualitative and quantitative approaches.

Scott, D. (2000). *Reading educational research and policy*. London: RoutledgeFalmer.
- Useful for providing a range of tools for reading documents critically.

Taylor, G. R. (Ed.) (2000). *Integrating quantitative and qualitative methods in research*. Lanham, MD: University Press of America.
- Promotes an integrated approach to research questions.

Wilkinson, D. (Ed.) (2000). *The researcher's toolkit: The complete guide to practitioner research*. London: RoutledgeFalmer.
- A useful introductory book for practitioner-researchers.

CHAPTER 2

Selecting a research design

What does it mean to be a researcher?

What are the decisions that all researchers make?

How do you choose a topic?

How do you develop a research question?

What kind of research design will best suit your purposes?

How do you choose who or what to study?

What does it mean to be a researcher?

We become researchers for different reasons. For some of us, it is a systematic choice, often linked to higher-level study. Others of us somehow stumble into it by being invited to participate in a project or because it is the only way we can see forward with a particular issue or problem. We all start with different levels of expertise, but one thing is clear, and that is (but do not be daunted by what I am about to say) it is never as straightforward as it might appear at the start. Here are what some researchers have had to say.

> Research is a dynamic activity that travels a long and winding trail from start to finish. It is not a single event, rather the act of doing research is a process. (Anderson, 1998, p. 27)

> Research can involve asking people questions, listening and observing and evaluating resources, schemes, programmes and teaching methods. It can also be messy, frustrating and unpredictable. (Wellington, 2000, p. 3)

> Given the multiplicity of qualitative research and the incredible varieties and possible permutations of human beings and what they do, interpretive researchers have little choice but to deal with complexity and variety. (Brizuela, Stewart, Carrillo, & Berger, 2000, p. *xiv*)

> Throughout this adventure, I kept a classroom journal that I have found to be useful as a researcher. The journal entries I made before the classroom research started reflected some of the concerns I had about my teaching and the class. The entries also set me up with some very high expectations . . . I was feeling very good about myself and my new adventure! Then as we proceeded through the uncertainty, my journal revealed my own misgivings. (Burnaford, Fischer, & Hobson, 1996, p. 122)

It appears, then, that you will face uncertainty and complexity on your research journey. As with any activity you undertake, a little forethought can help prepare you for the possibilities you might face and set you up with realistic expectations for success.

To be a successful researcher, you need:
1. knowledge of your discipline, field and/or topic, and the place of research within these;
2. knowledge of the craft of research to enable you to make sound decisions; and
3. understanding of the ethical responsibilities of a researcher.

We will look at the first two in more detail in this chapter and introduce ethics only briefly, as it has a chapter of its own later.

1. Knowledge of your topic, field, and discipline,

It is important to know a little more about your topic and where it fits in its particular field and discipline. Research does not happen in a vacuum. Researchers choose to follow up lines of interest and to build expertise in the field in which they work. To make sound decisions regarding your research question and method, you need to be up to date with ideas and issues in your line of work and field of research.

Let's say you are interested in the transition from early childhood education to primary school. First, you should understand a little more about the concept of transition. A quick Internet search or visit to your library will help you get clearer definitions of what exactly you mean by transition. From here, you can access articles that discuss research around this topic in various settings. Talking to colleagues or local people with expertise in the area is also a useful place to start. You also need to know about the field in which your topic sits. In this case, if you're an early childhood researcher, you need to be familiar with what the latest research in your area is and also what is currently happening in junior primary classrooms—don't rely on anecdote, assumption, and personal experience. The same is true if you are a primary school teacher-researcher. Just because the children in your class came from a certain preschool, you can't generalise that experience to all early childhood settings.

The second thing you need to know is where your topic and field sit within larger academic disciplines such as education, sociology, and psychology. Of the theoretical perspectives that people use to explain events and phenomena in these areas, which might relate to your topic? Who are the important theorists? This doesn't mean you immediately have to read Bronfenbrenner[1] or Vygotsky[2] in the original—this will come as you get seriously into your research project. However, you do need to be familiar with their key propositions and how their work is used in your area. Read research that has used their theories as frameworks for explaining research findings and delve into more complex material as you gain confidence with the terms and underlying concepts. Coming to grips with theory is one of the exciting—and essential—parts of educational research.

Table 2.1 offers a useful checklist of questions that you can ask yourself as you begin your research journey and that you can keep in touch with as you move along your chosen route. If you cannot answer a question, note down how (the ways) you might be able to improve your knowledge and understanding. Remember, you don't need to know everything immediately, but you do need to know your strengths and limitations and how to work towards enhancing your understanding. The more you know, the more excited about your teaching and research you'll become.

If you have difficulty accessing or evaluating the appropriate material, read (or reread) the section in Chapter 1 about making sense of research literature, and the relevant sections of Chapter 5 on reviewing the literature.

Table 2.1 Questions to ask yourself about your field of interest

How well do you know your field?	How can you enhance your knowledge and keep up to date?
1. Can you describe the field in which you work and how it relates to other fields? 2. Do you have an understanding of the history of your field? 3. Do you know the main theories and theoretical models discussed in your field? 4. Do you know who the "big names" in your field are? 5. Are you familiar with current topics, issues, and debates in your field? 6. Can you easily access research and literature related to your field?	1. Read some introductory texts (the kinds that are used in teacher education institutions or for qualification upgrades) and talk to your colleagues. 2. As above, plus more comprehensive works as you gain confidence. 3. Begin by skimming the reference lists of relevant articles and do an Internet search or find a reference book with summaries of key people and their ideas.[3] When you have gained a general overview, move to articles or books by reputable scholars or the theorists themselves and tackle more complex explanations. 4. As above in 1,2, and 3. 5. Read the practitioner and academic journals in your area. Skim other publications such as the *Education Gazette*, **set:** *Research Information for Teachers, Education Review,* or the *Times Educational Supplement*.[4] 6. Look in your staff library, go to the public library, join your nearest educational institution's library or "surf the net". Talk to colleagues and local experts. Attend conferences in your field, sector, or subject area.

2. Knowledge of the craft of research

You also need to know something about the craft of research before you begin. That is what this book is for. Now is probably a good time to stop and take stock of what you do know and where you might need to put your focus. Try the checklist below. You might find it useful to come back to after you have worked your way through the whole book.

How comfortable are you with the research process?
1. Can you write a focused and manageable research question?
2. Can you select appropriate methods to investigate your question?
3. Are you able to articulate where your main theoretical ideas and methodological choices have come from?
4. Can you place your research in the context of prior research?
5. Can you plan an appropriate research timeframe?
6. Can you fit your research alongside your work and other commitments in a manageable way?
7. Are you confident that you can deal with the ethical requirements?
8. Can you conduct research competently and confidently?
9. Can you use a range of strategies to ensure your research is reliable and valid (trustworthy and rigorous)?
10. Do you have the skills to analyse, interpret, display, and discuss your data?
11. Can you present your findings in a range of ways to suit different audiences?
12. Can you relate someone else's research findings to your own practice and/or the research and practice of others?

As I intimated earlier, research isn't a paint-by-numbers activity, but it is something that can be learnt. It's a little like learning to cook. Once you have mastered the key skills and some basic recipes, you can experiment with different ingredients, methods, and tools.

3. Understanding the ethical responsibilities of the researcher

A researcher also needs to understand the importance of acting ethically. As one writer in the field explains:

> Ethics begins and ends with you the researcher. A researcher's personal moral code is the strongest defence against unethical behaviour. Before, during and after conducting a study, a researcher has opportunities to, and *should*, reflect on research actions and consult his or her conscience. Ethical research depends on the integrity of the individual researcher and his or her values. (Neuman, 1997, p. 443, emphasis original)

Because researchers are in a position of power, it is imperative that they understand the ethical implications of their research. In general, as a beginning researcher, this means you are answerable to someone for the ethical decisions you make. It might be your board of trustees, the Ministry of Education, your research project advisory committee, or the ethical clearance committee (or equivalent) of an institution where you are enrolled in higher study. You will be expected to gain informed consent from the people you are researching (your research participants) and to have considered the possible effects of your study on them.

It is unlikely that your study will lead to physical, emotional, psychological, or cultural harm to yourself or your participants, but if we continue the journey metaphor, then consider it as "risk management". Before you embark on an outing with students, you are expected to complete some form of risk management matrix, to consider all the possible issues that might arise and put procedures in place to minimise them. Chapter 4 deals with ethical considerations in more depth, but, in my experience, it is important to cultivate an ethical sensibility right from the start of your research career. As Anderson (1998, p. 16) advises: "All human behavior is subject to ethical principles, rules and conventions which distinguish socially acceptable behavior from that which is generally considered unacceptable. The practice of research is no exception . . ."

What are the decisions that all researchers make?

Regardless of your approach, each requires similar decisions.

> If you are a beginning researcher, the problems facing you are much the same whether you are producing a small project, an MEd dissertation or a PhD thesis. You will need to select a topic, identify the objectives of your study, plan and design a suitable methodology, devise research instruments, negotiate access to institutions, materials and people, collect, analyse and present information and finally produce a well-written report or dissertation. (Bell, 1999, p. 1)

LeCompte and Preissle (1993) have a useful list of the decisions that all researchers make (1–7), and I have added an eighth one.
1. Formulating the problem;
2. Selecting the research design;
3. Choosing who and/or what to study;
4. Deciding how to approach participants;
5. Selecting a means to collect the data;
6. Choosing how to analyse the data;
7. Interpreting and applying the analysis; and
8. Disseminating the findings.

The following description summarises a piece of research that I conducted in the 1990s (see Mutch, 1998). The summary focuses on the decisions that I made. Use the list above to see if you can locate each decision within this summary.

> As a lecturer in a college of education, I watched the process behind the development of the new social studies curriculum. I wondered how the length of time that the development took and the changes that it underwent might have affected teachers and those who worked with the document. I decided to ask a small group of people in depth about their views, rather than survey a large group.

I thought that open-ended interviews might provide more detail of people's opinions and experiences. I wanted to include a range of views, so I tried to balance gender and ethnicity. I also wanted to talk to people from primary, secondary, and tertiary institutions. I initially sent letters to people who might fit my criteria, and received 15 positive responses. I set up interview times with these people, and all but one agreed to be tape-recorded.

After the first few interviews, I started looking for patterns and themes in the written transcripts. As I interviewed more people, I started to compare these themes with those from my literature review. I then chose the most coherent way of presenting my themes in relation to my four key questions and the major ideas that emerged from my analysis. My findings were reported in several different forums and were accepted for publication in a refereed journal.

At each stage, I could have made different decisions, but my overall design would still have been affected by my research question, the data sources, and data-gathering techniques that were the most appropriate for this question.

But let us return to the eight decisions adapted from LeCompte and Preissle (1993). The first three—"formulating the problem", "selecting the research design", and "choosing who and/or what to study"—are the focus of the rest of this chapter. I cover "deciding how to approach participants" in Chapter 4 and "selecting a means to collect the data" in Chapter 6. "Choosing how to analyse the data" and "interpreting and applying the analysis" are in Chapter 9. "Disseminating the findings" is the focus of Chapter 10.

How do you choose a topic?

Where does your research topic come from? In Chapter 1, I tried to show that researchable topics are all around us. As a beginning educational researcher, you'll probably find you become involved in research in one or more of three ways:

1. You are invited to participate in a larger project by a more experienced researcher or a team of researchers, for example, in the Teaching and Learning Research Initiative or Te Kotahitanga.[5]
2. You enrol in higher-level study and need to undertake a piece of research as part of your assignment work or to complete the qualification.
3. You are motivated to conduct your own research to improve your own practice, solve a teaching/learning problem, find a solution to a management issue, or evaluate a programme.

Sometimes, the topic, possibly even the question, is defined for you. Other times, you must define the topic and refine the question yourself. As an educator, you will find problems, issues, and questions of interest all around you. Before choosing the topic, however, you'll find there are other philosophical and practical factors to consider.

The next section encourages you to think carefully about your research topic and its ease of investigation before you refine it into a manageable research question. Marshall and Rossman (1999, pp. 9–10) suggest that a useful place to start is to ask yourself if your study has:
- should-do-ability;
- do-ability; and
- want-to-do-ability?

Should-do-ability is about the purpose, relevance, importance, appropriateness, and ethics of the research. Do-ability is about the manageability, skill required, prior experience needed, timeframe anticipated, and resource support available to conduct this research. Want-to-do-ability focuses on your own motivation, commitment, and perseverance.

Below is a useful checklist that gets you to consider the practical considerations (i.e., the do-ability) in relation to conducting a piece of research. Note how this checklist picks up many of the ideas we've already met and questions we've already asked. It also links to the two earlier sections on what it means to be a researcher and the decisions that researchers make.

Factors to consider when selecting a research topic

1. Size
- Is your topic or question carefully stated in a way that sets out the limits of your study?
- Have you focused your research in a way that will keep you on track?

2. Scope
- Have you defined the scope in terms of population and sample or setting and case?

3. Time
- Have you made a calculated guess at the length of time this study will take?
- Is the study manageable in the time you have at your disposal?
- Can you fit this study around your other work, family, or community commitments?
- Can you meet the necessary deadlines?

4. Resources
- Can you obtain the resources (financial, material, administrative, and personnel) required?
- Do you have easy access to these or the finances to support them?

5. Skill
- Do you have the data-gathering and analytic skills to conduct this study?
- Can you get help or training if it is beyond your expertise?

6. Access
- How easy is it to gain access to the site, the sample population, and/or cases you need to study?
- Have you considered whose permission you will require and how you will get it?

7. Prior knowledge
- How well do you know the field within which this topic sits?
- How familiar are you with the research, theoretical, and methodological literature around this topic?
- Do you know where to go for support or advice?

8. Motivation
- Will this topic hold your interest for the required length of time?
- Have you considered what intrinsic and extrinsic incentives might keep you going throughout the research?

Even if you don't know the answers to all these questions straight away, they will help you realise the scope of your undertaking and the commitment it requires so that you select something worthwhile, manageable, and do-able.

Here are some real-life examples of how research projects arose from events happening around the researchers (i.e., want-to-do-ability).

> Vikki suffered a death in her family that left young children motherless. In her effort to understand what it was like for the children, and to be able to help them cope, she interviewed children who had recently lost a parent and adults who had lost a parent when they were young. Her particular interest was in the transition from the trauma back into the school setting.[6]

> Barry took up a senior leadership role in an educational institution. He became interested in the difference between what the literature said leadership should be and what it was in reality. He conducted an in-depth case study that looked at leadership from multiple perspectives.[7]

Scanlon (2000) suggests there are three reasons for undertaking educational research (i.e., should-do-ability): to contribute to our knowledge within a particular discipline; to inform policy; and to address a specific issue or problem. If you don't have a burning question to answer or problem to solve, you might like to consider these as possible starting places for your topic. Here are some examples:

> Contributing to knowledge within a discipline: *Joce used the theory of symbolic interactionism to explain how early childhood teachers construct notions of curriculum. She spent concentrated time in an early childhood centre observing, analysing documents, and conducting open-ended interviews with the staff.*[8]

> Informing policy: *Ruth evaluated the effectiveness of Treaty of Waitangi workshops to inform future policy related to the teaching of Treaty issues in her institution. She found*

that the workshops were successful in raising issues, promoting discussion, and shifting attitudes.[9]

Addressing an issue or problem: *Concerned about the nature of silent bullying amongst girls, Tania set a research project in place to gain insights into how pre-adolescent and adolescent girls form friendships. Tania used video clips from popular media to stimulate discussion.*[10]

How do you develop a research question?

A research question is a way of explaining as sharply and pithily as possible to yourself exactly what you are going to research and what you might wish to find out. (Birley & Moreland, 1999, p. 7)

Probably one of the most important skills you can develop as a researcher is the ability to frame good research questions. (Anderson, 1998, p. 43)

These two quotes imply that time spent formulating an appropriate research question is time well spent. Some research questions start out as too broad in scope and have to be narrowed down, whereas others are too narrow or based on the researcher's untested assumptions.

To restate an earlier point, your question influences your research design. Your question will indicate the collection of quantitative data or qualitative data (or possibly a combination of the two). A quantitative research question begins with a proposition or theory that you set out to prove (or disprove), whereas a qualitative question requires you to gather data in order to describe a situation in detail from which you could formulate a theory. I'll consider each of these types of question in a moment, but first I want to assure those of you new to the following concepts and terminology that I will work through these ideas carefully and/or revisit them as necessary in later chapters. The further readings provided at the end of this chapter will also help you here.

Quantitative research

Quantitative research aims to numerically:
- describe a phenomenon of interest (descriptive research);
- explore relationships among variables (correlational research); or
- manipulate variables in order to measure the effects (experimental research).

To frame a quantitative research question, you need to understand some important concepts:
1. A *unit of analysis* is the object or event that you are counting or measuring, that is, the cases that make up your sample. These might be individual people

(as in a survey), interactions (as in an observation), or households (as in a census).
2. A *variable* is a concept that describes a phenomenon in a way that can be counted or measured (e.g., age, gender, IQ, mathematical ability, interest in sport). Variables can be:
   – independent, that is, influences, acts upon, or causes change in another variable; or
   – dependent, that is, is acted upon or is the effect of the prior variable.
3. *Attributes* are the categories into which you divide your variables. For example, gender might be "male" and "female"; age might be "below 20", "between 20 and 40", and "over 40"; and mathematical ability might use the stanines from a PAT test.

In *descriptive research*, measurable or observable data are collected to produce a categorisation or description of the variables or combinations of the variables. These can result in statements such as, "Twenty percent of girls between the ages of 10 and 15 read for pleasure for more than five hours per week."

In *correlational research*, researchers are interested in the relationship between variables. Researchers ask if one (the independent variable) links to or even causes a behaviour or reaction in another (the dependent variable). If, for example, we were interested in whether boys or girls choose more free-choice activities in an early childhood centre, we might ask how does the independent variable (e.g., gender) relate to the phenomenon of interest (e.g., free-choice activities in an early childhood centre)? Can we establish this by observing dependent variables, such as activity choices, length of time on task, individual or group play?

In *experimental research*, researchers manipulate one or more variable(s) to measure its/their effect on another. For example, they might decide to randomly assign a matching cohort of students to one of two groups. The experimental group receives a treatment (e.g., a new programme for learners with reading difficulties) and the control group does not. The researchers then compare the "before and after" results to see if the treatment had an effect. In classrooms, it is often difficult to control all the variables, that is, by trying to match for age, gender, ethnicity, ability, socioeconomic status, first language, time in school, number of schools attended, previous experience of a task, or the myriad other variables that might affect performance. As such, teachers are more likely to use quasi-experiments or single-case design (see Chapter 6), but these still require a unit of analysis and a set of variables.

- A quantitative research question takes a topic of interest and restates it in operational terms, that is, in terms of how you will gather the empirical data that will allow you to test your hypothesis in order to categorise or describe the relationships between your variables.

Figure 2.1 Developing a quantitative research question

RESEARCH QUESTION
Is [variable 1] related to [variable 2]?

STEP 1: HYPOTHESIS FORMULATION
Which is the independent variable (i.e., which comes first)?

STEP 2: HYPOTHESIS FORMULATION
What is the proposed direction of the relationship?

STEP 3: HYPOTHESIS FORMULATION
Phrase the hypothesis to answer the research question and make a testable prediction.

SEEK FEEDBACK
Does your research question need to be reformulated with a tighter focus?

EXAMPLE

RESEARCH QUESTION
Is [use of space in the playground] related to [chronological age]?

STEP 1: WHICH IS THE INDEPENDENT VARIABLE?
The independent variable is chronological age, as this logically precedes use of playground space.

STEP 2: WHAT IS THE PROPOSED DIRECTION OF THE RELATIONSHIP?
Increasing chronological age leads to a decreasing use of playground space.

STEP 3: PHRASE THE HYPOTHESIS TO ANSWER THE RESEARCH QUESTION AND MAKE A TESTABLE PROPOSITION
The lower the use of physical space in the playground, the greater the chance that the pupil will be older.

SEEK FEEDBACK: DOES THE RESEARCH QUESTION NEED TO BE REFORMULATED WITH A TIGHTER FOCUS?
Are older children less likely to make use of space in the playground?

Quantitative research requires you to restate your research question as a *hypothesis*. This is your best guess about the relationship between the variables that you will then set out to test. The following characteristics of hypotheses are adapted from teaching notes compiled by my colleague, Jean Rath.

A hypothesis:
- Is logically linked to your research question;
- Is a statement about the relationship between variables;
- Is clearly stated in a form that gives variables precise meanings;
- Is testable by means of gathering empirical data;
- Uses variables that are measurable in an acceptably accurate and reliable way; and
- Is falsifiable, that is, it must be possible to disprove the claim in the hypothesis.

Jean also has a very helpful flow diagram (Figure 2.1) that shows you how to relate your research question to your hypothesis. An example of the chart "in use" is included in the figure.

Later we will see that how you state your research question and your hypothesis influence the research methods and tools you select.

Many beginning researchers feel comfortable with quantitative research because once they have designed a clear and measurable research question and its companion hypothesis, the rest of the process follows logically. Other researchers find their interest is in what it is like for individuals within a setting or for groups of people coping with a particular phenomenon. They don't want to prove or disprove their original hunch; they simply want to find out what it is like from the perspectives of their participants. They might prefer to use qualitative methods.

Qualitative research

Qualitative research aims to uncover the lived reality or constructed meanings of the research participants.

Rather than using variables and their attributes as categories, and units of analysis by which to count or measure the occurrences of the variables, qualitative researchers gather rich description of the phenomenon of interest. This detail may come from careful observation, open-ended interviews with participants, or detailed examination of documents or artefacts. Any categorisation or theory building comes later as the data are thematically analysed and constantly revisited and reduced.

In *quantitative* descriptive research, such as in a survey, for example, many subjects may be asked the same questions. The findings are then generalised to all similar people or settings. In *qualitative* descriptive research, a few people (in some cases, only one person) may be asked many questions or allowed to tell their own stories in their own ways. The aim is to illuminate the experience or understanding for others but not to generalise from it. The case is considered to be bound by context and situationally specific. However, that is not to say that we cannot relate or compare what we find to other situations or settings if this enhances our learning or understanding.

My colleague, Jean, has also designed a format (Figure 2.2) for helping formulate qualitative research questions.

Now that you have a process for determining and refining an appropriate research question, we can move on to other research decisions.

Figure 2.2 Developing qualitative research questions

STEP 1
Select a phenomenon, issue, or event you want to know more about.

↓

STEP 2
Decide which key words or phrases will help you focus on your phenomenon.
(For example, *construct, interpret, understand, negotiate, perceive, make sense of*)

↓

STEP 3
Design a question based on one of the following patterns.

How do [the people] [in this setting] *key word* [the phenomenon of interest]?
or
In what way is [the phenomenon of interest or issue] [*key word*] by [the people] [in this setting]?

EXAMPLES

(adapted from some research projects we have already read about in this book)

How do teachers in early childhood settings *construct* notions of curriculum?
How do stakeholders in a New Zealand primary school *perceive* effective leadership?
or
In what ways are death and dying *made sense of* by children who have faced the death of a parent?
In what ways are the processes of educational policy making *described* by policy makers in high-profile positions?

What kind of research design will best suit your purposes?

To answer this question, I need to continue considering our two main approaches to research—quantitative and qualitative. I will again discuss them separately, not because I wish to promote a separatist way of thinking but for ease of understanding and because the two approaches arise from different research traditions and so have developed different research designs. Figures 2.3 and 2.4 give an overview of quantitative and qualitative research designs. I will work through the various stages in subsequent chapters in this book.

- *Quantitative research* design is more linear and sequential than qualitative. One step determines the next, and each is dependent on what has gone before. The logic is deductive in that it requires researchers to work from a theory or hypothesis and then gather data to describe it or test it.
- *Qualitative designs* are more evolving and often circular. The logic is inductive—from data to theory.

Once you have narrowed down your research-question problem or issue, you need to work through a further series of questions to help you select the most appropriate research design:
1. What will be the most suitable methodology, approach, or research style?
2. What kind of data do you anticipate gathering?
3. How might you gather this data?
4. From whom will you gather this data?
5. How might you analyse this data?
6. How might you display this data?

Figure 2.5 sets out these questions along with selected answers. These are not the only questions that you could ask at this stage, nor the only possible answers, but they are a useful place to start if you are less familiar with the research process. Although Figure 2.5 displays your choices as either quantitative or qualitative, you could design research that combines the two—they are not necessarily mutually exclusive.

How do you choose who or what to study?

When you have considered a suitable research design, LeCompte and Preissle (1993) suggest you next consider your data sources. You might choose to get your information from human sources (e.g., through a *quantitative* survey or a *qualitative* case study), or you might use non-human sources (e.g., existing

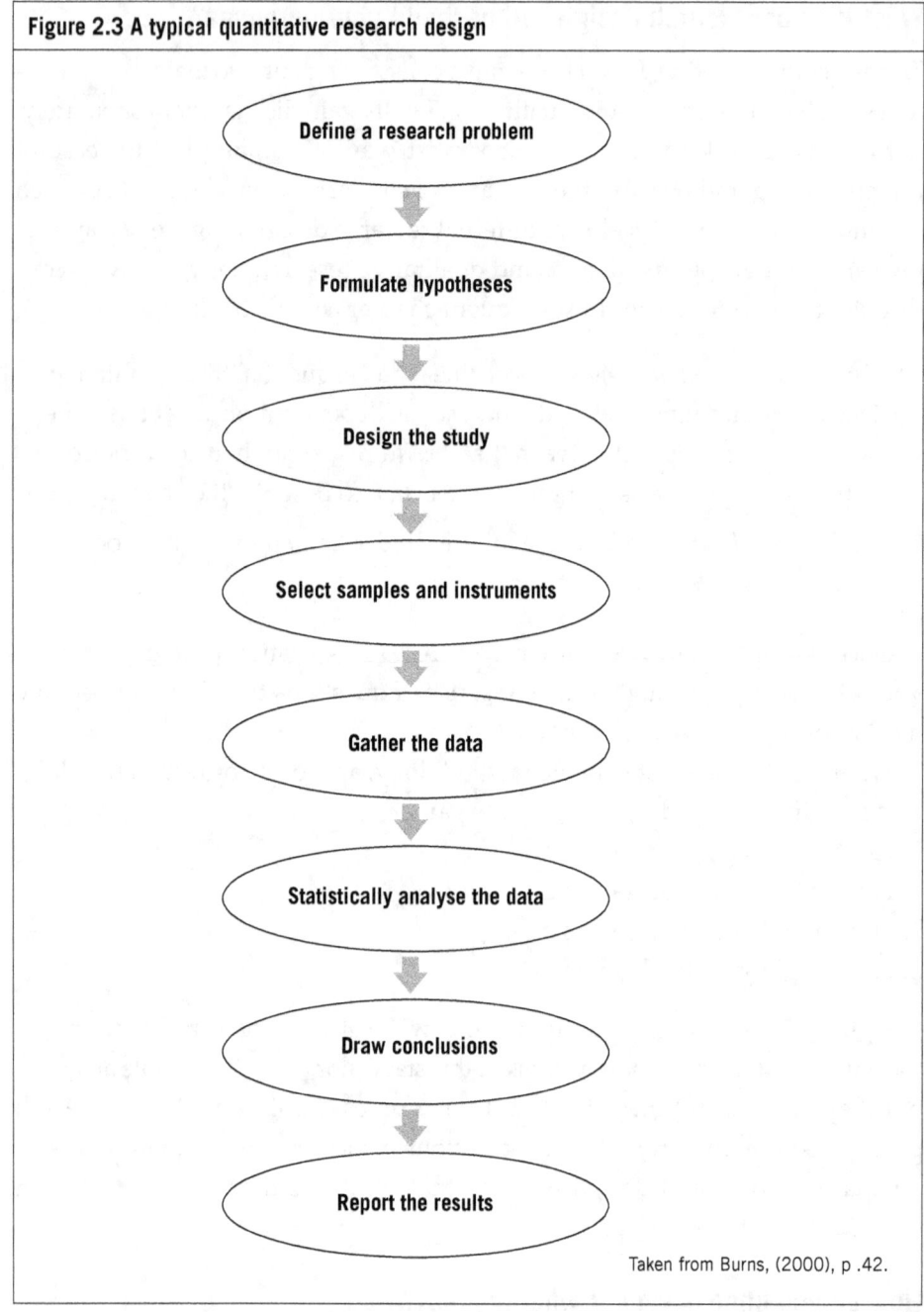

Figure 2.3 A typical quantitative research design

Taken from Burns, (2000), p .42.

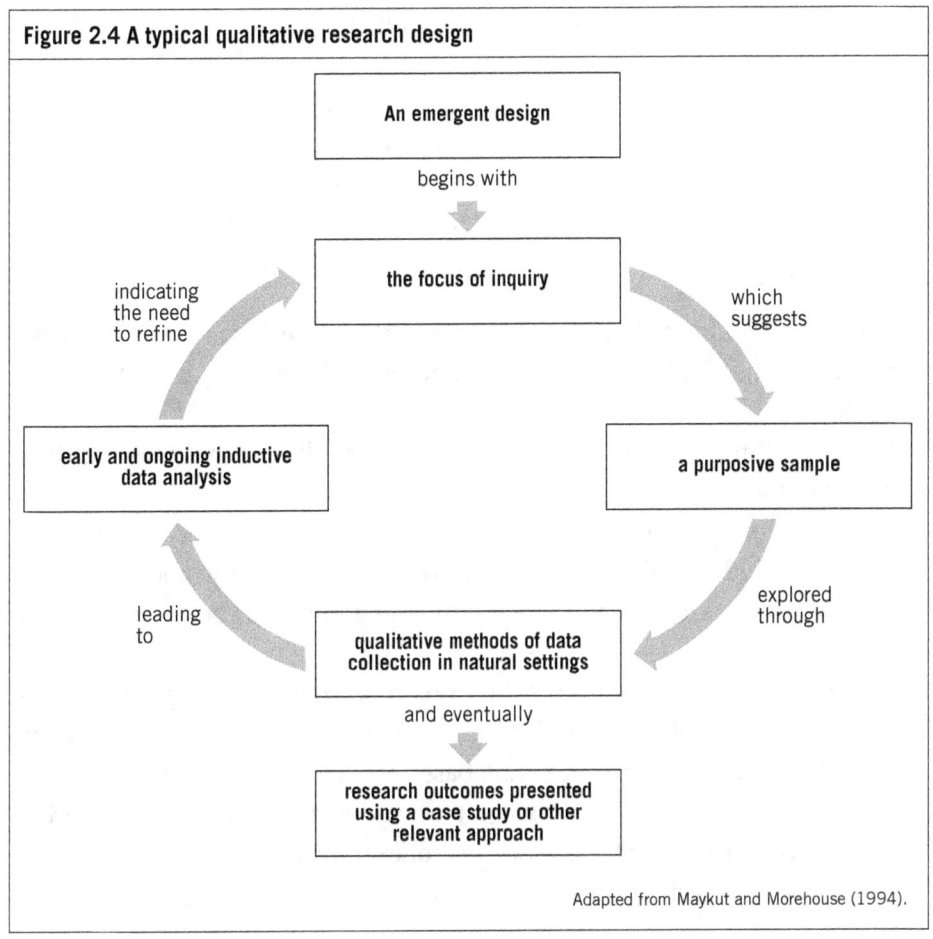

Figure 2.4 A typical qualitative research design

Adapted from Maykut and Morehouse (1994).

statistics or documents), or you might want to employ a combination of all three. This section gives guidance on choosing your sources and samples.

1. Human data sources

One of the decisions you need to make when using human subjects in research relates to the sample selected to represent your chosen population or the case(s) to illuminate your chosen phenomenon. There are two main sampling techniques:
- *probability sampling*, used mainly in quantitative research; and
- *non-probability sampling*, used mainly in qualitative research.

The aim, when employing descriptive quantitative research, is to make statements with confidence. To get the most accurate description of a situation or picture of a trend, you could ask every member of the relevant population, but this is not possible (the exception being the national census, and we can only guess at the amount of organisation and co-ordination that this entails). Instead, you ask a sample from that population that you expect will fairly represent it.

Quantitative research uses probability sampling because it allows us to estimate to a certain level of probability that our sample will be representative. It also ensures that our sample is free from researcher bias. One of the key traditions in this research approach is that of researcher objectivity.

Probability sampling

Probability sampling means that it is possible to specify the likelihood of any element that meets the criteria for the unit of analysis being included in the sample.

There are three main kinds of probability sampling techniques: random, systematic, and stratified.

- *Random sampling* means that any element has the same chance as any other of being included in the sample. The subjects are chosen by random, using a method such as a table of random numbers or a computer-generated random sample.
- A *systematic random sample* is based on some consistent way of selecting subjects, for example, every fifth name in the phone book or every 10th school from the Ministry of Education database.
- A *stratified random sample* selects subjects at random from a set of categories that represents the profile of the population, for example, so many males/females, a percentage of each ethnic group, a representative geographic spread.

As stated earlier, in line with the characteristics of quantitative research, probability sampling aims to reduce researcher bias and to extrapolate from the findings to the wider population. Great care therefore is taken to ensure that the sampling procedures are accurate and representative.

Non-probability sampling

In non-probability sampling, it is not possible—or even desirable—to generalise from the sample to the population. The sample is chosen for specific reasons to expand our understanding of the phenomena and not to make broad claims. The sample might, for example, be a sample of only one.

The three main kinds of non-probability techniques are purposive, theoretical, and quota sampling.

- *Purposive samples* are selected because they suit the purpose. They might be a typical example, an atypical example, an exemplar, or a well-rounded example of the case or phenomenon you wish to study.

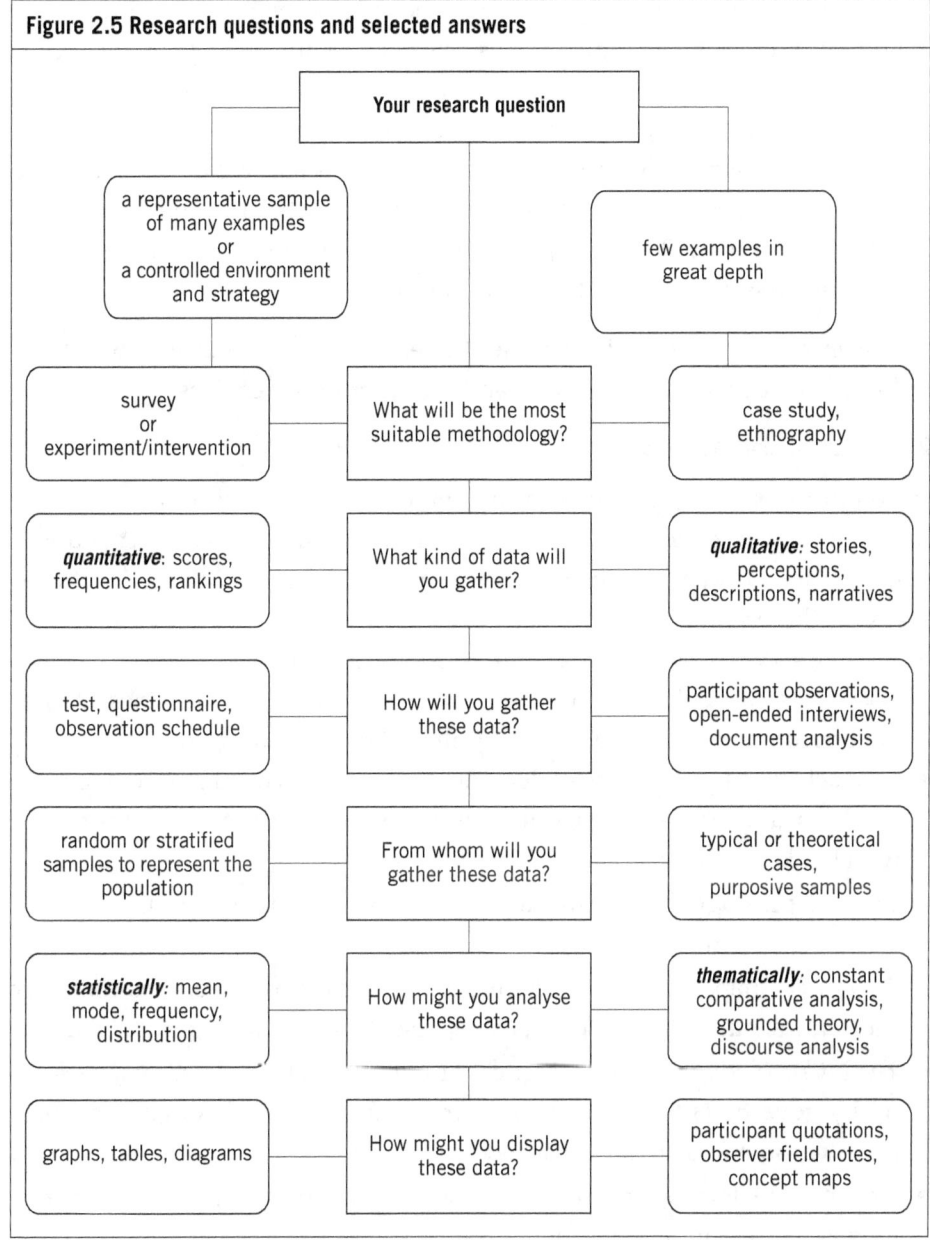

Figure 2.5 Research questions and selected answers

- *Theoretical samples* are guided by the theoretical framework you are using or the theory arising from the data analysis. If, for example, the theory describes four main categories, the sample might be examples of each.
- *Quota sampling* is similar to stratified sampling in quantitative research and is made up of quotas for each of the categories you wish to represent (e.g., age, gender, school decile rating).

Within these, you might also use convenience or snowball sampling.
- *Convenience sampling* simply means that you compromise your search for the perfect example and choose one that is easier to access but will provide useful data to illuminate your phenomenon of interest.
- *Snowball sampling* is often used when access to a particular group is more difficult. Your first subject recommends another subject, who recommends the next, and so on. These subjects still fit within your purpose or theory, but you have less control over the actual choices.

However you select your sample, the expectation is that you will have followed an appropriate procedure and can justify your choices.

2. Non-human data sources

If you are not using human subjects, or you are but also require further information, you could gather your data from existing sources, but you will still need to consider and justify your selection of these. Within educational research, these sources include:
- *Existing statistics:* sets of test scores, databases, yearbooks;
- *Documents:* curriculum or policy documents, school plans, timetables, teacher or curriculum plans, textbooks, portfolios of children's work;
- *Archival sources:* old published documents, unpublished personal documents (such as diaries, letters, ledgers, minutes of meetings), photographs, workbooks;
- *Visuals:* photographs, paintings or sketches, maps, symbols or logos, computer-generated images;
- *Audio-visuals:* tape recordings, video recordings, radio broadcasts, films, computer slideshows, musical items, dramatic representations, dance, performances;
- *The Internet:* educational sites, sites for children, sites for parents, sites set up by government departments or organisations, email communications, listservs, other discussion lists; and
- *Artefacts:* objects of historical or cultural significance, everyday objects, artworks, models, work samples, portfolios.

Chapter summary

- Successful researchers need knowledge of their discipline or field and topic, knowledge of the craft of research, and an understanding of the ethical responsibilities of a researcher.

- All researchers make decisions about formulating the problem, selecting the research design, choosing who and/or what to study, determining how to approach participants, selecting a means to collect the data, choosing how to analyse the data, interpreting and applying the analysis, and disseminating the findings.
- In choosing research topics, researchers need to consider should-do-ability, do-ability, and want-to-do ability.
- Researchers need to consider a range of factors when selecting a research topic, such as size, scope, time, resources, access, skill, previous knowledge, and motivation.
- Research questions need to be relevant, concise, and related to the choice of research design.
- Quantitative research designs are structured and linear.
- Qualitative research designs are more emergent and often recursive.
- Quantitative research uses probability sampling methods.
- Qualitative research uses non-probability, often purposive, sampling.
- Data sources in educational research are often human subjects in everyday settings, but researchers also use non-human sources, such as documents and artefacts.

Notes

1. Bronfenbrenner, U. (1979). *The ecology of human development*. Cambridge, MA: Harvard University Press.
2. Vygotsky, L., with Kozulin, A. (Eds.) (1986). *Thought and language* (rev. ed.). Boston: MIT Press.
3. Two books with useful summaries of theories and theorists for that initial overview are: Palmer, J. (Ed.) (2001). *Fifty major thinkers on education*. London: Routledge; and Palmer J. (Ed.) (2001). *Fifty modern thinkers on education*. London: Routledge.
4. *Education Gazette:* http://www.edgazette.govt.nz
   set: Research Information for Teachers http://www.nzcer.org.nz/journals
   Times Educational Supplement: http://www.tes.co.uk
5. Teaching and Learning Research Initiative research projects are funded by the Ministry of Education but managed by the New Zealand Council for Educational Research. See http://www.tlri.org.nz
   Te Kotahitanga research projects focus on Māori students in mainstream settings: http://www.minedu.govt.nz

6. Pink, V. (2003). *School re-entry after the death of a parent.* Unpublished Master of Education dissertation, University of Canterbury, Christchurch.
7. Brooker, B. (2004). *Effective school leadership: A stakeholder's perspective.* Unpublished manuscript, Christchurch College of Education.
8. Nuttall, J. (2004). *Why don't you ask someone who cares? Teacher identity, intersubjectivity and curriculum negotiation in a New Zealand child-care centre.* Unpublished doctoral thesis, Victoria University, Wellington.
9. Millar, R. (1995). *An investigation into students' perceptions of the successful aspects of Waitangi workshops.* Unpublished paper, Christchurch College of Education.
10. McBride, T. (2004). *Navigating the turbulent world of female friendships.* Unpublished manuscript, Christchurch College of Education.

References

Anderson, G. (1998). *Fundamentals of educational research* (2nd ed.). London: Falmer.
- Also has a useful diagram of the research process.

Bell, J. (1999). *Doing your research project* (2nd ed.). Buckingham: Open University Press.

Birley, G., & Moreland, N. (1998). *A practical guide to academic research.* London: Kogan Page.

Brizuela, B., Stewart, J., Carrillo, R., & Berger, J. (Eds.) (2000). *Acts of inquiry in qualitative research.* Cambridge, MA: Harvard Educational Review.
- Detail and examples of qualitative designs.

Burnaford, G., Fischer, J., & Hobson, D. (1996). *Teachers doing research: Practical possibilities.* Mahwah, NJ: Lawrence Erlbaum.
- Examples of teacher research.

Burns, R. (2000). *Introduction to research methods* (4th ed.). Melbourne: Longman.
- Thorough explanation of quantitative research design.

LeCompte, M., & Preissle, J. (1993). *Ethnography and qualitative design in educational research* (2nd ed.). San Diego, CA: Academic Press.

Marshall, C., & Rossman, G. (1999). *Designing qualitative research.* Thousand Oaks, CA: Sage.

Maykut, P., & Morehouse, R. (1994). *Beginning qualitative research.* London: Kogan Page.

Mutch, C. (1998). Current perceptions of the new social studies curriculum in New Zealand. *Children's Social and Economics Education, 4*(1), 65–80.

Neuman, W. L. (1997). *Social research methods: Qualitative and quantitative approaches* (3rd ed.). Boston: Allyn and Bacon.

Scanlon, M. (2000). Issues in research. In D. Wilkinson (Ed.), *The researcher's toolkit: The complete guide to practitioner research.* (pp. 1–12). London: RoutledgeFalmer.

Wellington, J. (2000). *Educational research: Contemporary issues and practical approaches.* London: Continuum.
- Details educational research in the UK context.

Other useful references and sources

Bouma, G. (1996). *The research process* (3rd ed.). Melbourne: Oxford University Press.
- Step-by-step quantitative research design.

Davidson, C., & Tolich, M. (Eds.) (1999). *Social science research in New Zealand: Many paths to understanding.* Auckland: Longman.
- Good explanations of important quantitative terms.

Liberty, K., & Miller, J. (2003). *Research as a resource for evidence-based practice.* Palmerston North: Dunmore Press.
- Useful sections on classroom-based research design in New Zealand settings.

CHAPTER 3

Considering the place of theory

What is theory?

What are the different types of theory?

Why do theories that explain the same phenomena vary so widely?

How does theory relate to research?

How do you begin to define your theoretical stance?

How do you prepare for working with people with different theoretical frameworks or in settings with different world views?

What is theory?

> Theories are statements about how things are connected. Their purpose is to explain why things happen as they do. Theories vary in size, density, abstractness, completeness and quality. (LeCompte & Preissle, 1993, p. 118)

As this quote from LeCompte and Preissle explains, theories are explanations. Theories can range from someone's hunch about something to a well-tested, well-respected explanation of the social or scientific world. Just because it is a "theory" doesn't mean it is necessarily a good theory. It is someone's best guess in relation to explaining particular phenomena or events at a particular point in time. Theories can be fluid. I recently read that the scientist who put forward the theory of the "black hole" in space is rethinking his ideas in the light of new evidence. Theories can be disproved. They can be contested, built on, ignored. Theories can be considered dangerous. And theories can go in and out of favour.

Understanding theory is of paramount importance when conducting and making sense of educational research, but we do need to view theories with a critical eye. We need to be aware of how theories come into existence, how credible they are, how they explain particular phenomena of interest, and how useful they might be to us in strengthening our explanations and validating our findings.

Most of the theories that you will deal with in educational research follow a consistent pattern. As LeCompte and Preissle explain (1993, p. 120): "Theories are created by developing a set of propositions, postulates or generalisations which establish relationships between things in some way."

Neuman (1994, p. 38) lists the key aspects of a social theory as follows. A social theory:

- contains a set of assumptions as a starting point;
- explains what the social world is like and how and why it changes;
- offers a system of concepts/ideas;
- specifies relationships amongst concepts (tells us what causes what); and
- provides an interconnected set of ideas.

However, not all theories are so all-encompassing. Some are more specific to certain settings; some are not as complete as others.

What are the different types of theory?

Walford (2001, pp. 147–148) attempts to explain why the notion of theory sometimes causes confusion.

The concept of theory often causes problems ... but there are clearly different types of theory that need to be recognised. At one extreme are 'grand theories' such as Marxism, functionalism, feminism or symbolic interactionism. These present a general way of interpreting the world; a framework within which various studies of phenomena can be situated ... At another extreme are the micro-level testable propositions that attempt to attribute causality to particular phenomena ... The [other] type of theory ... lies between those two extremes and might be called 'middle range' theory where a set of concepts is used to define, describe and suggest possible explanations for some phenomena or activities.

I have adapted Walford's ideas in order to investigate three levels of theory: macro-level theories; mid-range theories; and micro-level theories. The key questions to keep in mind when considering these theories are:
- In what ways do they establish a set of concepts and assumptions that describe and explain links, connections, causes and effects, and relationships?
- In what ways do they "act" as macro-level, mid-range, or micro-level theories?

1. Macro-level theories

These theories attempt to explain how societies and social systems function. They deal with large-scale interactions and complex relationships and are often used to underpin educational research. Because theories are based upon different assumptions, any one theory will focus on some aspects rather than on others. Consider the four theories that Walford mentions above.

- *Marxism* is a theory that highlights concepts of class, power, capital, labour, exploitation, and conflict. It is based on the assumption that society consists of groups competing for economic capital and, with that, political power. Those in power use a range of strategies to defend their position. The only way for those without power to gain it is to overthrow the system that perpetuates this inequality.
- *Functionalism* also focuses on concepts such as the division of labour but sees this as a necessary part of the structure, functions, and roles allocated to the individual parts of the system that enable it to operate as a whole. For society to function, highly specialised roles must be conducted in a complementary manner. When the parts are in disequilibrium, the term "dysfunctional" is used.

- *Feminism* also uses concepts of power and inequality but views these as historically, socially, and culturally gender based. The key assumptions are that social systems, organisational structures, gender roles, and social practices favour patriarchy to the disadvantage, even oppression, of women.

- *Symbolic interactionism* uses the concepts of role and role playing to explain people's behaviour and interactions. When people communicate, they use symbolic interactions based on their perceptions of self and others, and they take on different roles for different situations.

Mid-range theories

Most of the theories we use in our everyday educational discussions are mid-range theories. These theories can be formal or substantive.

- *Formal theories* are based on a broad conceptual area, such as theories of teaching and learning.
- *Substantive theories* are a subset of formal theories that focus on a specific area, such as language acquisition.

In Chapter 2, I referred to the theorists Bronfenbrenner and Vygotsky. We can use their theories as examples of *formal mid-range* theories.

Urie Bronfenbrenner (1917–present) is a human development theorist. His theory on the ecology of human development, which states that an individual develops within a context of micro-systems (e.g., families and communities), meso-systems (e.g., social institutions), and macro-systems (e.g., global changes) influenced the writers of *Te Whāriki*, the New Zealand early childhood curriculum.[1]

Lev Vygotsky (1896–1934) is a socio-cultural theorist. He believed that social interaction was a key factor in cognitive development. His concepts of the zone of proximal development (the distance between a child's functioning on a task without support and the child's potential achievement in that domain with support) and scaffolding (the use of peer collaboration or adult guidance, which is reduced as development proceeds) are commonly used in language acquisition and other learning theories.[2]

Substantive theories usually sit within specific fields of study. Each field has many of these theories. Some have become accepted as "common sense" while others are still contested. Here is an example. The lexical approach to second-language teaching is based on the assumption that repeated but meaningful chunks of language are used to construct most spoken text. The teaching of these chunks is therefore more useful than focusing on the mastery of grammar. Thus, learning fixed expressions such as "I'm sorry" in a relevant context is more beneficial than learning the rules of grammar ("I am, he is, she is, you are, we are …") out of context.[3] Some of us will see this premise as common sense; others of us will want to contest it.

Micro-level theories

Micro-level theories deal with particular phenomena, in specific situations in a more concrete manner. You will probably meet these as testable propositions in quantitative research projects or as tentative theories arising out of qualitative research. To give some examples:

> Hasan began his research with the proposition that although computers had been in use in schools for many years, they had not made a difference to mathematics teaching and learning. He conducted a wide-ranging survey across New Zealand secondary schools to test his theory and found that computers were used for mathematics teaching and learning for less than one percent of actual teaching time.[4]

> Maureen conducted research on women who became successful principals and concluded that the women's beliefs and practices had been influenced by their personal histories and various career experiences but altered by the way they individually interpreted or filtered these experiences. Her theory is that "Principals' knowledge bases are socially constructed through learning from experiences in the workplace, critical dialogue with peers, in-service education and formal postgraduate studies but mediated by their personal theories."[5]

Why do theories that explain the same phenomena vary so widely?

One question that puzzles beginning researchers coming to grips with theory is why theories vary so markedly when they are attempting to explain the same phenomena. This comes about because the theorists putting together the propositions on which their theories are based come from different perspectives or world views, or a mixture of these. Anderson (1992) drew up a table to show how people can view the world in completely different ways. He divided people into objectivists and subjectivists. While his approach might seem a little simplistic and dichotomous (and most of us actually lie somewhere in between), it helps make the point.

- *Objectivists* see the world as something tangible and real. It can be objectively described. Knowledge is attainable. There are universal laws that explain social behaviour, and the role of research is to uncover these explanations.
- *Subjectivists* believe the world is constructed by individuals on the basis of their experiences or socially through their interactions. This means there is a range of possible explanations. The purpose of research in this world view is to uncover how individuals or groups perceive their world and make sense of it.

Functionalism, as described earlier, is a theory set mostly in an objectivist world view, whereas symbolic interactionism is based on a range of possible explanations and is therefore set more towards the subjectivist end of the continuum.

Quantitative research, in general, comes from a positivist tradition that believes that rules and explanations can be uncovered by scientific research. *Qualitative* research, on the other hand, has generally (but not in all cases) moved away from positivist assumptions and does not attempt to generalise findings but instead focuses on the lived reality of the research subjects. As you come to understand a little more about world views, you will see how researchers take different research approaches and develop different theories to investigate and explain the same phenomena.

Let us now look at two mid-range theories used frequently in education that generally sit at different ends of the objectivist–subjectivist continuum (but take care, as this construction is just as contestable as many of the theories out there). Behaviourism has propositions that echo an objectivist stance, whereas constructivism is more subjective. Table 3.1 sets out some of the propositions that go with each theory.

Most New Zealand teachers are theoretically eclectic and borrow from different theories for different situations. Many teachers use behaviourist principles for classroom management (e.g., consequences, positive reinforcement, and rewards), but use constructivist principles for learning activities (e.g., developmental time, experiential learning, and inquiry processes). As you read more about educational theories, you will become familiar with their histories and come to understand their strengths and limitations.

Table 3.1 Propositions underlying the theories of behaviourism and constructivism

Behaviourism	Constructivism
The world is linear, rational, time bound, and controllable.	Reality is not fixed but constructed.
Human behaviour can be defined as a response to identifiable stimuli.	Knowledge and truth are created not discovered.
Behaviour can be modified if preceding causes can be identified and controlled.	Meaning is socially, culturally, and historically situated.
Learning is sequential.	We invent concepts, models, and schemes to make sense of our experiences.
Tasks can be reduced to smaller, achievable units.	We test and modify our models and schemes in the light of new experiences.
Repetition and mastery are important for success.	We recognise a plurality of symbolic and language systems.

How does theory relate to research?

> Theory without research is mere speculation; research without theory is mere data collection. (Davidson & Tolich, 1999, p. 17)

Researchers use theory in a variety of ways. It may influence the way they view society, their choice of topic, or the methodological choices they make. They might use a theoretical framework to analyse their data or explain their findings. They might also come up with their own theories based on their research. The following explanation might make this clearer, but be aware that the categories could easily overlap.

Macro-level theories often
- influence a researcher's theoretical position,
- determine a researcher's methodological choices,
- influence the choice of topic.

Mid-range theories are often
- used to analyse and interpret data,
- used to explain findings.

Micro-level theories often
- provide propositions to be further researched or tested,
- arise out of the research data.

How do you begin to define your theoretical stance?

Before you try to determine the most relevant theory to support your research or help determine your methodological choices, you should pause a moment and think about who you are and where your influences have come from. Here are some questions to consider:

- How does your cultural, social, and family background influence your choices?
- What childhood or later experiences have affected you?
- How did your schooling (formal and informal) influence who you are?
- What cultural, religious, and/or political views do you hold dear?
- How have your career choices and work experiences impacted upon you?
- What influences have your family, social, and personal relationships had?
- Has higher-level study or in-depth reading influenced your beliefs and values?

Qualitative researchers are very open about declaring their position. This means that they acknowledge how their age, gender, social class, ethnicity or culture, geographic location, life experiences, and current status influence their research decisions. Hertz (1997) calls this acknowledgement the researcher's "location of self". Denzin and Lincoln (1994, p. 24) talk of the researcher's "personal biography" and claim: "Any gaze is always filtered through the lenses of language, gender, social class, race and ethnicity. There are no objective observations, only observations socially situated in the worlds of the observer and the observed."

Quantitative researchers working from a positivist perspective would argue that it is possible to step outside who you are and maintain a neutral stance. They take great pains to ensure that their research design does this (e.g., through random sampling). My personal position on this is that who you are does affect the research decisions you make whether you work in a quantitative or qualitative paradigm, and that it is worth taking time to consider your values, beliefs, and assumptions and how they might influence what you do. (I talk a little more about my influences later in the chapter.)

Once you have established your key beliefs and influences, you need to start reading more widely to see how these ideas have found substance in social or educational theories. I have already briefly outlined a few theories. Did any of them resonate with you? Are you, for example, concerned about inequalities in education due to race or social class? If so, you might want to read more about critical theory,[6] which has its roots in Marxism. Do you think that women are still unable to achieve financial equality and job status with men? You might like to read some feminist theories.[7] Do you feel most comfortable with learning situations that allow the learner to build on prior experiences and make their own sense of the new experience? If you answered yes, consider reading some of the constructivist or experiential learning theories of Dewey,[8] Bruner,[9] or Kolb.[10]

Neuman (1994) considers there are three main theoretical groupings that influence research methodology (with methodology being the link between your theoretical approach and the overarching method of investigation you choose to follow). He terms these positivist, interpretive, and critical. Other writers group these differently, but they are a useful place for you to start to think where you fit theoretically and how they might influence you as a researcher. Neuman's definitions follow.

- A *positivist* approach is "an organized method for combining deductive logic with precise empirical observations of individual behaviour in order to discover and confirm a set of probabilistic causal laws that can be used to predict general patterns of human activity." (Neuman, 1994, p. 63)

Related theories are functionalism, exchange theory, systems theory, and behaviourism. Typical methodologies are surveys and experiments.

- An *interpretivist* approach is "the systematic analysis of socially meaningful action through the direct detailed observation of people in natural settings in order to arrive at understandings and interpretations of how people create and maintain their social worlds." (Neuman, 1994, p. 68)

Related theories are symbolic interactionism, phenomenology, social constructionism, and hermeneutics. Typical methodologies are case studies and ethnographies.

- A *critical* approach is "a critical process of inquiry that goes beyond surface illusions to uncover the real structures in the material world in order to help people change conditions and build a better world for themselves." (Neuman, 1994, p. 74)

Related theories are critical theory, feminist theory, queer theory, critical pedagogy, and post-colonial theory. Typical research methodologies can be borrowed from other approaches, for example, case study or survey (the distinction being the end purpose of the research), or they can be more action oriented, as with participatory action research, or more theoretical, as in discourse analysis.

Can you start to see the links between who you are and how you might conduct research? Can you see how a world view fits more comfortably with some theories than with others? Can you see how theories and methodologies relate to each other? Can you see how an overarching methodology will determine your research methods? We'll continue this discussion in Chapter 6, but for a summary in diagrammatic form, see Figure 3.1.

Figure 3.1 Link between world view and selection of research methodology/methods

How do you prepare for working with people with different theoretical frameworks or in settings with different world views?

In New Zealand, with our obligations under the Treaty of Waitangi to recognise Māori as tangata whenua, our growing familiarity with living in a bicultural setting, and the increasing multicultural nature of our population, we will, as researchers, conduct research in settings where the world view is different to our own. Also, because of our own "personal biographies", we will, as discussed earlier, conduct research with, on, and for people whose theoretical perspectives or frames of reference are different from our own.

Before beginning my discussion in this section, it is necessary that I "declare my position". I write from the experiences of a mature Pākehā woman, originally from a low socioeconomic background but now comfortably middle class. I am a wife and mother, and I work in education. You might think this information is superfluous, but these experiences have made me who I am and have influenced how I've written this book. This is the only position I can speak from. I cannot presume to speak for Māori, but I will share my experiences in learning from my wiser colleagues. I cannot speak for men, for young people, for the disadvantaged, the disabled, or for other cultures, but I can encourage you to challenge your own assumptions and approach your research with heightened sensitivity to such issues. Space does not permit a discussion of all these issues, and so I will keep within the framework of this chapter and focus on two world views which influence research methodologies—that of Māori and Pacific peoples.

Research in a Māori context

> In Māori communities today, there is a deep distrust and suspicion of research. This suspicion is not just of non-indigenous researchers, but of the whole philosophy of research and the different set of beliefs which underlie the research process. (Tuhiwai Smith, 1999, p. 173)

Given the history of research in New Zealand done *to, on,* and *for* Māori (but rarely *by* Māori), it is not surprising that there is a deep distrust among Māori of research and researchers. Linda Tuhiwai Smith (1999, p. 1) expands on the problem:

> The word itself, 'research', is probably one of the dirtiest words in the indigenous world's vocabulary. . . . It galls us that Western researchers and intellectuals can assume to know all that is possible to know of us, on the basis of their brief encounters with some of us. It appals us that the West can desire, extract and claim ownership of our ways of knowing, our imagery, the things we create and produce, and then simultaneously reject the people who created and developed those ideas and seek to deny them further opportunities to be creators of their own culture and own nations.

You may find these strong words, but if you are not Māori and wish to research in Māori contexts, you need to understand the history of research in these settings—the anger and disillusionment of Māori and their suspicion of you, the researcher. I suggest you do not embark on such research without finding a mentor from amongst your Māori colleagues or the local community who will provide you with wise advice and guidance for the local situation.

Tuhiwai Smith (1999, p. 197) also talks of the various strategies non-Māori researchers have adopted in relation to research in Māori settings:

1. The strategy of avoidance, "whereby the researcher avoids dealing with the issues or with Māori".

2. The strategy of personal development, "whereby researchers prepare themselves by learning Māori language, attending hui and becoming more knowledgeable about Māori concerns".
3. The strategy of consultation with Māori, "where efforts are made to seek support and consent".
4. The strategy of "making space", "where organisations have recognised and attempted to bring more Māori researchers and 'voices' into their own organisation".

If you have no knowledge or experience of such matters, I suggest strategy 1 (avoidance), that is, leave research in Māori settings to those who have, or have earned, the right to conduct such research. If you need or wish to pursue this at some time in the future, then begin on strategy 2 (personal development), knowing that you will follow strategy 3 (consultation) when the time comes. If you are in a position to offer support for strategy 4 (making space), then this is the best way you can foster Māori research development. As Cram (2001, p. 49) explains: "Research that is 'by Māori, for Māori' will encourage Māori participation in and Māori control over research processes." Cram (2001, p. 38) also expresses the view that despite the argument of some that non-Māori cannot conduct kaupapa Māori research, "non-Māori can support a Māori research kaupapa". In other words, they can support its development and ensure it happens in a way that works for Māori.

Cram (2001, p. 40) describes kaupapa Māori theory as "an attempt to retrieve space for Māori voices and perspectives . . . [that] opens up avenues for approaching and critiquing dominant, Western worldviews." Kaupapa Māori theory presupposes that the legitimacy of Māori is taken for granted, that the survival and revival of Māori language is imperative, and that autonomy of Māori over Māori cultural wellbeing is vital.

My mentor in matters Māori is my friend and colleague Marge Wong (Ngāti Kahungunu). She offers this advice:

> Like those of other indigenous peoples, the Māori world view is based on values and experiences that have evolved over time. Understanding the Māori cultural values of manaakitanga (caring and supporting), kotahitanga (unity), whanaungatanga (familiness), wairuatanga (spirituality), rangatiratanga (leadership) and mana (prestige) ensures a friendly, trusting passage for the non-Māori researcher. (personal communication)

How this plays out in research methodology relates to the selection of the topic, the purpose of the research, access to the site and/or the participants, conducting the research, and concluding the research.

1. *Selection of topic:* The topic should be of interest, relevance, and benefit to Māori and should sit comfortably within Māori values.
2. *Purpose of the research:* The ultimate purpose should be to improve systems and situations for Māori in a way that enhances self-determination. Māori should retain the right of ownership of their cultural knowledge, including the right not to share some information with the researcher.
3. *Access to site and participants:* Access should be done through the correct channels (e.g., kaumatua) and using appropriate kawa (protocol). Local advice should be sought.
4. *Conducting the research:* A hui (meeting) process that begins with a powhiri or whakatau (welcome), where all parties establish their identities and purposes, is important. Kanohi ki te kanohi (face-to-face) methodologies in whānau (family-like) settings are best.
5. *Concluding the research:* Feedback through a poroporoaki (concluding discussion) process and reciprocity on the part of the researcher are important concluding activities.

> Unuhuia te rito o te harakeke kei whea te komako e ko?
> Whakataerangitia—rere ki uta, rere ki tai:
> Ui mae koe ki ahau he aha te mea nui o te ao,
> Maku e ki atu he tangata, he tangata, he tangata!

> Take away the heart of the flax bush and where will the komako sing?
> Proclaim it to the land, proclaim it to the sea:
> Ask me what is the greatest thing in the world and I will reply,
> It is people, it is people, it is people!

Research in a Pacific context

Although the peoples of the Pacific represent many cultures, languages, and nations, my remarks here relate to Pacific Islands peoples who have come to live in New Zealand, and I use the term Pacific to cover them all while acknowledging their unique differences. Talofa lava! Kia orana! Malo e lelei! Fakalofa! Ia orana!

Diane Mara (1999) has a list of considerations for those wishing to conduct educational research in Pacific contexts: ownership of the research, methodologies, ethics, the role of the researcher, the participants in the research, and the intended (and unintended) outcomes.

1. *Ownership of the research:* Although acknowledging that the research often is "owned" by those who fund it, Mara (1999) makes a plea for Pacific peoples and researchers to be able to own the entire research process—"from framing the questions, development of the methodologies, analysing the data, designing the final documentation or presentation and ensuring the outcomes benefit our students and teachers" (p. 5).
2. *Methodologies:* Mara suggests that face-to-face methodologies, such as focus group interviews, where the participants are able to respond in their own languages, are the most appropriate. Advisory committees, "critical colleagues", and "cultural mentors" are also useful.
3. *Ethics:* As well as the usual ethical considerations important in any research, Mara suggests that Pacific research contains the dilemma of maintaining confidentiality (because of the small population from which participants can be drawn) while simultaneously giving public acknowledgement to the participants.
4. *The role of the researcher:* After listing the many and varied skills required by all researchers, Mara adds "cultural knowledges and a level of analysis which includes a realism about what research can and cannot do. For our communities the needs are great, the expectations are high and sometimes unrealistic within present constraints" (p. 9).
5. *The participants in the research:* Mara suggests that, for Pacific participants, provisions should be made for the use of their first languages (if preferred); the use of a prayer for opening and closing meetings; sharing food as part of the process; and some flexibility in time, method, and venue. She also stresses the importance of building mutual respect, trust, and credibility between researcher and researched.
6. *The outcomes:* The outcomes are usually negotiated at the beginning of the process, but some unintended outcomes (positive and/or negative) that researchers should be aware of include: focusing attention on particular issues or needs; raising questions for further study; facilitating communication; adding knowledge to the body of scholarship; increasing numbers of Pacific researchers; and altering the perception of educational research in Pacific communities.

Insider research in your own culture

Finally, for those of you who are Māori or Pacific researchers working in your own cultural settings, I offer Linda Tuhiwai Smith's (1999, p. 10) reminder about conducting research as an insider:

The indigenous researchers seeking to work within indigenous contexts are framed somewhat differently. If they are 'insiders' they are frequently judged on insider criteria; their family background, status, politics, age, gender, religion as well as their technical ability. . . . The point being made is that indigenous researchers work within a set of 'insider' dynamics and it takes considerable sensitivity, skill, maturity, experience, and knowledge to work these issues through.

Chapter summary

- A theory contains a set of assumptions that explain the relationships between concepts.
- Theories can exist at different levels (macro-, mid-range, or micro-levels) and can vary in detail and quality.
- Macro-level theories explain large-scale interactions and relationships within social systems.
- Mid-range theories relate to a field of study (e.g., education) and can be formal (more general) or substantive (more specific).
- Micro-level theories relate to particular phenomena, behaviours, or interactions in specific settings.
- Personal experiences and beliefs influence the researcher's world view.
- Theories can be informed by objective or subjective stances.
- Methodologies are the overarching links between theories and research practices.
- The three overarching methodologies in educational research are positivist, interpretive, and critical.
- Research conducted in a Māori context must take into account a Māori world view and the values of manaakitanga, kotahitanga, whanaungatanga, wairuatanga, rangatiratanga, and mana.
- Research conducted in a Pacific context must similarly respect Pacific world views and follow appropriate cultural processes.

Notes

1. Try Bronfenbrenner, U. (1979). *The ecology of human development*. Cambridge, MA: Harvard University Press. You might also like to read his work in the context of *Te Whāriki* (Ministry of Education, 1996).
2. Vygotsky is currently the most cited educational theorist. Try Vygotsky, L., with Kozulin, A. (Eds.) (1986). *Thought and language* (rev. ed.). Boston: MIT Press.
    - To get an initial understanding of these theorists, try any of the more general references listed below or type their name into an Internet search

engine such as Google. When it comes to your research project, however, primary sources are best, that is, the author in the original and reputable scholars using these theories in research contexts.
3. See Moudraia, O. (2001). *Lexical approach to second language teaching*. Retrieved from http://www.ericfacility.net/ericdigests/ed455698.html
4. Toubat, H. (2003). *The use of computer technology in secondary mathematics teaching in New Zealand: A survey of teachers*. Unpublished Master of Teaching and Learning thesis, Christchurch College of Education.
5. Doherty, M. (2002). *Sources of influence on professional practice: A study of five women principals in Aotearoa/New Zealand*. Unpublished doctoral thesis, Griffith University, Brisbane.
6. Critical theory: See, for example, the chapter by Vicki Carpenter in V. Carpenter, H. Dixon, E. Rata, & C. Rawlinson (Eds.), *Theory in practice for educators*. Palmerston North: Dunmore Press.
7. Feminist theory: Middleton, S. & Jones A. (Eds.) (1997). *Women and education in Aotearoa 2*. Auckland: Auckland University Press/Bridget Williams Books.
8. John Dewey (1859–1952). Try *The child and the school* or *The school and society*.
9. Jerome Bruner (1944–present). Try *The relevance of education* or *The culture of education* or *The process of education*.
10. David Kolb (1939–present). Try *Experiential learning: Experience as a source of learning and development*.

References

Anderson, G. (1992). *Fundamentals of educational research* (1st ed.). London: Falmer.
- Provides a more extensive discussion of the objectivist/subjectvist framework and its links to educational research.

Cram, F. (2001). Rangahau Māori: Tona tika, tona pono/The validity and integrity of Maori research. In Tolich, M. (Ed.), *Research ethics in Aotearoa New Zealand* (pp. 35–52). Auckland: Pearson Education.
- Further detail on issues in Māori research.

Davidson, C., & Tolich, M. (Eds.) (1999). *Social science research in New Zealand: Many paths to understanding*. Auckland: Longman.
- A useful chapter on competing traditions, which they term positivist and interpretive.

Denzin, N., & Lincoln, Y. (Eds.) (1994). *Handbook of qualitative research*. Thousand Oaks, CA: Sage.
- Extensive coverage of all aspects of qualitative research. I especially like the chapter by Valerie Janesick.

Hertz, R. (1997). *Reflexivity and voice*. Thousand Oaks, CA: Sage.
- An insight into qualitative methodologies.

LeCompte, M., & Preissle, J. (1993). *Ethnography and qualitative design in educational research* (2nd ed.). San Diego, CA: Academic Press.

Mara, D. (1999, April). *Why research? Why educational research for/by/with Pacific communities in Aotearoa-New Zealand*. Paper presented to the Pacific Island Educators' Conference, Auckland.

Neuman, W. L. (1994). *Social research methods: Qualitative and quantitative approaches*. Boston: Allyn and Bacon.
- Extensive discussion of knowledge, science, theory, and research.

Tuhiwai Smith, L. (1999). *Decolonizing methodologies: Research and indigenous people*. London/Dunedin: Zed Books/Otago University Press.
- Important reading for anyone wanting to understand indigenous research issues.

Walford, G. (2001). *Doing qualitative educational research*. London: Continuum.

Other useful references and sources

Abercrombie, N., Hill, S., & Turner, B. (2000). *The Penguin dictionary of sociology* (4th ed.). Harmondsworth: Penguin.

Audi, R. (Ed.). (1999). *The Cambridge dictionary of philosophy* (2nd ed.). Cambridge: Cambridge University Press.
- Both dictionaries and others like them are useful additions to your bookshelves as places to check concepts and get an initial overview of terms, theories, and people.

Bishop, R., & Glynn, T. (1999). *Culture counts: Changing power relationships in education*. Palmerston North: Dunmore Press.
- Has a chapter that focuses on research.

Bullock, A., & Trombley, S. (Eds.) (1999). *The new Fontana dictionary of modern thought* (3rd ed.). London: HarperCollins.

Cullen, J. (2001). An introduction to understanding learning. In V. Carptenter, H. Dixon, E. Rata, & C. Rawlinson (Eds.), *Theory in practice for educators* (pp. 47–69). Palmerston North: Dunmore Press.
- An introductory text for New Zealand students.

Seidman, S. (2003). *Contested knowledge: Social theory in the postmodern era*. Malden, MA: Blackwell.

Swingewood, A. (2000). *A short history of sociological thought* (3rd ed.). Basingstoke: Macmillan.

Wellington, J. (2000). *Educational research: Contemporary issues and practical approaches*. London: Continuum.

CHAPTER 4

Examining the ethical issues

Why are ethics important in research?

What are some key ethical concepts?

How do you prepare for ethical approval?

How do you approach your participants?

What do you need to consider when researching in your own workplace?

How do you act ethically in cultural settings other than your own?

Why are ethics important in research?

> Morals underpin ethics, but the two terms are not quite synonymous. An 'ethic' is a moral principle or a code of conduct which actually governs what people do. It is concerned with the way people act or behave. The term 'ethics' usually refers to the moral principles, guiding conduct, which are held by a group or even a profession. (Wellington, 2000, p. 54)

As discussed in Chapter 2, researchers are in a position of power. They enter the lives of, or gather personal information from, their participants. Even something as seemingly innocent as asking your class to complete a questionnaire carries with it possible issues related to trust, power, coercion, validity, repercussions for non-participation, and so on. My experience with teacher-researchers is that because they are used to gathering information as part of their everyday work, they do not often see the responsibilities and consequences of gathering data for research purposes. Let us look at this more closely.

From Table 4.1, we can see that teachers have the authority (and training) to collect and disseminate information regarding student learning as long as it is done within the relevant parameters. Laws protect teachers and students. In the research world, however, both researchers and their participants are more vulnerable. Apart from laws that govern all individuals in New Zealand, there are only codes of practice for those whose employment is in a research-related organisation or a higher education institution involved in conducting research. Teacher-researchers need to consider how to protect themselves and those they intend to research.

Teacher-researchers also need to consider when collecting information stops being about "teaching and learning" and starts becoming "research". If the information is gathered as part of a wider study to answer a research question, if it is used for a purpose that is different from the reason it was gathered, or if it is to be disseminated beyond the site where it was gathered, then it could be considered research. If it is research, then it must follow ethical principles. If you think I am labouring this point, consider these statements from my research students (all educational practitioners).

> "I won't bother asking my principal's permission. I'll just do the research without him knowing."
>
> "Should I phone the parents to tell them what T. [a participant] has just told me?"
>
> "I'll just use my own class and then I won't need to ask permission."
>
> "Somewhere I have children's work from last year; I'll use that."

Table 4.1 Data gathering for teaching and research purposes	
Information gathered for teaching purposes	**Data gathered for research purposes**
Purpose: to diagnose needs, evaluate student progress, plan next teaching step, or evaluate programmes.	**Purpose:** to answer a research question
Rights: Teachers have the right to collect information for valid teaching and learning purposes.	**Rights:** Researchers (except in cases such as gathering census data) do not have the right to gather information from others. It must be given voluntarily.
Skills: Teachers have undergone a training programme that includes assessment and evaluation skills.	**Skills:** There is no requirement that researchers undergo any training although many complete research methods or training courses.
Authority: Teachers have the authority to do this through the Education Act and are subject to checks and balances such as teacher registration or their employment agreements.	**Authority:** There is no registration of educational researchers. Authority generally comes from their status as educational professionals.
Ethics: Teachers are bound to act within the laws governing education. Those who are union members usually follow their union's code of practice.	**Ethics:** Higher education institutions and research organisations have codes of ethics and ethical approval systems for any research conducted under their auspices. There is no code of ethics for teacher-researchers acting on their own.
Dissemination: Teachers are bound by the Education Act and the Privacy Act. Within those frameworks they report individual progress to students, their parents or caregivers, and other professionals where the dissemination of the information is in the best interest of the students and their educational progress.	**Dissemination:** One of the aims of research is to disseminate the findings as widely as possible to communities of interest. As individuals, researchers are bound by the Privacy Act but if they wish to disseminate the research findings this should be done with the consent and understanding of those participating. Anonymity and confidentiality for participants should be assured.

Needless to say, these people received advice that had them considering things somewhat differently.

What are some key ethical concepts?

In general, if you treat your participants with consideration, fairness, and respect, you'll end up acting ethically, but it doesn't hurt to think about some issues or dilemmas in more depth. One of the general principles in the Christchurch College of Education's ethical guidelines (adopted from those followed by the New Zealand Association for Research in Education) states:

> The rights and welfare of students, research subjects and the public generally should take precedence over the self-interest of staff or the interests of employers,

colleagues or other special groups. In the conduct and reporting of research there should be thoughtful concern for the rights and interests of all the individuals, groups and institutions involved in and affected by it. (Christchurch College of Education, 2005, p. 1)

When embarking on a research project, you'll probably find it takes time to get your head around all the possible ethical considerations, but there are some generally accepted notions in research ethics you can follow.

- *Informed consent:* Participants in your research should be fully informed about the purposes, conduct, and possible dissemination of your research and should give their consent to be involved.
- *Voluntary participation:* Participants should be able to freely choose whether to participate in the research overall, or in aspects of it.
- *Right to withdraw:* Participants should be able to withdraw from your research without fear of consequences.
- *Permission:* Permission is required to gain access to some sites (e.g., from a board of trustees to conduct research in a school) or to use some participants (e.g., from the parents/caregivers of children).
- *Coercion:* Participants should not be coerced to participate in the research or to complete any part in a manner that makes them feel uncomfortable. This is especially important if the researcher is in a position of power over a participant (e.g., a teacher researching students he/she teaches).
- *Deception:* Participants should not be deceived about the purposes or methods of the research.
- *Confidentiality:* Participants should be assured that any data they provide will remain confidential to the researcher and be stored in a secure manner.
- *Anonymity:* Researchers should ensure that individuals, groups, and sites cannot be identified. This may require changing names or identifying features.
- *Privacy:* Participants should not be asked questions outside the scope of the research or made to feel that their privacy has been invaded or their time improperly used.
- *Participant safety:* Participants should understand the consequences of participation and not be subject to physical, psychological, emotional, or cultural harm. They should be informed of whom to approach if they have concerns about the conduct of the research.
- *Researcher safety:* Researchers should take care not to place themselves in positions of physical or emotional distress and should take steps to seek help if this occurs.

- *Dissemination:* Participants should be informed of the length of time the data will be kept and any anticipated venues or methods of disseminating the research findings. Findings should be fairly and accurately reported.

If you experience a need to go against one of these principles, only do so with the advice of your project advisory group, research mentor, or supervisor, and with the approval of the relevant ethical clearance committee. An example might be that you need to deceive participants about the purposes of your research because it might influence their behaviour, as was the case with Chuck:

> *Chuck was interested in the differences between girls' and boys' writing. He was interested in whether they chose to write about different topics and what these were and to what extent teachers influenced children's topic choices. To ensure that knowledge of the purpose of his research did not affect the choice of topics, he told the children and their teachers that he was interested in the qualitative aspects of creative writing.*[1]

Another example might relate to your inability to keep a person's identity anonymous because of their high-profile role. However, the person participating would understand and agree to this from the start. A third example might be that you state that participants only have until a certain time to withdraw from your study because after that it would affect the results or your ability to meet your deadlines. These changes are acceptable, but only if you consider them carefully and seek peer approval for them.

Another important aspect to consider is how ethical dilemmas might confront you throughout your research and how you should use whatever decisions you make about them to inform your research design.

> Ethical issues may stem from the kinds of problems investigated by social scientists and the methods they use to obtain valid and reliable data. In theory, at least, this means that each stage of the research sequence may be a source of ethical problems. Thus they may arise from the nature of the research project itself (ethnic differences in intelligence, for example); the context of the research (a remand home); the procedures to be adopted (producing high levels of anxiety); participants (emotionally disturbed adolescents); the type of data to be collected (personal information of a sensitive kind); and what is likely to be done with the data (publishing in a way that is likely to cause embarrassment). (Cohen, Manion, & Morrison, 2000, p. 49)

The examples that Cohen and his colleagues provide may seem a little extreme and outside the scope of anything you might want to undertake, but they make the point clearly: you need to consider ethics not just at the beginning of the research (when applying for ethical approval, for example) but throughout your research.

How do you prepare for ethical approval?

Now that you have the above principles to guide you, an ethical clearance form should not seem so daunting. Most forms follow a standard layout; as long as you complete all the boxes with accurate detail, your application should proceed smoothly. Most applications ask for two aspects—a form you are required to complete and copies of the material you have provided to your participants (I provide some samples later).

1. The ethical clearance form

You can expect to provide the following details:
- description of the project (title, aims, methodology, significance);
- information about the researcher or research team;
- whether you will be seeking ethical approval elsewhere;
- funding sources (if relevant); and
- any particular features of this research the committee should be aware of.

The form might require you to provide more detail about:
- sample selection;
- methods and tools; and
- proposed dissemination.

It will ask about:
- access to participants or sites requiring permission;
- anonymity of participants;
- confidentiality of, and restricted access to, data;
- voluntary participation/informed consent/right to withdraw;
- possible risks to participants;
- justifications for going outside accepted principles; and
- other issues that should be drawn to the committee's attention.

2. Supporting materials

You will be expected to attach a participant information sheet (or recruitment letter) and a consent form. Your *information sheet* will give:
- the name and position or affiliation of the researcher;
- a brief description of the nature and scope of the research (and who is sponsoring or supervising it if this is appropriate);
- the particular question or focus of interest;
- the way in which the participant(s) will be involved;
- a possible timeframe;

- your contact details; and
- another party the participant(s) can approach if they need more information or have concerns.

The *consent form* will include:
- the participant's right to voluntary participation;
- a statement that the participant can withdraw at any time;
- guarantees of anonymity and confidentiality;
- the participant's name;
- contact details;
- signature; and
- the date.

You will keep the original, but you might ask the participants to keep a copy for themselves.

How do you approach your participants?

> No researcher can demand access to an institution, an organisation or to materials. People will be doing you a favour if they agree to help, and they will need to know exactly what they will be asked to do, how much time they will be expected to give and what use will be made of the information they provide. Teachers, administrators, parents and keepers of documents will have to be convinced of your integrity and the value of your research before they decide whether or not to cooperate. (Bell, 1999, p. 52)

There are two aspects to approaching your participants. One is practical and the other is ethical.

Practical aspects revolve around:
- initial contact (personal, phone, email, letter);
- follow-up contact (information sheet, consent form, confirmation of dates and venues);
- amount and style of information to be provided (information for children will be tailored differently from that for adults);
- timeframes (between initial contact and agreement, between agreement and data gathering, between participant involvement in analysis and publication of findings); and
- costs involved (resources, transport, koha).

Ethical considerations have been discussed earlier, but on the next two pages you'll find some sample formats for you to adapt and use.

[Letterhead for project/ institution/ sponsoring body]

Address for contact and correspondence

Date

Dear Participant

I am [name] a [position] working with/at [organisational affiliation/ research team/ supervisor...] on a [research project/ Ministry-funded contract/ Master's thesis...].

My research focuses on [topic] and my particular interest is in [sub-topic/ research question/ context...]. To do this I am [sending out a questionnaire/ conducting interviews/ completing detailed observations...] of/on/to [sample/case/setting...].

I am approaching you because you [have been chosen randomly/fit my criteria for selection/ have been recommended as a suitable subject...]. This would involve you [completing a questionnaire that takes about 20 minutes/ participating in a focus group interview for 30–45 minutes/being visited on three separate occasions to complete concept maps...].

If you are willing and able to participate, could you read, complete, and return the attached consent form to [contact details including address, phone, fax and email...].

If you agree, a [questionnaire/interview schedule...] will be mailed to you by [date] /to be returned by [date] or

you will contacted by [person/ date...] to arrange [visit/venue...].

If at any time you have questions or concerns about the conduct of the research, please feel free to contact [ethical clearance committee chair/ advisory committee chair/ researcher project leader/mentor/supervisor...] at [contact details].

Thank you for your consideration. I look forward to your prompt response.

[Researcher's name].

[Project title] consent form

I [name of participant] have read and understood the nature of the research project and agree to participate as requested. I agree with the following statements (please tick):

I understand that my participation is voluntary and that I can withdraw ☐
at any time.

I understand that my identity and that of my [centre/ school/ ☐
workplace] will be kept anonymous and any information provided
will be kept confidential.

I understand that my responses will be kept in a locked filing cabinet for ☐
a period of three years before being destroyed.

I understand the findings of this research could be presented at
conferences and written up in academic journals. ☐

Signed _____ Date _____

When working with children and young people, you need to consider several matters. Ask yourself these questions. Who needs to give permission? When can children or young people give their own permission? What other ethical issues need careful consideration and approval (e.g., avoiding coercion, using deception appropriately)? How will I adapt the information sheets and consent forms so the participants can understand them? (For further discussion of working with children and young people, see Chapter 8.)

Finally, when approaching participants, do not, as Lovey (2000, p. 118) cautions, take them for granted:

> Educational or social research is essentially a parasitic occupation. We feed off our subjects, and without willing heads [principals], teachers, parents and, to a certain

extent, children, we cannot undertake our research. No one would attempt to research a distant, isolated civilisation without studying the history of the people, finding out something about the customs and beliefs of the people, and arming themselves with good maps, and perhaps some gifts.

What do you need to consider when researching in your own workplace?

Many beginning researchers choose to conduct research in their own settings because it is convenient, they lack the confidence to go elsewhere, the research they wish to conduct is sparked by a problem in their setting, or they are conducting action research and therefore focusing on their own practice. However, as Linda Tuhiwai Smith advised in Chapter 3, when researching as an "insider", there is a new set of issues to consider. Before working in your own setting, weigh up the advantages and disadvantages.

Advantages

- Easy access;
- No travel costs;
- You can fit your research around your other duties;
- Access to resources and materials;
- Knowledge of the history and culture of the organisation;
- Knowledge of the right channels to work through;
- Knowledge of whom to approach and how to approach them; and
- Credibility with the participants.

Possible disadvantages

- Role conflict (when are you a researcher and when are you a colleague or teacher?);
- Time commitments and keeping up with your regular duties;
- Trying to maintain confidentiality and anonymity;
- Having to keep promises made out of inexperience or enthusiasm;
- Insider knowledge and possible lack of objectivity;
- Discovering things about your colleagues you'd rather not know;
- Your colleagues may feel that you are judging them;
- Your colleagues may judge your research ability when you are just a beginner;
- You can't escape your mistakes; and
- You quickly use up all your favours.

If, on consideration, you think you can avoid or minimise the disadvantages and that your own setting is the most appropriate place, then continue with your plans. It does help, though, to have a critical friend or mentor outside the setting to debrief with. I'll leave the final words about insider research to Tuhiwai Smith (1999, p. 139):

> Insider research has to be as ethical and respectful, as reflexive and critical, as outsider research. It also needs to be humble. It needs to be humble because the researcher belongs to the community as a member with a different set of roles and relationships, status and position.

How do you act ethically in cultural settings other your own?

Indigenous methodologies tend to approach cultural protocols, values and behaviours as an integral part of methodology. They are 'factors' to be built in to research explicitly, to be thought about reflexively, to be declared openly as part of the research design, to be discussed as part of the final results of a study and to be disseminated back to the people in culturally appropriate ways and in a language that can be understood. (Tuhiwai Smith, 1999, p. 10)

In Chapter 3, we discussed working in settings with different world views. As I have worked alongside my colleague Marge Wong, we have discussed and devised our own set of principles for working in cross-cultural settings beginning with questions from Tuhiwai Smith's work but expanding these more fully. I have reproduced these in Table 4.2 as guiding questions that you can ask at each stage of your research to ensure you adequately consider cultural and ethical principles.[2]

Chapter summary

- It is important to act ethically to protect the researched, the researcher, and the credibility of the research.
- Teacher-researchers need to be aware of the difference between gathering data for teaching and learning purposes and gathering data for research.
- The key concept in ethical research is that of participants giving their informed consent.
- Other important ethical concepts are voluntary participation, the right to withdraw, protection of privacy, anonymity and confidentiality, and participant and researcher safety.
- Researchers should avoid deception, coercion, and causing harm.
- Tertiary institutions, research organisations, and funding bodies require researchers to gain ethical clearance before beginning their research.

Table 4.2 Principles for working in cross-cultural settings	
Research step	Questions to consider
1. Setting up the research	• What is the purpose of the research? • Why is it necessary? • Who is the research for? • Who controls the research? • Who owns the research? • Who funds the research? • Who has designed and framed the research? • Who benefits? • What are likely positive outcomes and for whom? • What are possible negative outcomes and for whom? • How can negative outcomes be lessened or eliminated? • Who needs to be consulted? • How will this consultation be done?
2. Selecting the research team and design	• Who will conduct the research? • What are their credentials and/or experiences? • Is the research team culturally competent and appropriate for the task? • Is the methodology one that sits within appropriate cultural knowledge and research frameworks? • How flexible is the design to emergent events? • Who will determine the research questions, methods, and analytic tools? • What parts do the participants or their communities have in determining these? • Who approves, oversees, and/or advises on the research? • Who gives ethical approval and through what mechanisms?
3. Preparing the way	• Do the participants and/or their communities fully understand the purposes of the research and give informed consent? • Do the participants and/or their communities know what will happen to the research findings? • Do the researchers meet with the approval of those being researched and/or their communities? • What processes are in place to support the research, the researched, and the researchers? • Is consultation time included in the timeframe?
4. Conducting the research	• Are appropriate cultural protocols followed? • Is the setting culturally and emotionally safe for all parties? • How is the concept of reciprocity catered for? • What parts do the participants play in the analysis or discussion of the findings? • How are the analytic frameworks determined? • Who writes up and disseminates the findings?
5. Sharing the results	• Can the results be returned to the participants and/or their communities in appropriate ways? • Who will undertake this? • Has funding been set aside for this? • What, if any, further action needs to be undertaken as a result of the findings? • How can this action be taken or supported?
6. Reflecting and refining	• How can all parties share their reflections on the process, its effects, limitations, and implications? • How can improvements be made? • Whose responsibility will this be?

- Consideration needs to be given to approaching participants in both the practical and ethical senses.
- When conducting insider research, researchers need to be aware of the advantages and disadvantages of this approach.
- Awareness of appropriate cultural protocols and using consultation and reflection at each stage of the process enhance research in cultural settings outside one's own.

Notes

1. Marriott, C. (2002, July). *Sex differences in primary school narrative writing*. Unpublished paper, Resource Teacher of Literacy Training Programme, Christchurch College of Education.
2. Wong, M., & Mutch, C. (2004, July). *Developing the koru model: Using an action research approach to reflect upon our practice as cross-cultural researchers*. Paper presented at the New Zealand Action Research Network Conference, Christchurch.

References

Bell, J. (1999). *Doing your research project* (2nd ed.). Buckingham: Open University Press.
- Has a chapter on negotiating access and insider research.

Christchurch College of Education. (2005). *Ethical guidelines for the conduct of research*. Unpublished paper. Author.

Cohen, L., Manion, L., & Morrison, K. (2000). *Research methods in education* (5th ed.). London: Routledge.

Lovey, J. (2000). Researching in schools: Case studies based on three research projects. In D. Wilkinson (Ed.), *The researcher's toolkit: The complete guide to practitioner research* (pp. 117–132). London: RoutledgeFalmer.
- Actual cases of in-school research in the UK.

Tuhiwai Smith, L. (1999). *Decolonizing methodologies: Research and indigenous people*. London/Dunedin: Zed Books/Otago University Press.
- A must for anyone considering working in indigenous or cultural settings different from their own.

Wellington, J. (2000). *Educational research: Contemporary issues and practical approaches*. London: Continuum.
- Useful section on ethics.

Other useful references and sources

Anderson, G., Herr, K., & Nihlen, A. (1994). *Studying your own school: An educator's guide to qualitative practitioner research.* Thousand Oaks, CA: Corwin.
- Helpful approach to working in your own setting.

Kvale, S. (1996). Interviews: *An introduction to qualitative research interviewing.* Thousand Oaks, CA: Sage.
- Discusses ethics through each step of the qualitative research process.

Mills, G. (2000). *Action research: A guide for the teacher researcher.* Upper Saddle River, NJ: Prentice Hall/Merrill.
- Useful examples of researching in own setting.

Tolich, M. (Ed.) (2001). *Research ethics in Aotearoa New Zealand.* Auckland: Pearson Education.
- Wise advice and useful examples for the New Zealand context.

CHAPTER 5

Reviewing the literature

- Why conduct a literature review?
- Where do you start?
- How do you keep track of everything?
- How do you write up a literature review?
- Why are referencing conventions important?

Why conduct a literature review?

> Successful research is based on all the knowledge, thinking and research that precedes it, and for this reason a review of the literature is an essential step in the process of embarking on a research study. A review of literature is a summary, analysis and interpretation of the theoretical, conceptual and research literature related to a topic or theme. (Anderson, 1998, p. 76)

The main reason for a literature review is to provide a context and justification for your study.
- Where does it fit?
- What has gone before?
- How does your study build on this?
- What research is lacking in this topic or in this field?
- How does your study address this gap?

The consumers of your research also need to know that there were reasons for your study and that you considered these carefully. Neuman (1997) outlines four goals of a literature review:
- To demonstrate familiarity with a body of knowledge;
- To show the path of prior research;
- To integrate and summarise what is known; and
- To learn from others and stimulate ideas.

I would add that, on occasions, you might use the review:
- To place your study within its relevant historical, political, social, and/or cultural context;
- To situate yourself as a researcher and/or your study theoretically; and
- To introduce your methodological choices.

Table 5.1 uses these goals and provides questions to guide your reading and thinking. These might also help you shape the writing of your review later on.

Where do you start?

When you want to gather the information available on a particular topic, it is often difficult to know where to start. Having an idea of what is available and how you might access it is very important.

There are three main sources—human, textual, and electronic. The checklist given in Table 5.2 might be helpful.

Table 5.1 Questions guiding what material to read when preparing a literature review

Literature reviews:	Questions to consider
1. Demonstrate familiarity with a body of knowledge	• Where does this topic sit in its discipline or field? • Who are key theorists, writers, and researchers on this topic? • What are the main concepts and ideas relating to this topic?
2. Show the path of prior research	• What are the seminal pieces of research relating to this topic? • What other research has been conducted and what has it found?
3. Integrate and summarise what is known, *and* 4. Allow us to learn from others and stimulate ideas	• What are the key themes, issues, and findings that come through in this literature? • What have prior literature reviews or meta-analyses shown? • How can your literature review contribute to a new perspective on this topic?
5. Place a study within its relevant historical, political, social, and/or cultural context	• Why is the topic important? • What key contextual factors affect this issue? • What is the current situation relating to this issue? • How can your study contribute to new understanding?
6. Situate the researcher and/or the study theoretically	• Where does your topic fit theoretically? • What theoretical perspectives have influenced you and your choice of topic? • What theoretical frameworks might you use to analyse or interpret your data?
7. Introduce methodological choices	• What methodologies have prior studies on this topic used? • How do these relate to the choices you will make?

Human sources

If you are starting with human sources, begin with people known to you. It helps if you already have a relationship with such people, but don't expect them to do your work for you. However, they might suggest (or even provide) useful readings. People are busy, and you might not be their current priority, but I have generally found people quite generous with their time and help, especially if they are passionate about their topic. Don't be afraid to contact people you don't know by email or letter, but don't wait for a response before moving on to other sources.

Textual sources

Cultivate your librarians. I find that the time spent in being personable and polite, in explaining exactly what I am looking for, and in appreciating their

Table 5.2 Questions guiding gathering of source materials for a literature review	
Human sources	• Who has written on this topic (locally, nationally, internationally)? • Who teaches in this field (and is easily accessible)? • Who has completed study or research on this topic? • Is there a research centre or organisation that focuses on this topic? • Who is referred to as an "expert" or as "knowledgeable" in this field?
Textual sources	• Are there books or book chapters on this topic? • Are there academic journals in this field? • Are there research summaries, indexes, digests, and/or handbooks on this topic? • Has anyone completed a Master's or doctoral thesis on this topic? • Has anyone presented at a relevant conference on this topic? • Does your library have a "clippings" file of newspaper or magazine articles or does it subscribe to a system that collects and collates such items?
Electronic sources	• What does a general search engine[1] turn up? • What further links can you go to from your initial responses? • Are there specific websites related to this topic or relevant organisations? • Are there useful New Zealand or international databases[2] available?

Note: Each of these sources requires a different approach.

efforts and expertise is well worth the effort. Take time to find out how your library works. Where is everything kept? Who is the expert in which aspect? How do you access regular, reference, archival, stack, visual, audio, electronic, and any other type of material? Ask for help when you need it, but also learn when to be independent and get on with it yourself. If you are at a distance from a library, don't let this put you off. I find libraries are especially helpful to distance customers. It also helps to understand the purpose of the library you are using. Different types of libraries (public, children's, academic, archival) function in slightly different ways and might offer slightly different services. Again, ask if you're not sure.

Electronic sources

Take time to become familiar with locating material electronically. To avoid wasting hours of your precious time, ask an expert to show you how to do this efficiently and effectively. Be very sceptical of what you find on the web; find out how to recognise authority and credibility.[3] Stick to tried-and-true websites and databases and follow links from those, although I have found a general search through a search engine sometimes turns up a gem that I couldn't have located any other way. As you become more knowledgeable in your field, you'll become more focused in your search terms. When you find items of interest, don't try to print off everything you find. Learn to bookmark, scan, skim, and be selective.

Other tips

Use the reference lists and bibliographies at the end of articles you have collected. Once I have located a few useful articles on my topic, I look to see who the authors are citing and try to get a feel for who are the "big names" or current experts in this field. I also check reference lists for currency and credibility. When the work is a seminal one in the field, currency is not so important. However, in general, I try to find articles published within about the past five years. A paper subject to peer critique (published in a refereed journal, for example) indicates some measure of credibility. I also look for critiques of the writers or viewpoints that I am uncovering. This helps me evaluate the arguments and the usefulness of the articles.

How do you keep track of everything?

An important task is to organise a recording and filing system so you can locate the materials and reference them accurately. You will probably do this manually or electronically. The three key steps at this stage are recording, filing, and evaluating.

Recording and filing (electronically)

Although you might need to record and file some material as hard copy, you can now do much of the work electronically. A computer program, such as Endnote,[4] allows you to build up your reference lists and article reviews or store articles and data tables electronically. Once that material is in the system, Endnote allows you to manipulate it easily. It is also a great help with referencing. Some of my colleagues insist that if you are beginning on a research project or new topic, you should first spend time becoming familiar with an electronic referencing system like Endnote, as it is much more efficient and helpful than manual methods.

Recording (manually)

For each book, chapter, journal article, conference paper, and other item that you have located or read, record the following:

- author(s) and/or editor(s);
- year of publication;
- title of paper or article;
- title of book or journal;
- edition or volume;
- place of publication;
- publisher; and
- page numbers.

(See the next section for comments on referencing conventions.)

> For each article you print off the Internet, ensure you have the full reference, pathway (URL, DOI), and date you retrieved it.

Don't shortcut this part. It will save you much time and anguish later. If, for example, you use a direct quote, you must be able to give a full reference and the page number. I once had to email a well-known academic because I had built an argument around a quote of his and then lost the reference. Together, we were able to trace the quote to its source.

If you have photocopied or scanned an article or chapter, check that this information is included on the pages somewhere (preferably at the front). Check photocopies or scans to make sure all the words fit on the page and the page numbers haven't been chopped off. Staple, clip, or hole punch to keep the pages together—finding a stray page and not knowing where it belongs is highly frustrating.

Filing (manually)

Once you have gathered and recorded your material, file it in some way. You could do this alphabetically by author, thematically, or chronologically. I find my material usually falls into three categories—content (or substantive), theoretical, and methodological, but sometimes articles have useful information on all three. In these cases, you need to develop a cross-referencing system. You need to experiment with a way that suits your logic and will be easy for you to find your way around. Some people use index cards, colours, codes, or keywords to help them.

Evaluating

The next step is evaluating the relevance of the material. At this stage, do not attempt to read every article from beginning to end! Learn to be economical with your time and effort. You need to scan and skim the articles. Scanning is glancing through to see if an article meets your purposes. Skimming is slowing down to focus on particular parts, perhaps searching for key words. Remember to use the signposts suggested in Chapter 1—title, headings, opening and closing paragraphs, illustrations or diagrams, statements such as " This study focuses on . . .", and so on. The decision you need to make here is whether an article will help you with this study. I organise my material into three groups—"very relevant to my topic", "might be relevant to my topic", and "of interest but not at the moment". Within those categories, I then prioritise again in terms of relevance (if I am pressured for time) or organise alphabetically. By this stage, my articles are often covered with pencil notes, post-its, and highlighted sections for me to come back to.

Whatever system you use—electronic or manual (or both)—ensure your filing systems are consistent and regularly updated. Also take care to keep full bibliographic details of each item so you do not inadvertently plagiarise.

- Plagiarism is where you use someone else's ideas, sections of text, visuals (or other media) and pass them off as your own (knowingly or unknowingly). It is a serious academic offence. To avoid this, you need to scrupulously acknowledge your sources, paraphrase material into your own words (with acknowledgement of the source of the ideas), and use a quotation convention (see section following on referencing).

How do you write up a literature review?

Once the recording, filing, and evaluating is underway, you can begin reading in earnest. LeCompte and Preissle (1993) explain that literature reviews are usually presented in three ways:
- A brief contextual section at the beginning of a study;
- A full chapter (as in many theses and dissertations); or
- Integrated throughout the study (more common in qualitative studies).

Some qualitative researchers prefer to read material as they go or even leave it until their research is completed, but, as a beginning researcher, you should practise reading ahead of time until you have the knowledge and skill to work this way. Whatever technique is best for your study, you must do more than simply list and describe what you have read (although that might be a useful place to start).

- The purpose of writing a literature review is to pull together the current writing and research on your topic and to present the findings, issues, and themes in a way that critically synthesises what is available in order to contextualise and justify your study. Writing a literature review (like all good writing) requires practice. Being able to synthesise ideas into a critical and coherent piece of writing is a skill. Table 5.3 offers a guide to producing a literature review based on some of the things we have already discussed but offering new advice as well.

A literature review is different from an annotated bibliography

An annotated bibliography has you follow all the steps in Table 5.3 to Step 5. You are then expected to structure your presentation with a clear summary and critical evaluation of each piece that you have read and to state its relationship to your topic. Unlike an annotated bibliography, a literature review requires synthesis in terms of grouping by common themes.

A literature review is different from a book review

A book review expects a much more detailed and critical analysis of one book (or more than one book if they are closely related). It takes more time to explore the author's purpose, the book's structure, the relevant audiences, and so on.

Why are referencing conventions important?

Beginning researchers and students groan at the complexity and pedantic nature of referencing conventions. There are no shortcuts, I'm afraid. You simply learn the conventions for your discipline and practise them until they become second nature.

- Referencing conventions are important for reasons of credibility and for clarity.

Credibility

In acknowledging that our ideas are not new but build on the research and writings of others, we adhere to a referencing convention. My institution has adopted the APA (the American Psychological Association) system. It is one of the "author-date systems". This simply means that with each reference or quotation you give in the text, you provide the surname of the author and the date the article or book was published. Other systems use footnotes or endnotes.

Table 5.3 Eight-step approach to writing a literature review

Writing a literature review

Step 1:	Define your topic	• The clearer you are about this, the easier it will be to locate relevant material. • Determine your keywords and define your terms.
Step 2:	Refine your search	• There is a lot of interesting material out there, but you need to focus on what will be relevant to your study. • Put limits around your search by narrowing the topic, timeframe of events, countries, or settings, to keep it manageable.
Step 3:	Locate your material	• Use human, textual, and electronic sources to locate your material. • Record all reference details, especially if you are photocopying from the original.
Step 4:	Collate your material	• Organise your materials in a way that helps you classify them and find them again easily. • Evaluate materials in relation to relevance to your topic
Step 5:	Summarise each article	• Read the materials and evaluate for credibility, clarity of writing, and usefulness (see Chapter 1). • Weed out any that are not substantiated, will not suit your purposes, and/or are too difficult to follow. • Summarise the rest using a set of consistent criteria (e.g., purpose of research, methodology, findings, themes, implications, relationship to your research, critiques).
Step 6:	Organise the review	• Use an organising technique (e.g., brainstorming, mind-mapping, grouping, and labelling) to draft common themes and make links or comparisons. • Try another method or refine your original method and compare the results. • Put your ideas into a logical, coherent structure.
Step 7:	Synthesise the review	• Use your structure from Step 6 and fill in the details as needed to summarise the key themes from the literature. • Show how this relates to and justifies your topic.
Step 8:	Shape the review	• Once you have a first draft—read, review, rewrite. • Any material you discard should be kept in case it has a purpose once the research is completed. • Whether the final purpose is as a contextual section, a full chapter, or is integrated throughout your study, it will need further crafting, shaping, and refining before it is ready for publication.

I will use APA as an example, but you will come across other systems in your reading (and later in your writing). I will not go into the detail of APA here because this is where it gets complicated, but you can find the full details in the APA manual[5] or in a summarised version from a library or study skills support unit.

An electronic referencing tool like Endnote is very helpful in setting up reference conventions.

1. In-text referencing

This is where you acknowledge someone else's ideas within the text of your writing. (The following examples relate to historical research that I have done on education at the time of the Great Depression.[6])

> Factors that prevented ideological confrontation turning to class war, were first, that class differences were less acute in New Zealand than elsewhere (Simon, 1994), second, that the emerging leaders on the left sought to promote solutions through more political means (Bassett & King, 2000) and third, New Zealand's involvement in World War I.

This signals to the reader that I have:
- Read widely on my topic
- Synthesised the key ideas
- Acknowledged the ideas of others; and where I have not acknowledged them that I have
- Used my own ideas or the ideas are public knowledge.

2. Acknowledging quotations

A quotation of fewer than 40 words is integrated into the text. It gives the author, date, and page reference. The actual quote is put inside quotation marks.

> But as Green (2000, p. 18) states, "still firmly tied to Britain's imperial apron-strings, New Zealand's economy was buffeted by volatile world commodity prices."

A longer quotation is indented from the original text and does not use quotation marks.

> The Reverend Scrimgeour (Uncle Scrim), a popular radio commentator and humanitarian during the Great Depression, agrees and explains how these international events were only to exacerbate problems already apparent within New Zealand:
>
> > A lot of people believe that the Depression was caused by the collapse of Wall Street. It was a creeping affair. It came with terrible gradualness. It

simply was a fact that mankind had produced abundantly and nobody paid attention to the fashioning of a distribution system—a social security, if you like. (Scrimgeour, Lee, & Simpson, 1976, p. 19)

Clarity

The use of in-text referencing also aids clarity. Use of the author-date system instantly tells readers your source and its currency without disturbing the flow of the reading. If they wish to find this source, they can turn to the reference list at the end for full details.

Reference lists and bibliographies

At the end of your report or article, you must provide full details of the source documents you've cited or quoted from. This is why it is important to keep accurate details right from the start. The list takes the form of a reference list or a bibliography, and the two are often confused. (Your literature review will generally require a reference list.)

- A *reference list* contains only the works referred to in the report or article. These may be people whose ideas you cited or work you paraphrased, or people from whom you took quotations, diagrams, and/or statistics.
- A *bibliography* lists all the works you read in order to put this piece of writing together, whether you refer to them in your text or not, or lists all the potentially useful texts that support the topic.

Again, the specific conventions for setting out each work in the list or bibliography are complicated. Rather than explain them here, if you look at the end of each chapter in this book, you will see conventions used for books, book chapters, journal articles, conference papers, theses, and electronic sources. You simply need to find good models to copy until you become familiar with the rules yourself. If using an electronic referencing system, you will find it especially helpful at this stage.

Chapter summary

- A literature review shows familiarity with the field, summarises prior research, and contextualises and justifies the proposed research.
- There are three main sources of material for a literature review—human, textual, and electronic.
- Once materials are located, they need to be recorded, filed, and evaluated for usefulness.

- Full reference details should be accurately recorded.
- Care must be taken not to plagiarise other people's work, especially when using electronic sources.
- A process to follow when writing a literature review includes defining the topic, refining the search, locating and collating the material, summarising and synthesising the material, and organising and shaping the review
- Bibliographic referencing conventions are important for credibility and clarity.

Notes

1. A search engine will find all the electronic references to the words that you type in the search space. Your home page will default to a particular search engine, such as Yahoo. Different search engines search and sort differently. I find Google and Google Scholar the most helpful search engines for my purposes.
2. There are many useful websites, databases and indexes. You can find these through a web search or by asking a local librarian.
3. It is hard to sort out what is credible and authoritative on the web. In general, sites with "ac" (academic) or "edu" (education) in the address are recognised academic institutions and those with "org" are government, non-government, or non-profit organisations, whereas "com" or "co" indicate a commercial enterprise.
4. http://www.endnote.com
5. American Psychological Association. (2009). *Publication manual of the American Psychological Association* (6th ed.). Washington, DC: Author. See also http://www.apastyle.org
6. Mutch, C. (2006). The sugarbag years: Politics and education intersect at the time of the Great Depression. In D. Hicks & T. Ewing (Eds.), *Education and the Great Depression: Lessons from a global history* (pp. 200–232). New York: Peter Lang Publishing.

References

Anderson, G. (1998). *Fundamentals of educational research* (2nd ed.). London: Falmer.

LeCompte, M., & Preissle, J. (1993). *Ethnography and qualitative design in educational research (2nd ed.)*. San Diego, CA: Academic Press.

Neuman, W. L. (1997). *Social research methods: Qualitative and quantitative approaches*. Boston: Allyn and Bacon.
- All three of these books have useful sections on literature reviews.

Other useful references and sources

Bell, J. (1999). *Doing your research project* (2nd ed.). Buckingham: Open University Press.

Burns, R. (2000). *Introduction to research methods* (4th ed.). French Forest, NSW: Pearson Education.

Birmingham, P. (2000). Reviewing the literature. In D. Wilkinson, (Ed.), *The researcher's toolkit: The complete guide to practitioner research* (pp. 25–39). London: RoutledgeFalmer.

Liberty, K., & Miller, J. (2003). *Research as a resource for evidence-based practice*. Palmerston North: Dunmore Press.

Wellington, J. (2000). *Educational research: Contemporary issues and practical approaches*. London: Continuum.

- All the books listed above have sections on locating sources, filing, taking notes, and preparing literature reviews.

CHAPTER 6

Choosing methods, strategies, and tools

What is the link between theory, methodology, and method?

How does your research question link to your research design?

What are common methodologies used in educational research?

How do you ensure your research can be trusted?

What are common methods, strategies, and tools used in educational research?

What is mixed methodology?

What is the link between theory, methodology, and method?

When you have decided on a topic, refined it and specified objectives, you will be in a position to consider how to collect the evidence you require. The initial question is not 'Which methodology?' but 'What do I need to know and why?' Only then do you ask 'What is the best way to collect information?' and 'When I have this information, what shall I do with it?' (Bell, 1997, p. 63)

By the time you reach this chapter, you (hopefully) will have sorted a topic, narrowed it down to a manageable research question, and considered your sources of data. You will be ready to think about which methods might help you gather the most useful data. You will also have an understanding of why some research questions fit best with particular methodologies. Figures 2.1 and 2.2 in Chapter 2 will remind you that your research question drives the process, and Figure 3.1 in Chapter 3 will remind you that your research question is often influenced by your view of the world.

Figure 6.1 combines these two sets of ideas to give you a practical example. It shows you that although a general research interest might sit most comfortably within the subjective view of the world and, in general, these questions tend to qualitative methodologies, you could rephrase the research interest as a question (and hypothesis) that would allow you to gather quantitative data. The point I am trying to make is that you choose your methodology and/or method as the one (or ones) that will best answer your question. You might also choose to use a combination of approaches.

- *Methodologies* link theoretical frameworks to methods. They usually comprise a selection of related methods and strategies.
- *Methods* are a coherent set of strategies or a particular process that you use to gather one kind of data.

Confusingly, writers often use these terms interchangeably or replace them with other terms such as paradigm, research approach, or research style. I have given you one definition for each and then used these consistently, but be aware that you might meet different definitions in your reading. Your task is to choose definitions that best explain your understanding and then use these as consistently as you can.

How does your research question link to your research design?

Your research question, once carefully formulated, will determine your research design. To review research designs, revisit Chapter 2.

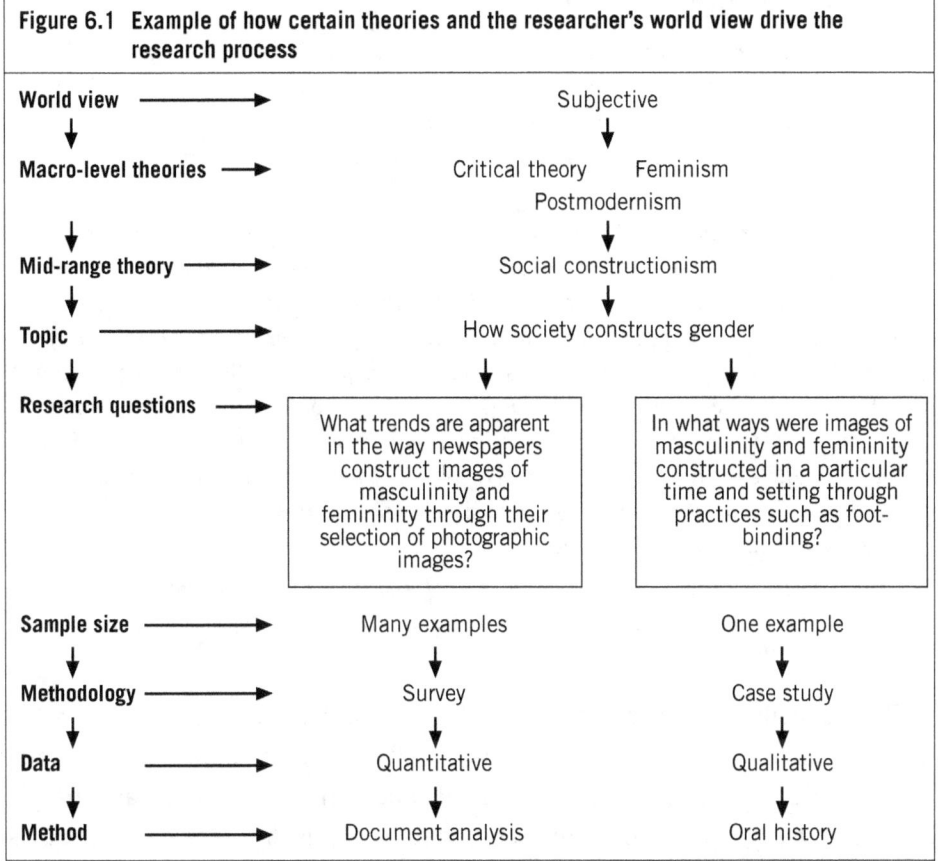

Figure 6.1 Example of how certain theories and the researcher's world view drive the research process

- If your research question requires gathering quantitative data, your research design will follow a linear "path" in which your unit of analysis, variables, and categories are determined ahead of time.
- If your research question requires gathering qualitative data, you will use an emergent design, which means you determine your categories once you have gathered your data.

Let us look at two brief examples. For the quantitative example, return to Figure 2.3 in Chapter 2 that outlined the process this way: define a research problem; formulate hypotheses; design the study; select samples and instruments; gather the data; statistically analyse the data; draw conclusions; and report the results.

1. A quantitative design

Diane was interested in the concerns raised by the Literacy Taskforce that there is a lack of information about the best strategies for underachievers in spelling. A literature review showed the advantages of various programmes but none compared a structured spelling approach with a whole-language approach and none was set in New Zealand classroom settings.

Diane chose to examine the effects of a daily 10–15 minute structured spelling programme in addition to a regular whole-language based programme. She used an experimental design, which she described as "single -case, combined multiple-baseline and reversal design". Single case means that each student's progress was compared against their baseline data. Multiple baseline means that several types of data were gathered (e.g., SRA spelling mastery test results, children's writing behaviours—number of words written in 20 minutes, accuracy of phonological and phonetic spelling—and generalisation of mastery words to free writing). Reversal meant that there was a period of baseline (regular class programme), followed by regular programme plus treatment (mastery programme), reverting to regular programme, and so on, for five cycles.

Diane gathered data and graphed them daily. She then turned this information into weekly means and analysed all data at the end of the study to see if any improvements could be attributed to the treatment.[1]

For the qualitative example, return also to Chapter 2 and review Figure 2.4 that outlined the process as a focus of inquiry that suggests a purposive sample, explored through qualitative methods of data collection in natural settings, leading to early and ongoing inductive data analysis and research outcomes presented as a case study.

2. A qualitative design

Karen was interested in the role of itinerant music teachers (ITMs) in schools. As she wanted to get a detailed description of this role from those closely involved, she chose a qualitative research design. To gauge interest, she attended one of the ITMs' regular meetings. Their interest gave her the confidence to proceed. After completing research and ethical approval formalities, she embarked on her data gathering. She conducted participant observations, semi-structured interviews, and document analysis. She coded and analysed the data to produce tentative themes. She returned her transcripts to participants and shared preliminary findings with two groups of ITMs. The feedback helped her reconsider her analysis, and she finally selected three central themes—temporality, invisibility, and adaptability—to report upon.[2]

What are common methodologies used in educational research?

The next question is how do methodologies, methods, and strategies link? Table 6.1 uses four methodologies common in educational research—two quantitative and two qualitative.

Table 6.1 Methodologies common in educational research		
Methodology	**Related methods**	**Possible strategies**
Survey—a survey gathers large scale data in order to generalise to a population.	• Questionnaire • Observation • Interview • Document analysis	• Mailed questionnaire • Time-sampling observation • Telephone interview • Content analysis
Experiment—an experiment compares variables under controlled conditions.	• Controlled experiment • Quasi-experiment	• Randomised trial • Intervention • Single-subject design
Case study—a case study focuses on providing rich description of a bounded case. The case could be a person, a setting, or a concept.	• Observation • Interview • Document analysis • Oral history	• Non-participant observation • Semi-structured interview • Discourse analysis
Ethnography—an ethnography portrays the lived reality of people in a particular setting.	• Observation • Interview • Artefact analysis	• Participant observation • Open-ended interviews • Interpretation of visuals

From this table, you can see that some methods are common to both kinds of methodologies, for example, interviews and observations. Where they differ is in their research design and the kind of data they gather. A survey interview will ask a large number of respondents the same questions and analyse the responses statistically, whereas an ethnographic interview will ask a few people very open-ended questions that could lead in different directions.

Let us look now at common research methodologies in educational research. Note that these are not totally discrete groupings; there is some overlap between them.

Common research methodologies in educational research and some examples

- **Survey**—gathers large-scale data in order to generalise to a population.
  Hasan surveyed secondary school teachers in New Zealand to find out about the use of computers in secondary mathematics teaching.[3]
- **Experiment**—compares variables under controlled conditions.
  Diane *measured the effects on seven Year 2 children of a spelling mastery programme as part of a whole language writing approach.*[4]
- **Case study**—focuses on providing rich description of a bounded case.
  Cathy conducted a case study within her early childhood teacher education programme that focused on the transition from face-to-face to distance delivery.[5]

- **Ethnography**—portrays the lived reality of people in a particular setting.
  Karen worked with itinerant music teachers to find out exactly what they did, how they viewed their role, and how the schools that used them viewed them.[6]
- **Historical research**—sets out to gather information on a historical event, person, or phenomena.
  Marie was interested in how the distance learning projects Cantatech and TOSItech came into being, and what the issues and impacts around them were.[7]
- **Policy research**—focuses on the creation, dissemination, interpretation, and implementation of educational policy from national to institutional levels.
  Murray wanted to know who determined who participated in National Educational Monitoring Project activities, and how and why, especially in relation to students with special needs.[8]
- **Action research**—focuses on one's own practices for the improvement of teaching and learning or management purposes.
  Sue worked with a team of staff in her school as they examined their approach to delivering the new arts curriculum, with the aim of improving their teaching and assessment practices.[9]
- **Programme evaluation**—uses a range of methods to evaluate the success of a particular programme or innovation.
  Elaine investigated the success of the Early Numeracy Project on changing the mathematics thinking and practices of junior primary school teachers.[10]

A range of methods, strategies, and tools is available under each of these methodologies.

- *Strategies* are a subset of methods and usually focus on a specific process. For example, a survey is a quantitative methodology, and you could conduct it via a questionnaire. Your specific strategy, then, could be to use a series of telephone interviews. A case study is generally a qualitative methodology, but you could use observation as your method and non-participant observation as your particular strategy.
- *Tools* (or instruments) are the actual things that you use to collect the data, for example, your questionnaire form, your observation matrix, or your list of interview questions. In qualitative research, the phrase "researcher-as-instrument" is sometimes used because it is the researcher who gathers the information through their descriptive field notes.

Rather than skip lightly over all the possibilities, I have chosen five methods to focus on in a little more depth later in the chapter, and I will discuss different strategies and tools within each of these. The five methods are quasi-experiment, questionnaire, observation, interview, and document analysis.

How do you ensure your research can be trusted?

Of the methods mentioned above, apart from the quasi-experiment, which works only with quantitative data, the other four methods could gather quantitative or qualitative data, or both. Before gathering your data, you need to address a major consideration. People reading or referring to your research need to be sure they can trust your design and decisions. In quantitative design, you need to convince the reader that your study is valid and reliable. In qualitative research, you need to convince the reader that your study is trustworthy and credible.

- *Validity* means that your study actually measures what it sets out to measure. This means that you must take special care that you clearly define your terms, variables, attributes, and units of analysis. Your research question should be sharp and focused, and your research design should allow you to gather and analyse data that will confirm or refute your hypothesis as it is stated. For example, if you set out to measure children's scientific understanding and you provided your subjects with some paragraphs to read and questions to answer, a reader would need to be sure that this measured scientific understanding, as per your definition, and not reading comprehension.
- *Reliability* means that you or someone else could replicate your study with similar results. If other researchers took a similar-sized sample from a similar population and reapplied your research strategy, they should be reasonably confident that their study would yield similar results.
- *Trustworthiness* means you have clearly documented the research decisions, research design, data-gathering and data-analysis techniques and demonstrated an ethical approach. Because of the nature of qualitative research, it is not possible to replicate a study and achieve similar results. The point of qualitative research is that you want each of your cases or participants to represent themselves, and although you might see parallels with other cases, you are not setting out to generalise your findings to a broader population. Your readers still need to be sure, however, that they can trust your processes and believe your findings.

- *Credibility* means that you have used some way of ensuring that your findings resonate with those in, or who are familiar with, the case or setting. One common technique is *triangulation*, where you use more than one data source, data-gathering technique, or researcher to give other perspectives on the case or setting. Another technique is *member checking*, where you return your transcripts, field notes, data analyses, or findings to the participants to see if they fit within their understanding of the phenomenon or situation

What are common methods, strategies, and tools used in educational research?

In his action research book, Geoff Mills (2000) helpfully divides data collection techniques into "Three Es"—experiencing, enquiring, and examining (see Figure 6.2).

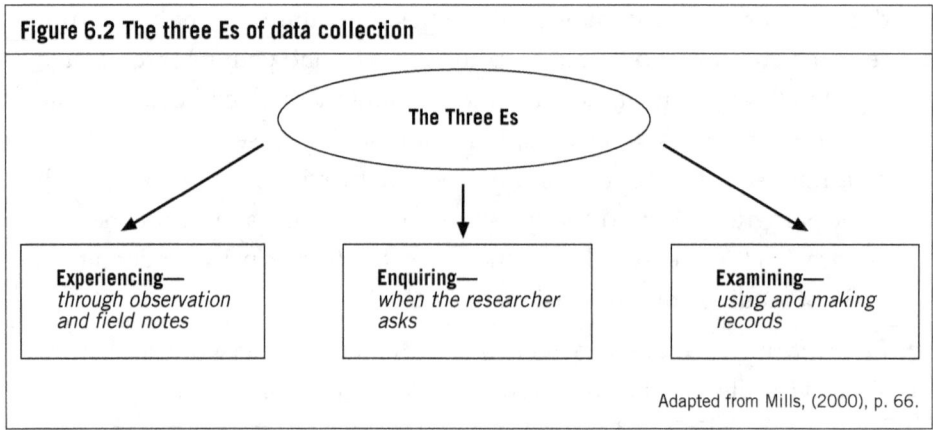

Figure 6.2 The three Es of data collection

Adapted from Mills, (2000), p. 66.

As teachers, you are already familiar with a range of data-gathering techniques that fit under Mills' headings and could be used as part of a research project under a particular research method. Here are some examples:

Experiencing

- Informal observations;
- Skills checklists;
- Behaviour monitoring;
- Time sampling; and
- Children's learning stories.

Enquiring

- Interest inventories;
- Individual conferences;
- Questionnaires;
- Pre- and post-tests;
- Running records; and
- Formal interviews.

Examining

- Students' written or art work;
- Student journals;
- Portfolios of work;
- Oral or dramatic presentations; and
- Existing statistics (student grades, attendance figures, subject choices).

Now it is time to look in depth at the five selected research methods.

Quasi-experiments

As explained earlier, an experiment needs controlled conditions to measure the effects of a treatment on selected variables. This is usually done through the use of two matching groups: a control group that does not receive the treatment, and an experimental group that does. If the groups are carefully matched in terms of various factors (e.g., gender, ethnicity, socioeconomic status), it is then presumed that the differences at the end of the treatment are due to the treatment and not to other factors.

An experiment is not an easy option for a busy classroom teacher. For a start, how can you continue teaching the whole class while this is going on? For another thing, how can you be sure, given the life experiences, home backgrounds, and learning differences that your students bring, that you can evenly match your groups? And is it even ethical to provide a treatment (that you anticipate will be beneficial) to some children in your class and withhold it from others?

For these reasons, less controlled versions of experiments are conducted. Here, the outcome of the group's treatment is compared with its starting point and not with the outcome for another group. (This is often called an intervention.) Alternatively, an individual's skill development or academic progress is compared with the baseline data gathered before the new programme was put in place (called single-subject or single-case design). All of these are quasi-experiments. A teacher working with larger groups of children in schools or early childhood centres is more likely to use a group-sized intervention. A teacher working one to one, such as a resource teacher of learning and behaviour (RTLB), might find a single-subject design more useful.

A quasi-experiment follows a quantitative research design (see Figure 6.1 earlier in this chapter) and has three key stages within this process: establishing the baseline data; providing the intervention; and measuring the results. The process, using the quantitative research design proposed by Burns (2000) (see Chapter 2), is outlined in Table 6.2.

Questionnaires, observations, and interviews can be used to gather either quantitative or qualitative data (or both), so the research design steps can be taken from either the quantitative or qualitative approaches provided in Chapter 2. What follows are specific tips—not for the design itself but for the unique aspects of each method.

Table 6.2 Key stages of a quasi-experiment research design

Stages of the design	Points to remember	An example
Define the research problem	• Narrow your research interest to something manageable. • Conduct your literature review. • Define your terms. • Determine your unit of analysis. • Determine your independent and dependent variables.	Carolyn is a Resource Teacher of Literacy working with children with reading difficulties. After conducting an in-depth literature review, she chose an individual and intensive reading tutoring programme that she hoped would improve children's reading strategies and attitudes to reading.
Formulate the hypothesis	• Write your research question. • Rewrite it as a hypothesis.	Would the "Parent Tutors in Reading" programme raise the literacy levels of children with reading difficulties?
Design the study	• Determine what your baseline data will be and how you will collect this (Stage 1). • Set out timeline and process clearly. • Apply for funding and/or ethical clearance.	To collect her baseline data, Carolyn decided to use a "Burt Word Reading Test" and "running records". These would determine the students' current reading level. Four schools were approached for parental permission for student participation and for parent volunteers.

Select samples and prepare instruments	• Decide on and justify your sampling technique. • Prepare your intervention strategy. • Prepare your data-gathering instruments. • Determine how you will record the data.	Twenty-seven children reading at least two years behind their chronological ages were chosen to participate. Twenty-two parent volunteers were trained in the "Pause, prompt, praise" method. Towards the end of the intervention, 10 parents and 10 teachers were selected randomly to complete a questionnaire.
Gather the data	• Gain access to the sample. • Put your intervention strategy in place (Stage 2). • Gather the data systematically. • Record accurately. • File carefully.	Each child received tutoring for 15 minutes per day, four days per week, for 10 weeks (in addition to their normal reading instruction). The Burt Reading Test was taken before and after the intervention and running records were taken at the baseline stage, six weeks into the intervention and at the end. Questionnaires were administered towards the end of the programme.
Statistically analyse the data	• From your raw data grid, reduce data using your categories. • Using descriptive statistics, put your data into manageable and useful states.	Carolyn compared the reading levels (from running records) at the three determined points and the Burt raw scores at baseline and completion.
Draw conclusions	• Compare final results with baseline data (Stage 3). • Use measures of significance to determine whether the results are more than chance. • Make statements about the findings in relation to your hypothesis.	All but two students increased their reading levels, with 13 students gaining three levels. This represented average gains of 2.25 levels or between 6 and 12 months reading age. Parents who completed the questionnaire rated the programme (on a 1–5 scale) an average of 4.7 for enjoyment and 4.9 for effectiveness. The teachers of the children rated the effectiveness of the programme for their students with an average of 4.3.
Prepare the results	• Display your findings as graphs or tables.	Carolyn concluded that, although this programme might not work for all children, with this group reading gains did take place and confidence levels, motivation, and general use of reading skills did increase.
Disseminate the results	• Make sure your claims are consistent with your data. • Prepare a report for relevant audiences.	Carolyn was able to share her results with the participating schools and other resource teachers of literacy.[11]

Questionnaires

Questionnaires are useful tools for collecting data from a large number of respondents. Designing a good questionnaire can be a skilled and challenging technical activity. Therefore think very carefully before deciding to use one; in your case it may not necessarily be the most appropriate tool for data collection. (Hinds, 2000, p. 42)

A questionnaire is one method of conducting a survey. A survey aims to gather enough *quantitative* data to be able to generalise to a population. Hinds (2000, p. 43) suggests that a questionnaire is best when:

- Information is sought from large numbers over a relatively large geographical area.
- The information sought is not complex.
- You are seeking information about facts, either in the present or, because of the influence of memory, in the recent past.
- You want to study particular groups, or people in a problem area, because you want to generalise about them, make comparisons with other groups or use their responses or comparisons for development.
- You are certain that a questionnaire will produce the type of information you need.
- You are certain that barriers such as language and literacy do not apply to your population.

After following the usual stages in a quantitative research design, you reach the stage where you must devise the actual instrument (or tool) itself—the questionnaire. This requires an understanding of question design.

- *Closed questions* allow respondents to select from pre-determined categories. These can be pre-coded by the researcher to save time during analysis.
- *Open questions* allow respondents to state their responses in their own way. The responses need to be coded and categorised after the questionnaires are collected.

Youngman (cited in Bell, 1997) suggests the following types of quantitative questions, and I have included examples.

- **List**: a list of options is given and respondents select the most suitable option. These can be pre-coded for ease of analysis, that is, using the example below, "Certificate" is given the code (1), "Diploma" (2), "Bachelor's" (3) and so on.
  <u>Which is your highest academic qualification? Please circle.</u>
  Certificate Diploma Bachelor's B(Hons)/PGCert/PGDip Master's Doctorate

- **Category**: a set of categories is provided and respondents select one.
  Please indicate which age category you fit into with a tick in the appropriate box.
  Under 20☐ 20–29☐ 30–39☐ 40–49☐ 50–59☐ 60–69☐ 70+☐

- **Ranking**: respondents are asked to rank items in a particular way.
  <u>Please rank the following study skills in order, with your highest preference = 1:</u>
  time management☐   critical thinking☐   organisation☐   planning☐
  preparation☐   note taking☐   summarising☐   attentive listening☐
  filing☐   memorisation☐   reading☐   participation in class☐
  group work☐

- **Scale**: scales can be nominal, ordinal, interval, or ratio (see Chapter 9 for further explanation of these terms). Likert scales are common in questionnaires. Here, respondents show their agreement with a statement along a continuum with a certain number of choices.
  Please indicate your agreement or disagreement with the following statements. Circle one.
  (SA = strongly agree; A = agree; N = neutral; D = disagree; SD = strongly disagree)
  Boys are better at mathematics than girls
  SA   A   N   D   SD
  Girls are better at reading than boys
  SA   A   N   D   SD

- **Quantity**: respondents supply the number, measure, or amount relating to the item requested.
  How many years have you been teaching? _____

- **Grid**: a matrix or grid is provided for the respondents to fill in one or more items.

Estimate the time per week that you spend in your class on the following strands of the arts curriculum and mark the correct box:	Less than 30 mins	30–60 mins	60–90 mins	90–120 mins	More than 120 mins
Music-related activities					
Drama-related activities					
Dance-related activities					
Visual arts					

Qualitative or open questions ask the respondents for their ideas, preferences, or opinions in narrative or descriptive form and are then analysed thematically (see Chapter 9).

Give your opinion about the impact of NCEA on student learning

_____

_____

_____

Advice for setting out successful questionnaires
- Keep your questionnaire to a reasonable length.
- Keep the layout clear and uncluttered.
- Keep your instructions simple and precise.
- Word your questions with care:
  - Avoid questions with in-built assumptions;
  - Avoid double-barrelled questions;
  - Avoid leading questions;
  - Avoid questions with negatives; and
  - Frame questions in a socially and culturally sensitive way.
- Consider how to maximise ease of completion for the respondent and ease of analysis for the researcher.
- Pilot (trial) your questionnaire to ensure your questions are clear and unambiguous. Ask for critical feedback. Consider reframing questions or layout if necessary.
- Set up a raw data grid or spreadsheet and trial your analysis.
- Consider how to determine and approach your sample (see Chapter 2).

- Code your questionnaires so you can keep track of your returns.
- Organise clear labelling, distribution, and filing systems.
- Prepare a timeline, including follow-up of non-returns.
- Enter data as soon as returns come in.

Finally, Bouma (1996, p. 64) offers the following advice for quantitative surveys:

> I cannot over-emphasize the fact that interview schedules and questionnaires are devices for measuring variables. Each question must have some bearing on one of the variables you are studying. These techniques are not 'fishing' expeditions in which all sorts of 'interesting' questions are asked.

Observations

Observations can be quantitative or qualitative, can focus on specific behaviours or broader descriptions, and can be one-off activities or ongoing immersion in a setting.

- A quantitative observation has a schedule with pre-set categories.
- A qualitative observation records "rich description" and later uses a thematic analysis to determine categories and themes.

A *quantitative* observation systematically records observable and measurable behaviours, occurrences, or events. If, for example, your research project had the following hypothesis, "Boys show more aggression than girls in the classroom," you might need to consider (along with everything you already know about research design and ethics):

- What concepts and terms are involved in this hypothesis (e.g., aggression, gender, classroom)?
- What kind of method might help you collect this data (e.g., quantitative observation)?
- What kind of instrument would gather the best data (e.g., observation schedule)?
- What limits will you place on your observation (i.e., classrooms only, with or without teacher, mixed- or single-sex classrooms, particular subjects/times/schools)?
- What are your variables (i.e., how will you measure aggression)?
- What is your unit of analysis (i.e., what will you count, e.g., aggressive acts)?
- How will you keep track of the subjects (e.g., sampling, multiple observers)?

You could then devise an observation schedule (similar to the one given as Figure 6.3) that is based on observable and countable aggressive acts.

Figure 6.3 Observation checklist for classroom aggression

Observer		Date	
School		Class	
Teacher			
Subject			
Period		Time	
Behaviour		Boy	Girl
1. Talking loudly or shouting			
2. Swearing			
3. Jeering or taunting			
4. Staring aggressively			
5. Physically blocking			
6. Rude gestures			
7. Flailing with arms or legs			
8. Punching or kicking			
Total aggressive acts			

Adapted from Bouma, (1996), p. 59.

Qualitative observations are more common in case studies and ethnographies. This is where observers go "into the field" (the school, classroom, staff room, work setting, marae, community meeting) to take detailed notes of everything they see and hear (and touch, taste, and smell, if relevant). They might draw plans of the layout, describe the environment, record the discussions, collect samples of the documents, and/or observe interactions and behaviours. (See also the section on writing field notes in Chapter 8.) A researcher might be distanced from the events being observed or might, in fact, participate in them.

- *Non-participant observers* do not take part in the activities they are observing. An example would be an outside researcher observing a teacher working with a class.
- *Participant observers* are involved in some way in the activities that are part of the observation. Examples would be a teacher taking notes for research purposes at one of his or her staff meetings or an early childhood worker observing in his or her own centre.

Qualitative observations, like qualitative interviews (below), need good interpersonal skills. Lofland and Lofland (1995) remind qualitative researchers that they must enter, remain in, and leave the field with sensitivity and respect.

Interviews

> Interviewing people of any age can be one of the most enjoyable and interesting activities in a research study. Interviews can reach the parts which other methods cannot reach. (Wellington, 2000, p. 73)

Anderson (1990, p. 222) defines an interview as "a specialised form of communication between people for a specific purpose associated with some agreed subject matter". Cohen and Manion (1994) suggest that research interviews serve three purposes:

- They are a principal way of gathering information relating to the research objectives;
- They can be used to test hypotheses (or suggest new ones); and
- They can be used to support other methods (e.g., to triangulate data or go deeper into elements uncovered by other methods).

Interviews have an advantage over written questionnaires in that reading ability is not a concern—the researcher can check the respondent's understanding of the questions—and once the respondent has agreed, there is a higher chance of successful completion. Telephone interviews can ensure access to a wide geographical area and, because the format is set, the interviews can be conducted by someone other than the researcher—a research assistant, for example. However, they are time intensive and, unless follow-up or further discussion of issues are likely, they might not be the most practical strategy for a busy practitioner.

- *Structured interviews* follow a questionnaire format or a set of prescribed questions.
- *Semi-structured interviews* have a set of key questions that are followed in a more open-ended manner.
- *Unstructured interviews* begin with a single open-ended question or a broad theme, and the respondent plays a bigger part in determining the direction.

Wellington (2000, citing Maykut & Morehouse, 1994) outlines the following process for preparing interview questions:
1. *Brainstorming:* jumbled, unjudged list of ideas, areas of interest.
2. *Classifying and categorising:* areas, topics and questions are grouped into classes

or categories ("categories of inquiry").
3. *Interview guide:* selection and judgement on which areas/questions will actually be explored.
4. *Interview schedule:* phrasing of all questions into meaningful language, for example, for school pupils, removing ambiguity, carefully sequencing questions, identifying and ordering open and closed questions.

An interview guide is a list of broader topics or questions to be covered that is usually used in semi-structured and unstructured interviews. It might include starter, prompt, probe, and follow-up questions. An *interview schedule* is a carefully ordered set of questions used in structured and some semi-structured interviews.

- Quantitative interviews are a verbal form of a survey because the questions and categories are pre-determined.
- Qualitative interviews are generally semi-structured or unstructured, of longer duration, and conducted one to one. This is because the researcher wants to get a more in-depth understanding of the topic or issue from the participant's perspective.

As Kvale (1996, p. 2) suggests: "The qualitative research interview is a construction site of knowledge. An interview is literally an inter view, an interchange of views between two persons conversing about a theme of mutual interest."

Qualitative interviews require the interviewer to establish a relationship with the interview participant. If the subject matter is not contentious, this may involve just a brief discussion at the start to put the participants at ease. Remind them of the purpose of the research, reassure them of the confidentiality of their contributions, and explain your approach (i.e., whether you will tape-record, write notes, keep to an interview schedule, or let the interview take its own course). You will have given them the research information sheet and consent form before the interview, so these matters should not come as a surprise, but busy people often like a reminder. Also, part of establishing an empathetic rapport is to have a conducive environment in which to conduct the interview—one that is quiet, comfortable, and free from interruptions is best.

If the interviews cover contentious or emotionally charged content, then other aspects might need to be considered—privacy, support, or follow-up counselling for the participant, debriefing for the interviewer, and the need to go at a different pace, perhaps with breaks or even stopping the interview to continue at a later time. I have been surprised that a topic that does not look contentious to begin with can often provoke strong emotional responses from the participant, so it is best to be prepared.

- *Focus group interviews* are generally of the structured type with pre-set questions but some negotiation of responses, depending on the purpose and the composition of the group.

Hinds (2000) explains *focus group interviews* as:
- Based on the principle of self disclosure;
- Set in a comfortable environment;
- Using a particular type of questioning;
- Occurring after establishing a set of focus group rules;
- Generally numbering between seven and 10 participants; and
- Gathering information about people's perceptions, ideas, and experiences.

Focus group interviews can be a useful tool for busy practitioners because they can combine the best of surveys (a broader sample) and interviews (an in-depth response). They are not as time intensive as a series of individual interviews or labour intensive as sending out a set of questionnaires. They do, however, require skill in conducting the interview and are difficult to record and transcribe. Hinds (2000, citing Kreuger, 1994) suggests two people conduct the interview, one as facilitator and the other as recorder.

Before leaving the discussion on interviews, it is useful to remind you of the ethical issues (see Chapter 4), cultural considerations (Chapters 3 and 4), practical aspects (Chapter 8), and preparation for analysing the data (Chapter 9). In relation to cultural considerations, note that the qualitative semi-structured interview sits comfortably with the Māori concepts of kanohi ki te kanohi (face-to-face) and hui (meeting). Bishop and Glynn (1999, p. 25) suggest that:

> . . . in indigenous research contexts, rather than the interview being a research tool primarily used by the researcher to gather data for subsequent processing, interviews should be developed to position the researcher within co-joint reflections on shared experiences and co-joint constructions of meanings about these experiences, a position where the stories of the research participants merge with that of the researcher in order to create new stories.

Document analysis

Document analysis is an easily accessible way to gather data to answer a question.

It is useful in historical research, in comparative research, as part of a case study, or for its own sake. It doesn't require informed consent from participants, although gaining access to or permission to use some documents might still be required. You can analyse documents quantitatively or qualitatively.

Documents can be classified as primary (coming from the original source) or secondary (having been filtered in some way—through a summary, interpretation, or second-hand account). Scott (2000) suggests that documents can be evaluated for authenticity, credibility, representativeness, and clarity of meaning before they are selected for analysis, but this would depend on the purpose of the research.

1. Content analysis

Approaching documents (or "text" in its broadest sense) in a quantitative manner by counting or measuring is called content analysis. You might count the number of times certain phrases, words, or concepts appear in a document. You might time sequences on television. You might measure the amount of printed or visual space items take up. (Do you remember the example of gender construction in Chapter 6? See also the example of quantitative analysis in Chapter 9.) Table 6.3 provides a simple strategy to follow, with an example alongside.

2. Thematic analysis

Analysing text qualitatively uses a thematic approach (see also Chapter 9). The important thing is to approach the text with an open mind and try to have it "speak for itself". What are the text's key messages? How are words used? What important themes emerge? Table 6.4 outlines this process, along with a brief example.

Mary conducted a document analysis of music curriculum documents. Here is an excerpt from her thematic analysis that focused on a comparison of the language used.[12]

Table 6.3 Process to follow when conducting a content analysis

Current analysis process	An example
1. Write research question and hypothesis. (See Ch.2)	My hypothesis is that as English is the most commonly spoken language in New Zealand, it will have more references to it in the policy document the *New Zealand Curriculum Framework* (1993).
2. Determine unit of analysis. (What exactly are you counting or measuring? People in photographs, words in print, square centimeters of type?)	I will count single words or word clusters as each occurrence (e.g., "English" or "the English language").
3. Determine sample. (Are you looking at one page, one document, a month's worth of daily newspapers? How representative of your population is your sample?)	For the purposes of this example, I will limit myself to page 10 of the *New Zealand Curriculum Framework*. This is the page that focuses on the "Language and Languages" policy statement.
4. Determine categories. (What different categories does your hypothesis suggest? What are the criteria for what is included and excluded in each category? What will you do with items that don't fit your categories?)	I will use the categories: English; Māori; Other languages; and Neutral (e.g., the word "language" without any indication that it is, or is not, English).
5. Collect data. (Record every occurrence on a raw data grid or spreadsheet. These can later be tallied, reduced and interpreted by using descriptive statistics.)	Here is my tally: English　Māori　Other languages　　　　　　　　Neutral ////　　///　　/// (Pacific Island)　　　　　　　　　 ////-////-//// 　　　　　　 // (other/another language) 　　　　　　 / (community language) 　　　　　　 / (mother tongue) 　　　　　　 / (Asian) 　　　　　　 / (European)
6. Report findings. (Display your data as graphs, and/or tables. Explain your findings in relation to your hypothesis and possible implications.)	I could display these as a bar graph in order to show a comparison across categories or I could display the results as a pie graph where each category is displayed as a percentage of the total results. My results show that of the named languages English was mentioned most (although only once more than Māori or Pacific Island languages). There were more references to languages other than English than to English itself. If these are the intentions of the policy writers, what are the implications for curriculum development in schools?

Table 6.4 Process to follow when conducting a thematic analysis	
Thematic analysis process	An example
1. Browse	Skim read the section you wish to analyse. Try to approach with an open mind. Don't go in expecting to find something—try to see what the document is telling you. Stop and consider if particular aspects have caught your attention—what and why?
2. Highlight	Read more closely, underlining or highlighting anything of interest—a repeated concept, a common word, a recurring theme, an image, a metaphor, a particular literary device, a comparison, an argument, a contradiction.
3. Code	*Coding* is what qualitative researchers call the first step in determining categories. At this stage, your categories are still quite loose. When coding, you write key words or themes in the margin as you read.
4. Group and label	You are now ready to look at patterns emerging from your coding more closely. You might look specifically at similarities between this document and others, or between this section and other sections of the same document. You might write your ideas down on strips of paper or cards so that you can physically move them around. What are all the different ways you can group your codes or themes? What concepts seem to go together? How would you label these groups? What criteria determine what goes in a particular group or category? What do you do with words or concepts that don't fit?
5. Develop themes or categories	From your grouping and labelling exercise what bigger themes or categories are apparent? Are there some themes that are stronger or more important than others? Are there any links between the themes? Do they suggest a particular format—timeline, matrix, flow diagram?
6. Check for consistency and resonance	Once you have decided on themes that you want to explore further or discuss in more depth, look back at the original text of the document. Do the themes seem valid and consistent? Using your experience, knowledge, reading, and common sense, do your findings "ring true"? Would they "resonate" with other researchers working in this field or with the relevant research and theoretical literature?
7. Select examples	When you are comfortable with your thematic analysis, revisit the original text to select quotations to exemplify what you are describing. You might choose typical examples (or an atypical example and then explain why it was so).
8. Report findings	Your findings are presented by summarising the key themes, providing relevant examples, suggesting a possible theoretical explanation for why this has occurred and, as with other types of research, raising issues, highlighting implications, and suggesting further research.

1970	1992
Many sentences are verbose, detailed, emotive, directive, and difficult to follow and leave no room for teacher/pupil initiative and divergent thinking."A more fruitful and psychologically sound approach applicable to the introduction (p.87) ... may even give the modicum of attention necessary for the evocation of a pleasurable but rather vague emotional response (p.18)... a classroom teacher spends inordinate amounts of time creating a climate. He will probably expedite the growth of his insight into the piece (p.21)."	Sentences are shorter, specific, to the point, easier to follow and allow individualism in teacher input, choice, and creativity."The difference between hearing and listening is that listening is active (p.23) ... each music lesson should have a focus ... be careful not to explain too much (p.25) ... provide games which develop musical skills (p.175) ...plan the physical environment to ensure the lesson will flow smoothly (p.175) ... make your evaluations descriptive rather than judgemental (p.177)."

Before using any of these strategies, you might like to read Chapter 8 on implementing research, and Chapter 9 on analysing data.

What is mixed methodology?

Up to this point, we have dealt with quantitative and qualitative research designs, methodologies, and methods separately for ease of understanding. In fact, it is quite common for researchers to mix their methodologies in order to best answer their research questions. Mixed methodology research can follow several different approaches:

- The approach has one main research design, either quantitative or qualitative, but includes methodologies/methods from the other paradigm to expand or enhance data collection.
- The approach uses the two designs in a complementary manner using a purpose-built design.
- The approach uses a series of smaller studies under the umbrella of a larger project.

Following is an example of the last of these mixed methodology approaches.

Veronica and Sue have been working with the "Project on Learning" under the direction of the late Emeritus Professor Graham Nuthall. This three-year research project consisted of a series of eight classroom-based studies of children's learning. The focus was on how students, aged between 9 and 11 years, learn from their classroom experiences and the kinds of learning involved. The project was also interested in the relationship between teaching and learning. The project used a comprehensive and extensive mixed methodology approach, including the following data collection strategies:

- *running record observations;*
- *audio and video-taped recordings;*

- *pre- and post-tests related to content;*
- *extended interviews that explored student knowledge and thinking about curriculum content and feelings and beliefs about learning;*
- *interviews with teachers related to unit planning, evaluation, pedagogy, and perceptions about student learning;*
- *photocopies of all work produced by students; and*
- *photographic records of key resources used by students.*

As Veronica and Sue explain, "Transcribing and detailed coding of these data have enabled tracking of the moment-by-moment experiences of students as they negotiate the academic and social life of the classroom."[13]

Chapter summary

- Your research question should drive the research process by suggesting a particular methodology and method.
- Your research question is often influenced by your view of the world, which in turns fits best with a certain methodology.
- Methodologies link theoretical frameworks to methods, and methods are a coherent set of strategies or a particular process that is used to gather data.
- Common research methodologies in educational research include surveys, experiments, case studies, ethnographies, historical research, policy research, action research, and programme evaluation.
- Methods are a coherent set of strategies or a consistent process that gather one main form of data.
- Strategies are a subset of methods and usually focus on a specific process.
- Tools (or instruments) are the actual things that collect the data.
- Useful research methods for busy practitioners are quasi-experiments, questionnaires, observations, interviews, and document analysis.
- Many educational research projects use mixed methodologies.

Notes

1. Walker, D. (2003). *The effects of the spelling of Year 2, 6 year old children when SRA spelling mastery is added to the whole language process writing approach to written language.* Unpublished Master of Teaching and Learning thesis, Christchurch College of Education.
2. Carter, K. (2003). *Itinerant teachers of music: A state of flux.* Unpublished Master of Teaching and Learning research project, Christchurch College of Education.

3. Toubat, H. M. (2003). *The use of computer technology in secondary mathematics teaching in New Zealand schools: A survey of teachers.* Unpublished Master of Teaching and Learning thesis, Christchurch College of Education.
4. Walker (2003).
5. Hide, C. (2002). *Tutor perspectives on the transition to distance delivery in teacher education: A case study.* Unpublished Master of Teaching and Learning research project, Christchurch College of Education.
6. Carter (2003).
7. Langley, M. (2003). *Case study of the Cantatech and TOSItech distance learning projects.* Unpublished Master of Teaching and Learning thesis, Christchurch College of Education.
8. Overton, M. (2003). *NEMP assessment and children with special needs.* Unpublished Master of Teaching and Learning research project, Christchurch College of Education.
9. Rose, S. (2002). *How do we improve the delivery of the Arts curriculum in our school?* Unpublished Master of Teaching and Learning research project, Christchurch College of Education.
10. Bolitho, E. (2003). *The Early Numeracy Project: A study of teacher change.* Unpublished Master of Teaching and Learning research project, Christchurch College of Education.
11. Boland, C. (2002). *Adult assisted in-school tutoring of children experiencing difficulties in reading.* Unpublished paper, Resource Teacher of Literacy Training Programme, Christchurch College of Education.
12. Fenwick, M. (1999). *A comparison of the 1970 and 1992 music curriculum documents.* Unpublished assignment completed for HA646, Investigating Issues in Curriculum, Christchurch College of Education.
13. Collins, S. (2004). *The relationship between what the teacher does and how that causes children to think and behave as they do in the classroom context.* Unpublished manuscript, Christchurch College of Education; and O'Toole, V. (2004). *The role of mood or emotion in children's learning task engagement in the elementary classroom.* Unpublished manuscript, Christchurch College of Education.

References

Anderson, G. (1990). *Fundamentals of educational research* (1st ed.). London: Falmer.
- See also the second edition, 1998.

Bell, J. (1997). *Doing your research project*. Buckingham: Open University Press.
- Useful chapters on questionnaires, documents, interviews, diaries, and observations.

Bishop, R., & Glynn, T. (1999). *Culture counts*. Palmerston North: Dunmore Press.
- Useful chapter related to research in Māori contexts.

Bouma, G. (1996). *The research process*. Melbourne: Oxford University Press.

Burns, R. (2000). *Introduction to research methods* (4th ed.). Melbourne: Longman.

Cohen, L., & Manion, L. (1994). *Research methods in education* (4th ed.). London: Routledge.
- Very detailed chapters on research methods. See also the fifth edition, 2000.

Hinds, D. (2000). Research instruments. In D. Wilkinson (Ed.), *The researcher's toolkit: The complete guide to practitioner research* (pp. 41–54). London: RoutledgeFalmer.
- Helpful tips on different methods.

Kvale, S. (1996). *InterViews: An introduction to qualitative research interviewing*. Thousand Oaks, CA: Sage.
- Very thorough approach to qualitative interviewing.

Lofland, J., & Lofland, L. (1995). *Analysing social settings: A guide to qualitative observation and analysis* (3rd ed.). Belmont, CA: Wandsworth.
- Useful guide to qualitative methods.

Mills, G. (2000). *Action research: A guide for the teacher researcher*. Upper Saddle River, NJ: Prentice Hall/Merrill.

Scott, D. (2000). *Reading educational research and policy*. London: RoutledgeFalmer.

Wellington, J. (2000). *Educational research: Contemporary issues and practical approaches*. London: Continuum.
- Includes chapters on interviewing, document analysis, and surveys.

Other useful references and sources

Bassey, M. (1999). *Case study research in educational settings*. Buckingham: Oxford University Press.

Bennett, J. (2003). *Evaluation methods in research*. London: Continuum.

Cox, J. (1996). *Your opinion please! How to build the best questionnaires in the field of education*. Thousand Oaks, CA: Corwin Press.

Davidson, C., & Tolich, M. (1999). *Social science research in New Zealand*. Auckland: Longman.
- Case studies of a broad range of research methods.

De Laine, M. (2000). *Fieldwork, participation and practice: Ethics and dilemmas in qualitative research*. London: Sage.

Denzin, N., & Lincoln, Y. (Eds.) (1994). *Handbook of qualitative research*. Thousand Oaks, CA: Sage.

Gillham, B. (2000). *Developing a questionnaire*. London: Continuum.

Gomm, R., Hammersley, M., & Foster, P. (Eds.) (2000). *Case study method*. London: Sage.

Jenkins, P. (1999). *Surveys and questionnaires*. Wellington: New Zealand Council for Educational Research.

Kellehear, A. (1993). *The unobtrusive researcher*. St Leonards, NSW: Allen and Unwin.

McCulloch, G., & Richardson, W. (2000). *Historical research in educational settings*. Buckingham: Oxford University Press.

Robson, C. (1993). *Real world research*. Oxford: Blackwell.

Statistics New Zealand. (1995). *A good guide to survey design*. Wellington: Author.

Vaughn, S., Schumm, J., & Sinagub, J. (1996). *Focus group interviews in education and psychology*. Thousand Oaks, CA: Sage.

CHAPTER 7

Writing research proposals

- What is the purpose of a research proposal?
- What is a common format for a research proposal?
- At what stage do you write a research proposal?
- How much do those who approve your proposal influence its content and format?
- How do you set a budget?

What is the purpose of a research proposal?

The research proposal is a central feature of the research world. Typically, the presentation and approval of a formal proposal is required before a piece of research can proceed. (Punch, 2000, p. 1)

As Keith Punch reminds us, someone needs to approve a piece of research before it is undertaken to protect both the researcher and the researched. A research proposal is the mechanism by which we can clarify what we want to do and by which someone else can consider our intentions and give approval. Table 7.1 sets out some reasons we might have to write a research proposal and to whom we might be accountable.

Members on any of the authorities given in Table 7.1 will have questions similar to the following in mind as they read your proposal:
- What are you intending to do?
- Is the research worth doing?
- How can they be sure you know what you are doing?
- How carefully have you thought through the issues?
- What more do they need to know before they feel comfortable giving approval?

Table 7.1 Research proposal approvals

Purpose	Research approval mechanism
• To complete research as part of an academic qualification	• The degree programme or higher education institution's research approval panel
• To win funding for research to be undertaken	• The funding body's research approval committee
• To tender for an advertised research contract	• The body letting the contract (e.g., the Ministry of Education)
• To undertake research within a classroom or school/centre/institution	• The board of trustees or equivalent (e.g., local iwi) or their nominated representative (e.g., the principal, supervisor, or kaumatua)
• To undertake research that does not require approval from any of the above	• Your own organisation's approval system or • A research project advisory committee constituted by the researcher

Punch (2000, p. 22) suggests your proposal must deal with the following main themes, which he calls the "what", "how", and "why" of the research:
- *What* the proposed research is about;
- *What* it is trying to find out or achieve;

- *How* it will go about doing that;
- *What* we will learn from that; and
- *Why* it is worth learning.

In terms of clarifying for yourself and your readers exactly what you are proposing to do, I have found a research matrix is a useful place to start. Table 7.2 is an example of the headings you might use. I have put it together with reference to my research on educational policy making (discussed earlier in the book).[1]

Table 7.2 Example of a research matrix

Research question(s)	Sources of data	Selected data-gathering strategies	Selected analytic and interpretive strategies	Other issues to be considered
How are educational policy decisions made in New Zealand?	• Document sources—published and unpublished documents, accounts, commentary • Human sources—élite policy makers, key observers	• Historical and archival research • Literature search • Semi-structured interviews	• Summarising and synthesising • Constant comparative thematic analysis of transcripts • Constructing a flow diagram of the process	• Access to documents and records • Authenticity • Triangulation • Access to individuals • Ethical considerations

What is a common format for a research proposal?

Punch (2000, p. 67) goes on to provide a basic template for a research proposal that can be adapted to suit your purposes. I've altered some of the wording to be consistent with the terms used in this book and also added a few extra items.

i. Title and title page
ii. Abstract
iii. Introduction
- Area and topic
- Background and context
- Statement of purpose (or aims)
- Significance of the study
- Researcher or research team experience (if relevant)

iv. Research questions
- General
- Specific

v. Conceptual framework, theory, hypothesis (if appropriate)
   vi. Literature review
   vii. Methodology
   - Design—overall methodological framework and methods
   - Sample, case(s), and/or data sources
   - Data collection strategies and tools
   - Data analysis techniques
   - Limitations (and how these might be addressed)
   - Timeline
   - Ethical considerations
   viii. Proposed dissemination
   ix. Budget
   x. References
   xi. Appendices

An *abstract* summarises the key points of the research in 100–200 words. In this case, it could include topic, purpose, theory, methodology, and significance. (Yes, that is no more than a sentence or two on each aspect!) In finished research, it would also include important findings and implications. Most people write the abstract last, when they have worked those ideas through thoroughly.

Appendices are items that support the ideas in the main document but are too detailed to be included in the text. Examples in the proposal could be the participant information letter, a sample consent form, a full budget breakdown, or a copy of the actual research tool (e.g., a questionnaire). Other examples in completed research reports include fuller data tables from quantitative analysis or samples of coding used in qualitative analysis.

At what stage do you write a research proposal?

This will depend, of course, on whom it is for and what the timeline is. If you are putting in an expression of interest or tendering for a contract and you only have a two-week turn-around, then you will be completing it immediately. If it is for a qualification, then you will be expected to know the theoretical, substantive, and methodological literature to some extent and to have worked on your research question and research design. You might be expected to complete ethical approval requirements at the same time as the proposal or separately, either before or subsequent to research approval.

The following suggestions are for a research proposal process that allows you sufficient time to prepare a coherent document:

1. Define the research topic and refine the research question through reading, discussing, thinking, and writing.
2. Read around the literature—theoretical, substantive (content), and methodological.
3. Consider the research design and the subsequent decisions flowing from that.
4. Work through the practicalities of access, cost, implementation, and analysis.
5. Consider the ethical issues involved.
6. Do some more reading, writing, and talking.
7. Sketch a research design and possible timeline. Try to make a realistic estimate of the time involved and note that most of us underestimate the time our study will take, so add a little extra to compensate for this.
8. If the approval body hasn't provided a set of headings, set up a template based on those suggested above.
9. Complete a first draft.
10. Have the draft reviewed by a peer or "critical friend".
11. Complete a final draft, and then carefully proofread (including spell-checking) it, and read for comprehensiveness, coherence, and clarity of content.

How much do those who approve your proposal influence its content and format?

The answer to the above question depends on whether you are a novice or experienced researcher.

Novice researchers

Novice researchers apply to conduct research under the supervision of an institution or experienced researcher, usually towards the completion of a qualification. In this case, the researchers are completing a kind of apprenticeship in research. On successfully completing this undertaking, they can conduct research in the future without such close supervision.

If you are a novice researcher, a research approval body will want the following assurances from your research proposal.
- Your topic is appropriate and manageable given the constraints of time, skill, and resources.
- You are adequately supported by an experienced mentor (supervisor or committee) and will have adequate resource support (e.g., library access).
- You are conversant with the relevant literature and can demonstrate how the study will contribute to the field.

- You have carefully thought through the topic, question, research design, and ethical issues. (With novice researchers, there is often a need to be more explicit about theoretical frameworks and methodological decisions.)

Some institutions also require an oral defence of a research proposal. This allows candidates to clarify their thinking with a group of peers and experienced researchers who can offer useful critique in a supportive atmosphere before the research gets underway.

Experienced researchers

Experienced researchers have completed a qualification or gained practical experience that gives them the credibility to conduct research as an individual or as part of a team. Researchers in this category often apply for research contracts or funding with set specifications. If you are an experienced researcher, your proposal needs to provide not only a clear purpose, sound research design, consideration of ethical issues, and so on, but also the following:
- Details of your experience or, if you are part of a team, the team members' experience and areas of expertise, and how these cover the range of aspects in the research proposal.
- Evidence that you have consulted with an advisory committee, groups representing the interests of the participants (e.g., local iwi, teacher unions, principals' associations, community groups), and experts in the field (if relevant).
- Evidence of peer review within the process, or referees who can vouch for your (and your team members') abilities and experiences.
- Thorough knowledge of the literature, especially prior research on the topic and articulation of what this research will contribute to the field.
- Thorough detail of the practical aspects, such as timeline, consultation schedule, budget, and reporting frameworks.

Some funding agencies or research bodies expect the researcher or team to demonstrate how they will keep within the expected parameters of the research framework, how they will meet milestones or reporting deadlines, and how they will manage relationships, conflicts of interest, and other potential issues.

How do you set a budget?

My former colleague, Missy Morton, has very sound advice when preparing a research budget.[2] Some initial questions to consider are:
- Is a budget figure or range given?

- Is GST included?
- What does your institution expect in the way of overheads (to cover room usage, access to facilities, and so on)?
- Does your institution have a budget template?
- Is there a formula or set of guidelines to assist you?
- Is there a protocol for preparing, consulting, and signing off on a research budget, proposal, or contract?
- Have you considered all the obvious, hidden, and unexpected costs related to your research?

Missy suggests that you use the framework given in Table 7.3 to identify the key tasks and costs. After putting in initial estimates, work both across and down to trim or expand as needed. Ask yourself if you are trying to do too much in the allotted time and with the allocated budget.

Table 7.3 Research budget—key tasks and associated costs				
Research questions	Tasks required and strategies proposed to answer questions	Project phases and timeframe	Resources required	Estimated costs
Take these from the RFP (research funding proposal), contract guidelines, or your own research proposal. Include sub-questions.	Write down everything you will do from the proposal through ethical clearance, and all aspects of your research design through to presenting the final report.	Identify the best sequence and clearly outline each stage, including what needs to happen before and after each stage. Determine how long each stage will take. Assign milestone-writing targets, if required.	Match each task with the necessary resources. Researcher time is usually the biggest resource required. Consider also: literature review costs, materials, equipment, communication, travel, accommodation, consultation, koha, and institutional overheads.	Put a figure on each resource. Remember in salaries to include ACC contributions and holiday pay. Are salaries direct or indirect costs? In materials and equipment, remember to include room rental, phone, Internet access, a business margin or increases/overruns line.

If a budget format is not supplied, Table 7.4 provides one you can use, or amend to suit.

Table 7.4 Research budget—a suggested format	
RESEARCH BUDGET	
Item	**$**
Salaries *Direct costs*—usually expressed as $ per hour or FTE (full-time equivalent) *0.2 FTE = one person for one day per week*	
Indirect costs	$xxx
Total salary costs	$xxx
Search and document retrieval *Include number of items and cost per item (ask your library)*	$xxx
Printing and copying *Check with your copy centre*	$xxx
Stationery and postage *Check with your mail centre*	$xxx
Telecommunications *Estimate number of calls, cost per call, including video/audioconferences*	$xxx
Travel and accommodation *Estimate where and how often, check with travel agent or on the web, include rental cars or mileage allowance if using own car*	$xxx
Consultation and koha *If researching in a context where you need to return to present research findings, include these costs*	$xxx
Sub-total *Find out what the maximum allowable/possible is for this figure (less GST)*	$xxx
GST (15%)	$xxx
Total cost	$xxx

Chapter summary

- A research proposal is completed for two reasons: to clarify the research intentions and to gain approval for the research to proceed.
- Research proposals should outline the "what", "why", and "how" of the proposed research.
- A basic template includes an abstract, the topic, question, context, theoretical framework, literature review, research design, ethical considerations, and relevant appendices.

- As a research proposal is a complete document in itself, it should receive as much time and care as possible.
- Proposals should be tailored to the audience and the specifications of the approval body.
- A proposed budget should be clear, detailed, and realistic in terms of task and timeline.

Notes

1. Mutch, C. (2004, November). *Who pays the piper? Educational policy making in New Zealand*. Paper presented at New Zealand Association for Research in Education Conference.
2. Morton, M. (2004, August). *Preparing a budget for a research proposal*. Presentation given at Christchurch Polytechnic Institute of Technology.

Reference

Punch, K. (2000). *Developing effective research proposals*. London: Sage.
- A detailed look at research proposals; especially useful for larger projects.

Other useful references and sources

Bushaway, R. (2003). *Managing research*. Maidenhead: Open University Press.
Wilkinson, D. (2000). Planning the research. In D. Wilkinson (Ed.), *The researcher's toolkit: The complete guide to practitioner research* (pp. 15–23). London: RoutledgeFalmer.
- Both books have useful sections on planning research projects.

CHAPTER 8

Conducting the research

What factors make for successful implementation?

What equipment do you need and how do you manage it?

What are field notes and why do you take them?

How do you manage all that data?

What is a research journal and why is it helpful?

What do you need to be aware of when conducting research with children?

What factors make for successful implementation?

> We all learn how to do research by actually doing it, but a great deal of time can be wasted and goodwill dissipated by inadequate preparation. (Bell, 1999, p. 1)

As Judith Bell points out, the most important factor in successful research is adequate preparation. Steinar Kvale (1996) has two metaphors for research. The positivist (usually quantitative) researcher is a miner who sets out to unearth gems of truth. The interpretive (usually qualitative) researcher sets out on a journey, with the story constructed according to the people the researcher interacts with and the events that happen along the way. Whichever kind of researcher you are—a miner or a traveller—these metaphors reinforce the point that research needs a range of factors, such as adequate preparation and appropriate equipment, for the outcome to be successful.

As I mentioned in the previous chapter, we often underestimate the time taken to conduct research. Dividing time into thirds (one third preparation, one third implementation, and one third concluding activities) is a useful structure to follow. If you have followed the suggestions in this book, then you will already have considered and implemented many of these aspects. However, it is worth outlining them again in more depth. In Table 8.1, I follow this three-stage structure, but you might find that for some research it is a little artificial because the stages might overlap or steps from one stage might also appear in others.

What equipment do you need and how do you manage it?

Your equipment, of course, depends on your research design. When conducting my recent research in Wellington (away from my home town), you might have thought I was preparing to go mountain climbing because I took so much care over my preparation. But the analogy is not inappropriate—sitting in a busy official's office with a voice recorder that isn't working is a little like arriving at a certain point on Mt Everest without an oxygen tank. I couldn't say, "Excuse me while I just pop out and get some new batteries."

For my interviews, I took:
- A full set of copies of the research details—research proposal, ethical clearance sheets, and participant information sheets.
- Two copies of the itinerary, with appointment times, participant contact details, and a map of how to get from one place to another. One copy I pasted in my diary and the other went in my research folder.
- Two pearlcorders (handheld dictaphones) and spare batteries.

Table 8.1 Factors to consider when implementing research

Stage of the research process	Factors to consider
1. Preparation	• Research design—including purpose, question, theoretical framework, methodology, method, strategies, and tools (see Chapters 1, 2, 3, and 6) • Literature access and review (Chapters 1 and 5) • Research approval and funding (Chapter 7) • Ethical clearance (Chapter 4) • Cultural considerations (Chapters 2 and 3) • Access to data sources, participants and/or settings (Chapters 2 and 4) • Resources needed—materials, finances, research support (Chapter 7) • Practical considerations—travel arrangements, storage, back-ups, equipment (see Table 8.2)
2. Implementation	• Arrival at site (if appropriate)—location, introductions, explanations • Distribution of data-gathering tools—by mail, email, in person, through research assistants • Practical data-gathering requirements—tools, equipment, back-up, intervention materials • Changing circumstances that necessitate amended research decisions or ethical considerations • Concluding data gathering—expressing thanks, gathering and collating (and transporting) data, materials and tools, providing information to participants on next steps in the process
3. Conclusion	• Storage and filing of raw and processed data • Access to and use of analytic tools (Chapter 9) • Practical data-analysis considerations—time, location, support (Chapter 9) • Meeting deadlines • Report writing and dissemination (Chapter 10)

- Cassette tapes with the participants' research codes printed on (and spare tapes). With the advent of digital technologies, this is no longer necessary but labelling digital files for easy storage and retrieval still is.
- One plastic A4 zip-lock bag per participant containing a copy of the signed consent form, the information sheet, the question starters, coded notepaper, and the participant's tape.
- My research kit—pad, pencils, highlighters, watch, stapler, business cards.

All this I kept in one bag—the kind you get when you go to a conference is ideal. If you have more than one project on the go at any one time, put all the materials needed for each project in a different bag, as this saves a lot of reshuffling.[1] (Just make sure you pick up the right bag!) Table 8.2 offers some more general suggestions for you to consider at each stage.

Table 8.2 Tips for managing collection of data	
Stage of the research process	Equipment or materials needed
1. Preparation	• Filing systems, both physical and electronic • Back-up systems • Resource access—computer, printer, photocopier
2. Implementation	• Your research kit (see above) • Your research details (see previous page) • Research tools—questionnaires, observation schedules, interview questions • Research materials—resources or artefacts used for the research activity, intervention, discussion or interpretation with participants • Recording materials and appropriate spares and back-ups—writing materials, video recorder, camera, digital recorder • Koha or tokens of appreciation as appropriate
3. Conclusion	• Secure storage facilities for raw and processed data • Transcribing equipment • Access to analytic tools—computer packages such as SPSS, NVivo, Statview[2] or materials needed to physically code and manipulate data as appropriate to your research design

What are field notes and why do you take them?

Researchers often refer to carrying out their research as "going into the field". Field notes, therefore, are the formal and informal notes that you make before, during, and after this "immersion" in the field. Bogdan and Biklen (1992) suggest three types of field notes—descriptive, reflective, and analytic.

1. *Descriptive field notes* answer the questions, "Where am I?" and "What's going on here?" They are particularly important in case study and ethnographic research, but they might also be useful in setting the scene for other types of research. If I am conducting research in a school, I often stop for several minutes outside, considering what the buildings, layout, signs, and items on display tell me about the school. I do the same with classrooms, the principal's office, staff rooms, even people I might be interviewing. It all adds to the gathering of data, especially in qualitative research where our aim is "rich description". Here is an example from descriptive field notes that I later used as part of my evidence in a research article:[3]

   As I enter the classroom foyer, I am met by a welcome sign and a series of coloured labels: "This is an inquiry classroom. Are you an independent learner? Are you excited by learning? Then this is the place for you. Your teachers are here to help you." The foyer is set out as an extension of the classroom, containing posters and displays. A digital photo of every child is accompanied by a statement about what makes them a good friend. Examples of work from their rules and responsibilities unit, photos from their science trip and a written language unit, and a collage of children's personal symbols and mottoes are on display.

2. *Reflective field notes* answer the questions, "What is my response to what I see? and "What does this remind me of?" These are more personal responses. They are particularly important in observations and interviews when, for example, the voice recorder can't show the participants' expressions or body language and your responses to these. Such nuances are lost even more when interviews are turned into transcripts.
3. *Analytic field notes* answer the questions, "What patterns and themes are emerging?" and "What do I think this means?"

Table 8.3 shows how I set out my field notes.

Table 8.3 Example of taking different types of field notes		
Reflective field notes	**Descriptive field notes** (main column)	**Analytic field notes**
What is my response to what I see?	Where am I?	What patterns and themes are emerging?
	What do I see (hear/smell)?	
What does this remind me of?	What's going on here?	What do I think this means?
In this space I record, using shorthand words and symbols, reactions to items appearing in the main column.	In this space the main data is gathered. This might be my detailed observations of a setting or my notes taken during an interview.	This space is for my first impressions of key words, recurring images, repeated phrases, and emerging themes.
	Note: Examples developed from research conducted by Mutch (2003).	

How do you manage all that data?

Managing data should not be a problem if you have set up a good filing system. It helps to keep each step of the process together—and to have back-up copies of all important material. We have all heard stories of people who have had their laptop computers stolen and not had back-ups! I keep my material together in sections, such as:

- Background material (filed articles, literature review);
- Research details (research proposal, ethical clearance application, research instruments);

- Raw data (completed research instruments, e.g., questionnaire returns, interview transcripts, observation sheets, field notes); and
- Processed and reduced data (spreadsheets, graphs, tables, and tentative findings or codes, themes, categories, and selected examples).

As I process and reduce data, I label and file raw material and earlier versions until I am left with a manageable summary. Sometimes I do this reduction process electronically, using a spreadsheet program such as Excel or a statistics package like Statview. These allow you to input, store, and manipulate data from quantitative studies. There are also packages that allow you to do the same with qualitative data, such as NVivo, but some qualitative researchers prefer to physically cut and paste (i.e., with scissors) and move chunks of data (such as cut-up interview transcripts, or codes and categories written on cards) so they can see it all spread out before them. Chapter 9 gives more detail about the actual analysis process. In this section, I simply want you to plan a way of filing, managing, and retrieving your data easily.

What is a research journal and why is it helpful?

> In recent years, the idea of teachers keeping a record of their own professional and career development has gained in currency. People have spoken variously of professional journals, logs and portfolios . . . It is possible therefore either to opt for a record of outlining events and activities or aim for a collection of reflections on practice—or a combination of both. (Craft, 1996, p. 174)

Keeping a research journal is one way that you can become reflexive and reflective. These are attitudes towards yourself and your conduct as a researcher that this book has tried to foster. Wellington (2000) explains the difference between the two.

- *Reflexivity* is about interrogating yourself—who you are, what your influences are, where you stand theoretically, how this impacts on what you do (see Chapter 3).
- *Reflectivity* is about reflecting critically on your decisions and actions.

Many beginning researchers find keeping a research journal helps them chart their development as they face challenges, learn new skills, and come to new understandings. Many experienced researchers continue this practice for both personal and professional reasons. At a personal level, this practice helps the researcher articulate frustrations and work out problems as well as highlight the joys and rewards of conducting research. In professional terms, the journal becomes a kind of audit trail that lets the researcher document decisions and the justifications for these. Do you ever find that a great idea comes to you in the middle of the night and you have nowhere to write it down? A research journal provides a place for important emerging ideas to be articulated, refined, reshaped, and, later, retrieved.

Keeping a research journal is a very personal thing. Find a way that is easy to manage and that suits your needs and way of operating. One of my colleagues carries a spiral-bound notebook and regularly records insights and ideas. (For her, everything is data!) I keep a hard-covered exercise book in which I write—less frequently than my colleague!—details of each particular research project and the big decisions I am facing or the key ideas that are emerging. If you are writing in a journal for the first time, you might feel a little self-conscious, but as you gain confidence, you'll find it a useful (if not indispensable) tool. Here are some questions to ask yourself before you get started:

- What kind of format is best for me (notebook, electronic, daily diary)?
- How often will I write (regularly, daily, weekly, when the mood takes me)?
- How will I record my thoughts (notes, narratives, stream of consciousness, bullet points, mind-maps)?
- What will I record (problems, research decisions, brainstorms of solutions, SWOT[4] analysis, emerging ideas, anything and everything)?

What do you need to be aware of when conducting research with children?

Before leaving this chapter on conducting research, I want to consider situations that might require a different way of operating. In Chapters 3 and 4, I discussed the care needed when researching in cultural contexts outside your own. In this chapter, I focus on researching with children and young people.

> To be able to interview a child, one must first have a basic understanding of how a child thinks and communicates. A child's thinking is dependent on a number of factors including memory, conceptual development and language formation. (Wilson & Powell, 2001, p. 1)

The above quote alerts us to some of the considerations when researching with children and young people. McDonald and Topper (cited in Vaughn, Schumm, & Sinagub, 1996) classified types of research conducted with children they had observed. These were an adult-oriented approach, a creative-drama approach, and a structural approach.

The first approach did not alter the research approach from that used with adults. The second promoted more creative open-ended responses (usually in a simulated setting), and the third had children perform structured tasks or answer questions relevant to their experiences or understandings. Each of these might have a purpose in relation to the research question. However, in general, our experience as educators would have us take account of developmental levels. Factors to consider when researching with children or young people follow.

- *Children and young people as data sources:* Are they necessarily the best data sources in relation to your research interest or question? Will there be limitations due to language, emotional, or conceptual development? If so, how will you overcome these?
- *The choice of the research question:* How will you frame the research question to take account of the particular needs, interests, and developmental levels of the children/young people?
- *Ethical issues:* Is the question appropriate for children/young people? Who needs to give permission? Will there be any deviation from usual ethical practices (e.g., voluntary participation or avoiding deception)? How will you justify these and who will approve them?
- *Research implementation:* What methods will be appropriate for the developmental levels and allow you to gather the data required? What modifications might you need to make to the research tools (to cater for language or skill levels)? What setting will the research take place in, and will you need to modify it? If you intend using recording equipment, what will be the advantages and disadvantages of this? What allowance do you need to make for concentration span, interruptions, distractions, and so on?
- *Concluding the research:* What kind of closure, summing up, reporting back, and debriefing might you need at the conclusion of each stage or at the end of the project?

Chapter summary

- Careful planning and preparation are the keys to successful research implementation.
- Equipment needs to be accessed and managed at all stages of the research (preparation, implementation, and conclusion).
- There are three types of field notes—descriptive, reflective, and analytic.
- Careful collating, labelling, and filing are central to data management and retrieval.

- A research journal is both a personal learning tool and a professional audit trail to encourage reflexivity and reflectivity.
- Research with children needs to be ethically justified, sensitive to their stages of development, and open to modification of methods, setting, and tools.

Notes

1. Thanks to my former colleague, Derek Wenmoth, for this invaluable suggestion, which I have used for many years.
2. SPSS (see http://www.spss.com); StatView (see http://www.statview.com).
3. Mutch, C. (2003). Citizenship education in New Zealand: Inside or outside the curriculum? *Citizenship, Social and Economics Education: An International Journal*, 5(3), 164–179.
4. SWOT = Strengths, Weaknesses, Opportunities, and Threats.

References

Bell, J. (1999). *Doing your research project* (2nd ed.). Buckingham: Open University Press.

Bogdan, R., & Biklen, S. (1992). *Qualitative research for education: An introduction to theory and methods* (2nd ed.). Boston: Allyn and Bacon.

Craft, A. (1996). *Continuing professional development*. London: Routledge.
- Contains useful discussion on teacher reflection and development.

Kvale, S. (1996). *InterViews: An introduction to qualitative research interviewing*. Thousand Oaks, CA: Sage.

Mutch, C. (2003). Citizenship education in New Zealand: Inside or outside the curriculum? *Citizenship, Social and Economics Education: An International Journal*, 5(3), 164–179.

Vaughn, S., Schumm, J., & Sinagub, J. (1996). *Focus group interviews in education and psychology*. Thousand Oaks, CA: Sage.
- Has a chapter on interviews with children and young people.

Wellington, J. (2000). *Educational research: Contemporary issues and practical approaches*. London: Continuum.
- Discusses the concepts of reflectivity and reflexivity.

Wilson, C., & Powell, M. (2001). *A guide to interviewing children: Essential skills for counsellors, police, lawyers and social workers*. Crows Nest, NSW: Allen and Unwin.
- Although designed more for disclosure or evidence interviews, contains points to think about.

Other useful references and sources

Davidson, C., & Tolich, M. (Eds.). (1999). *Social science research in New Zealand: Many paths to understanding*. Auckland: Longman.

Wilkinson, D. (Ed.) (2000). *The researcher's toolkit: The complete guide to practitioner research*. London: RoutledgeFalmer.

CHAPTER 9

Analysing the data

How do you analyse quantitative data?

How do you display quantitative data?

How do you analyse qualitative data?

How do you display qualitative data?

How do you interpret your findings?

What is the place of tentative theorising?

You have collected your data. What are you going to do with the stacks of questionnaires, data sheets, or completed interviews? You will have made some tentative decisions about this when you prepared dummy tables earlier. Nonetheless, when confronted with a pile of data, new problems emerge, and further decisions will have to be made. (Bouma, 1996, p. 145)

How do you analyse quantitative data?

Quantitative data are those types of data that can usually be reduced to numerical form. The analysis of these data types involves manipulating them in some way and/or applying some form of statistical test. (Wilkinson, 2000, p. 81)

If you set up your data-gathering and recording processes effectively, then the process of analysis should be relatively straightforward. Although quantitative analysis requires some mathematical knowledge, this chapter deals mainly with descriptive or inferential statistics, which are easily understood. If more complex inferential statistics are needed, then a course in statistics or a more detailed textbook is required.

- *Descriptive statistics* do not aim to generalise beyond the particular group investigated.
- *Inferential statistics* generalise to the population from which the sample is selected.

In Chapter 6, I gave examples of questions that could gather quantitative data. These questions will help you unpack some important statistical concepts. You will also be able to see the link between how you gather your data and how you analyse and interpret them. Bouma (1996) suggests that data organisation follows this process:
- Select categories;
- Code data; and
- Present data.

To *select categories*, you need to have some idea of what you are measuring. The sample scale question in the section on questionnaires in Chapter 6 noted that there are four types of measurements—nominal, ordinal, interval, and ratio.

- *Nominal* measurements use numbers to name or identify something. For example, the number on a rugby player's jersey has no numerical value. If the player wears number 22, it does not mean he is the twenty-second player, is 22 years old, or has scored 22 tries!
- *Ordinal* measurements use numbers to indicate the order of something, for example, to come first, second, or third in an Olympic event.
- *Interval* measurements mean that the numbers can be compared and the interval between the numbers has some value. Interval measures have an arbitrary zero. This means that the numbers 1, 2, 3, 4, and 5 on a Likert scale relate to each other, but that 0 has no meaning in this context.
- A *ratio* is similar to an interval measure, but zero has a value—it is called "absolute zero". This means that if you were asked how many times you watched television this week, 0 will have a particular meaning in relation to the other numbers you could have chosen.

Consider again our sample questions in Chapter 6. The list and category questions are nominal measures. If we assign numbers to the possible responses, then there are only certain ways we can analyse and interpret the responses. We cannot, for example, give the average of the qualifications, but we can give the frequency with which a category was selected.

Which is your highest academic qualification? Please circle.

Certificate   Diploma   Bachelor's   B(Hons)/PGCert/PGDip   Master's   Doctorate

Please indicate which age category you fit into with a tick in the appropriate box.

Under 20 ☐   20–29 ☐   30–39 ☐   40–49 ☐   50–59 ☐   60–69 ☐   70+ ☐

The *quantity* question is an example of a ratio measurement. It assumes an absolute zero. With this type of measurement, we could, for example, determine the range, the mid-point, and/or the average number of years that our respondents had been teaching.

How many years have you been teaching? _____

The sample *scale* question is an interval measurement. If we assign the numbers 1–5 to the choices, then zero has an arbitrary value. We can use these data to determine the frequency of particular responses and compare responses between groups.

Please indicate your agreement or disagreement with the following statements. Circle one.

(SA = strongly agree; A = agree; N = neutral; D = disagree; SD = strongly disagree)

Boys are better at mathematics than girls

SA   A   N   D   SD

Girls are better at reading than boys

SA   A   N   D   SD

The *ranking* question is an example of an ordinal measurement where 1 equalled our first (or most preferred) choice. We could determine, for example, which skills most frequently received a higher or lower ranking.

Please rank the following study skills in order, with your highest preference = 1:
time management ☐ critical thinking ☐ organisation ☐ planning ☐ preparation ☐ note taking ☐ summarising ☐ attentive listening ☐ filing ☐ memorisation ☐ reading ☐ participation in class ☐ group work ☐

By designing questions as we have done above or by setting up a grid (either manually or using a computer package such as Excel or SPSS[1]) to count occurrences of selected variables, we have determined the categories into which we will sort our raw data.

Bouma's (1996) next step is *coding*, which requires determining which data go into which category and how you keep track of them all. A table or spreadsheet that holds all the raw data in an unreduced form is called a *raw data grid*. Although a little cumbersome, this can be useful for looking for patterns or comparisons that might be lost later when data are recategorised and reduced. In Chapter 6, I suggested that you could undertake a content analysis of daily newspapers to determine portrayals of masculinity and femininity. Figure 9.1 presents an example of this. It shows part of the raw data grid for one section of one day's newspaper in which I counted which pictures portrayed mainly males or females according to pre-determined stereotypes.[2]

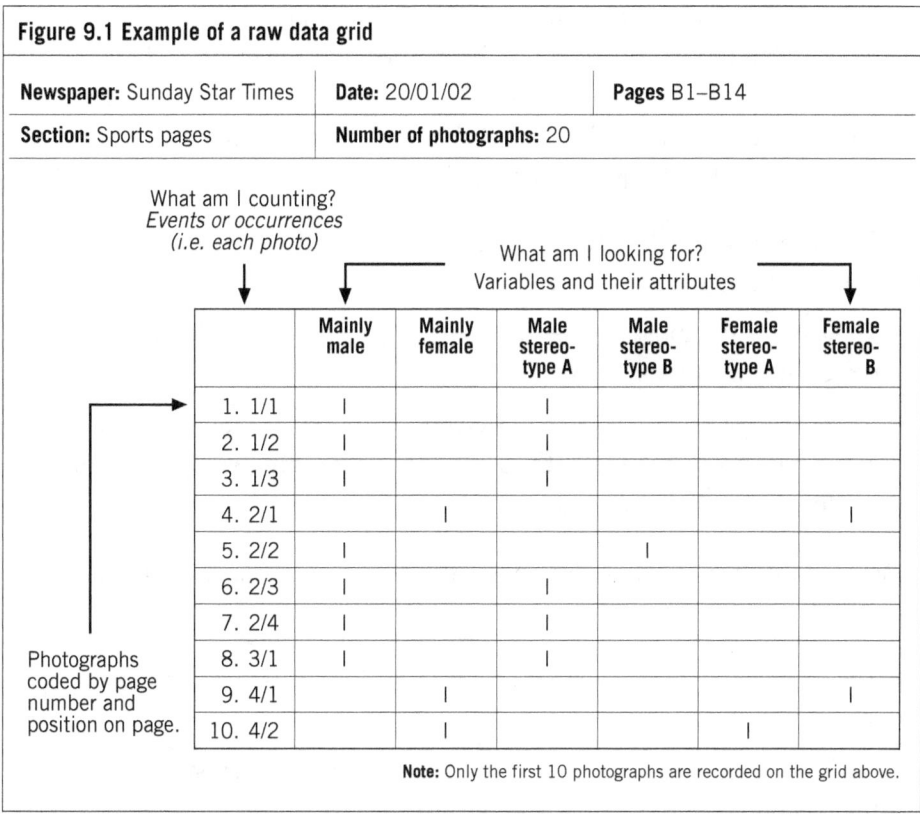

Figure 9.1 Example of a raw data grid

From this grid, I could discuss not only whether the photographs depicted pictures of mainly males or females and which stereotype they portrayed but also which page they were on and how prominently they sat on the page. If I had reduced my data too soon, that is, if I had gone straight to a tally chart of mainly male and mainly female, some of these other data would have been lost.

Once you have a raw data grid, it is no problem to reduce data to totals or to combine columns and so on. From here, you can determine the frequency of occurrences of variables, turn totals into a percentage of the whole or, depending on whether the data are nominal (as above), ordinal, interval, or ratio measures, find the best statistical measures to interpret the data. You could find:

- The mean, median, or mode, known as measures of central tendency;
- The range, variance, or standard deviation (measures of dispersion);
- Standard scores or percentile ranks (measures of relative position); or
- The correlation coefficient (a measure of relationship).

While I do not intend giving examples of each of these measures, an understanding of their meanings will help when reading quantitative research reports.

1. *Measures of central tendency* are based on the normal curve. A normal curve assumes that the data are equally distributed and the mean and median are the same. This curve is sometimes called a "bell curve" because when graphed it takes the shape of a bell, with the majority of scores clustered around the centre and the less frequent scores tailing out from there.

   - The *median* is the mid-point when the scores are all arranged in ascending or descending order.
   - The *mode* is the most frequently occurring score. A set of data can have more than one mode.
   - The *mean* (commonly referred to as the average even though it is, in fact, only one type of average) is the sum of the scores divided by the number of scores.

2. *Measures of dispersion* describe the distance from the mean. They also are based on the normal curve.

   - The *range* indicates the spread between the highest score and the lowest score.
   - *Variance* is a measure that describes how all the scores are spread around the mean.
   - The *standard deviation* is a more commonly used measure of the dispersion of scores in a distribution.

3. *Measures of relative position* give a score to describe the distance from the mean.

   - *Standard scores* use standard deviation units. Common standard scores are z scores and derived from these are T scores.
   - *Stanines* divide the normal curve into nine parts.
   - *Percentile ranks* describe the point in the distribution below which a percentage of scores fall.

To find the formula for each of these measures, you need to refer to a simple statistics textbook or you can put the data into a computer program such as Excel or SPSS and work from there. Figure 9.2 shows how these measures are based on the normal curve and how they relate to one another.

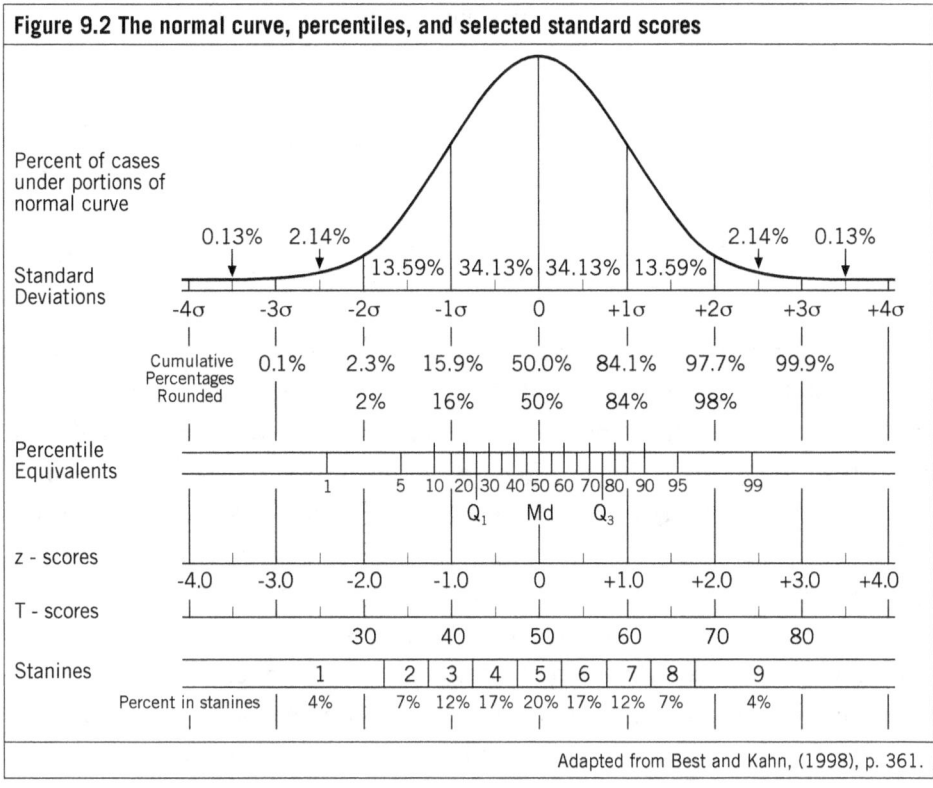

Figure 9.2 The normal curve, percentiles, and selected standard scores

Adapted from Best and Kahn, (1998), p. 361.

4. *Measures of relationship* are the final set of important measures I want to mention here. Educational researchers often use these when looking for links between variables such as a relationship between Listening PAT scores and spelling ages.

- Measures of relationship, such as correlation, show the relationship between two or more paired variables or two or more sets of data.

How do you display quantitative data?

Bouma's (1996) final step is to *present data*. As explained earlier, a common first task here is to enter all your data into a raw data grid. The next task is to tally the items in each column. From this stage, data can be displayed visually.

- A *table* presents reduced numerical data under appropriate headings.

Let's use the data gathered in our content analysis example because it easy to work with.

	Mainly male	Mainly female	Male stereotype A	Male stereotype B	Female stereotype A	Female stereotype B
Totals ($n=10$)*	7	3	6	1	1	2
			Note: *I am using the 10 results displayed earlier, not the full study.			

There are various ways we could display this, for example, as above or with the sub-totals under their totals, that is, under "mainly male" show the sub-total for each male stereotype. If our overall sample (n) was large enough, we could turn each sub-total into a percentage of the whole. (Note that smaller numbers, that is, under 10, make little sense as percentages, and it is helpful to show your sample size (n) so your readers can get some sense of the validity of your interpretation. N (capital n) is your population; n (small n) is your sample.) Alternatively, we could turn our data into graphs.

A graph presents data in a two-dimensional form. Each score is interpreted as a point made up of two items, with the first item located along the x (horizontal) axis and the second item along the y (vertical or frequency) axis. The point on the graph represents the intersection of the two items. Following are some examples of common graphs (done on Excel) you might come across.

A *scattergram* or *dot plot* displays all the intersecting points (see Figures 9.3 and 9.4). The patterns shown by the clusters of points can be interpreted in various ways. A simple scattergram could show a trend (or lack of one), or sets of paired scores could show the relationship between two variables. Figure 9.3 shows a child's increasing skill in softball throwing over one week, while Figure 9.4 compares children's listening PAT scores and their spelling ages. A spread of dots pointing to the upper right-hand corner indicates a positive correlation and a spread of dots pointing to the lower right-hand corner indicates a negative correlation. The fictional data in Figure 9.4 indicate a definite link between children's PAT listening scores and their spelling ages.

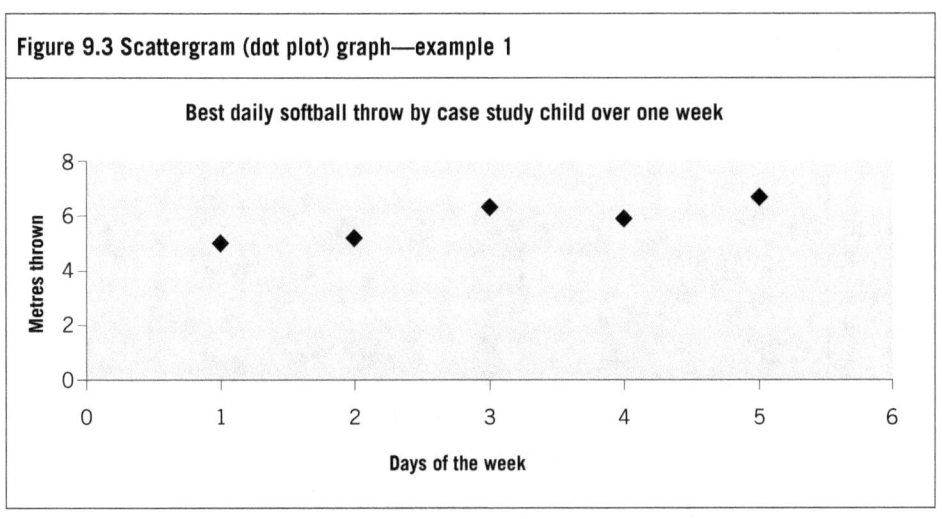

Figure 9.3 Scattergram (dot plot) graph—example 1

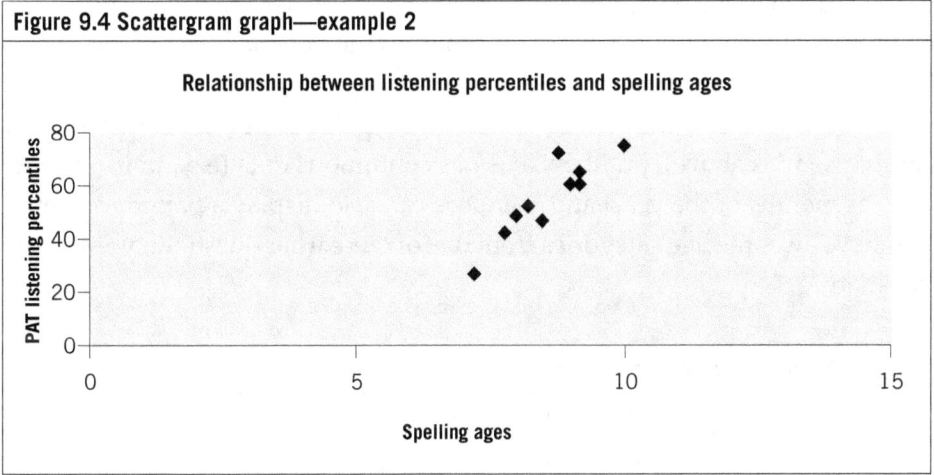

Figure 9.4 Scattergram graph—example 2

A *bar (or column) graph* uses bars drawn from the x axis to the point of intersection where the size of the bar is proportional to the size (frequency) of the variable (see Figure 9.5). The main purpose is to compare variables or groups with each other. The x axis has the original variables, attributes, or categories. These are not necessarily related to each other, that is, we could locate the labels for the variables in any order and our graph would still make sense. Figure 9.5 uses the sample questionnaire question focused on qualifications.

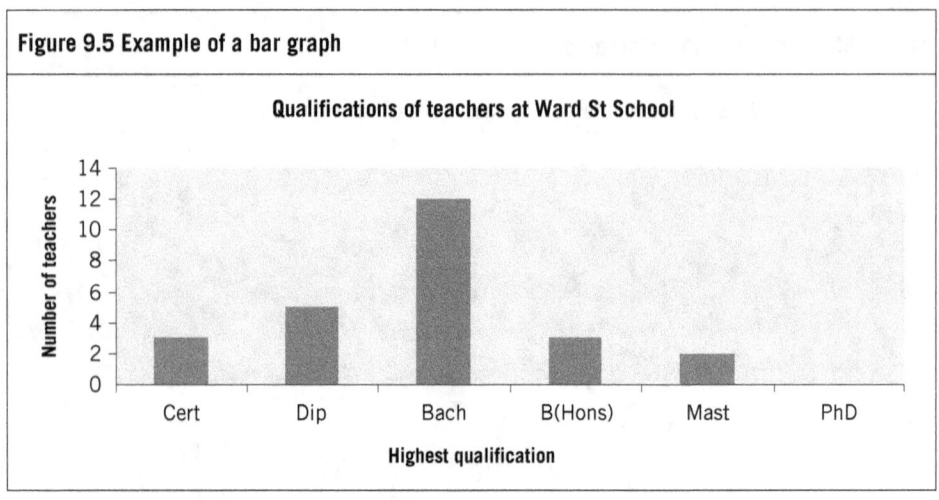

Figure 9.5 Example of a bar graph

A variation of the bar graph can also show data as percentages. Figure 9.6 is an example of a *horizontal bar chart* that shows the fictional response to one of the Likert-scale questions.

A *histogram* uses bars from the x axis to the point of intersection to show a comparison (as above), but the x axis has continuous data (e.g., units of time, such as months of the year) and therefore can also display a pattern or trend. Figure 9.7 uses the age categories from one of our earlier questionnaire sample questions.

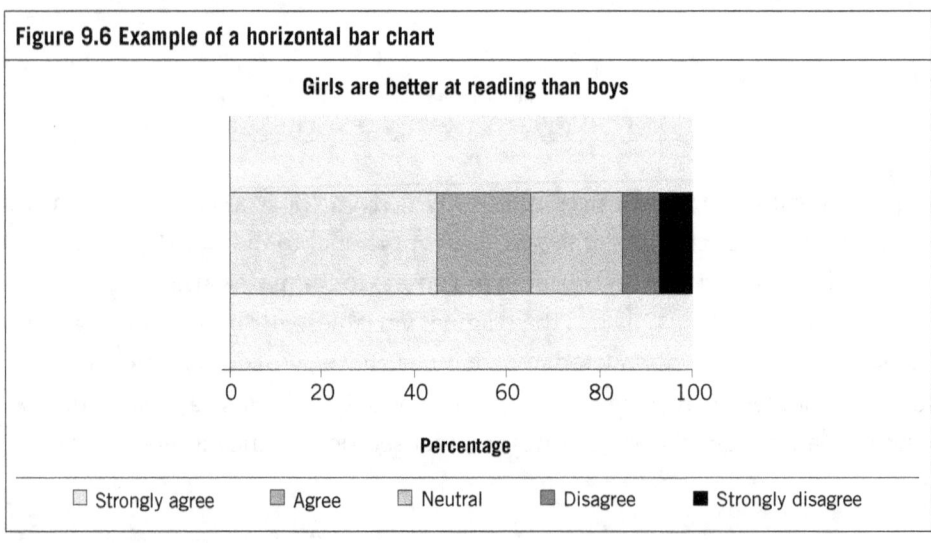

Figure 9.6 Example of a horizontal bar chart

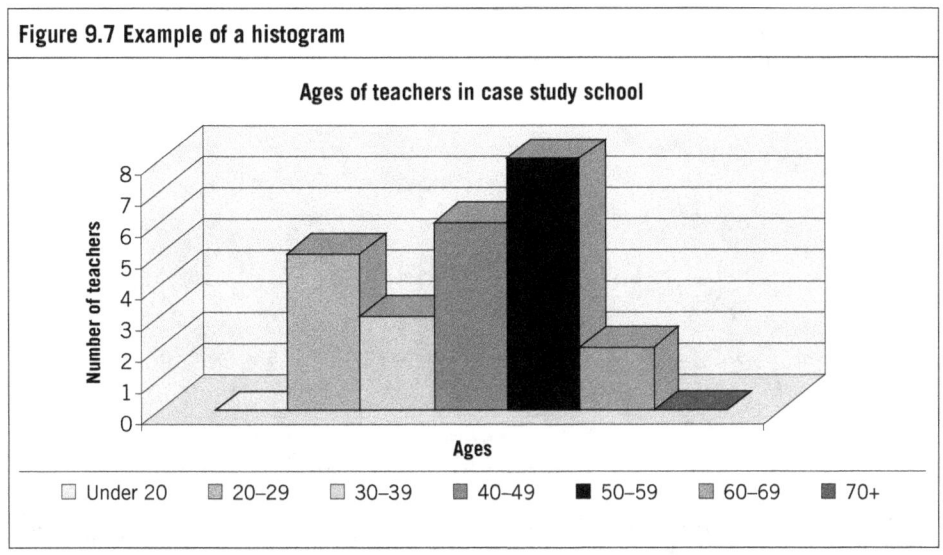

Figure 9.7 Example of a histogram

A *line graph* joins a set of points to show the frequency of scores or the relationship between two variables as a progression, pattern, or trend (Figure 9.8).

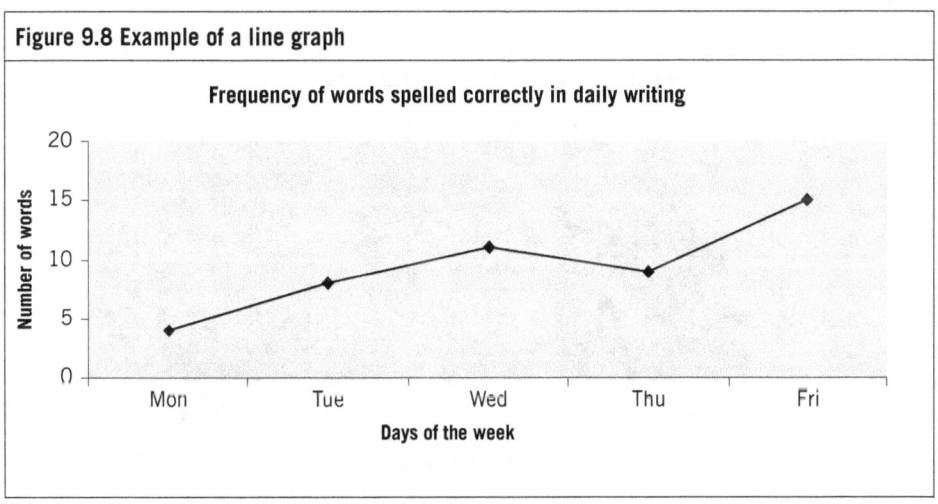

Figure 9.8 Example of a line graph

A *box plot*, or "box and whisker" graph, shows the data in quartiles (Figure 9.9). The mean is shown by a line across the box and the extent of the range is indicated by the "whiskers".

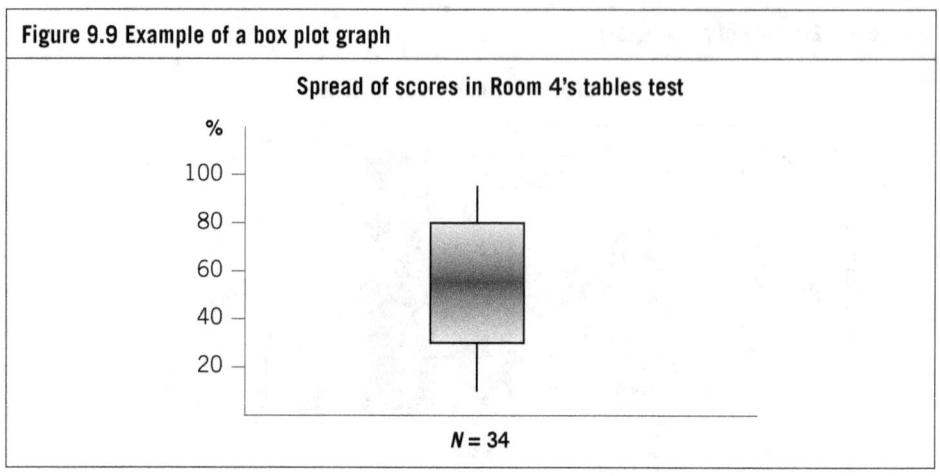

Figure 9.9 Example of a box plot graph

How do you choose which graph is best? Let's go back to our gender stereotyping exercise. The data pairs (with x axis first and y axis second, which are then represented as a points on a graph) look like this: (mainly male, 7), (mainly female, 3). These data are best displayed on a bar graph that shows a simple comparison between the two genders (Figure 9.10).

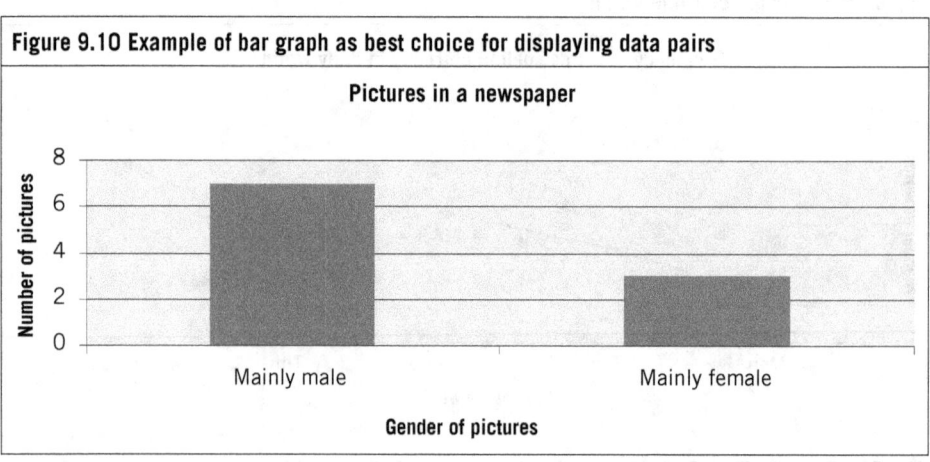

Figure 9.10 Example of bar graph as best choice for displaying data pairs

If we turn the same raw data into percentages of the whole sample, then it has most impact when displayed as a *pie graph* (Figure 9.11). A pie graph displays the proportion of a variable or category in relation to the whole. Each part of the whole resembles the wedge of a pie.

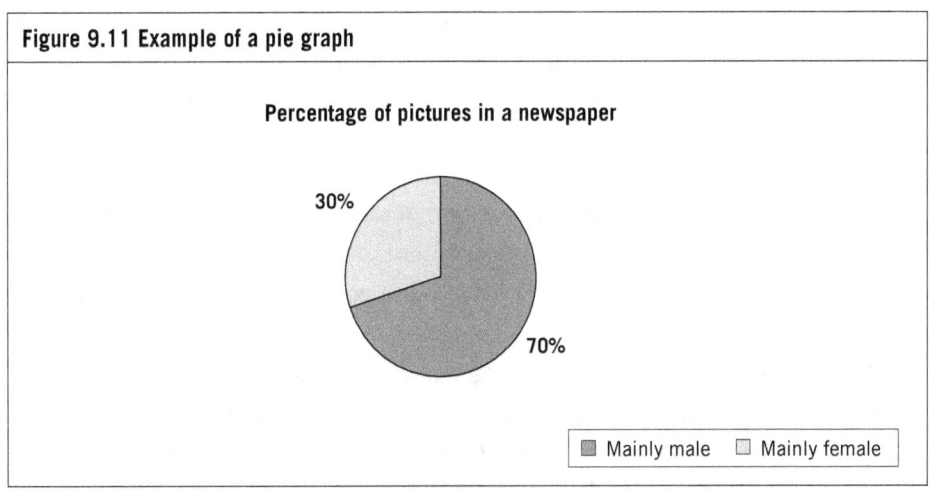

Figure 9.11 Example of a pie graph

If working in this way excites you, you needn't stop here. This is where working with quantitative data becomes fun. You could, for example, investigate the variability of the data by calculating the standard deviation. This would show you how much a particular score or group varies (or deviates) from the mean. You could also compare any score to the rest of the scores by grouping the data into percentiles (hundredths) or other relevant groupings. If you want to go further into inferential statistics, you could test for significance or correlation and so continue to display data in very interesting ways, but you'll need a little more understanding of statistics than I can give you here. I've listed some useful references at the end of the chapter.

How do you analyse qualitative data?

> Identifying salient themes, recurring ideas or language, and patterns of belief that link people and settings together is the most intellectually challenging phase of data analysis and one that can integrate the entire endeavour. (Marshall & Rossman, 1999, p. 154)

If you set out your raw qualitative data as suggested in the section on field notes (Chapter 8), then you have begun the process of data analysis already. If not, you might want to consider doing this in order to approach your data in an easy-to-manage form.

- Raw qualitative data are usually in textual form, either as original text (i.e., not created by the researcher, such as policy documents) or researcher-created text (e.g., interview transcripts or field notes).

The most common approach to analysing text is *thematic analysis*. Other approaches include semiotic analysis and discourse analysis. Qualitative analysis sometimes involves examining the visual as well as the textual.

Thematic analysis

Thematic analysis is a qualitative strategy that takes its categories from the data, unlike quantitative strategies (such as content analysis), which pre-determine categories. This way of working is also called constant comparative analysis or grounded theory.

What is of importance is the emergence of themes. Kellehear (1993, p. 39) cautions, "Subjective as it is, thematic analysis is more demanding on the personal resources and intellectual art and craft of the individual researcher." One method of thematic analysis (suggested in Chapter 6) relates to document analysis. Another method I use is a form of constant comparative analysis after LeCompte and Preissle (1993). Their steps are:

- *Perceiving:* What am I looking for? What are my first impressions? What is capturing my attention?
- *Comparing:* What can I see that is similar to something else? What things go together? What do different parts have in common?
- *Contrasting:* What can I see that is different to other things? What things don't go together? What things don't fit my emerging categories?
- *Aggregating:* What groupings are evident? Why do these things go together? What are suitable labels for my groups?
- *Ordering:* Does any pattern or order appear with these groups? Are some themes stronger or more important than others? Are there categories and sub-categories?
- *Establishing linkages and relationships:* What does this remind me of? How do my categories relate to one another? How do these relate to the literature? How do they relate to everyday practices?
- *Speculating:* What is my tentative explanation or theory? What is the significance of this? What other research does this study indicate needs to be done?

As mentioned in the examples in Chapters 6 and 8, coding in qualitative research involves looking for patterns and themes. The text is initially examined and labels or key words are used to capture items of interest that are found in the text. These might be repeated words, strong emotions, metaphors, images, emphasised items, key phrases, or significant concepts. A computer program such as or NVivo³ will also help you sort qualitative data into your suggested categories. In the following example, Karen, the teacher-researcher investigating itinerant music teachers, sorted her codes and categories manually.⁴

> *I transcribed my field notes but the interviews were professionally transcribed, then checked and corrected by me and returned to the interviewee for final comment. I made photocopies of everything and filed the originals. Initially, I used a highlighter to mark any ideas or key words that interested me from the interview and observation transcripts. From this "open coding", I sought repeated patterns in the data. I also used prior codes such as "disadvantages" or "status", which derived from the research question. Increasing familiarity with the data and its richness led to some codes being renamed or subdivided.*
>
> *On completing the coding, I manually cut up the transcripts and taped coded chunks onto labelled sheets of paper. Some of the data belonged to multiple codes and appeared more than once. Throughout this process, I created a series of concept maps to categorise the codes in various combinations, in an attempt to make sense of what I was reading. I did this either by writing key words on pieces of paper and shuffling them from category to category, or by constructing diagrams on paper. Finally, when I had a "fit" between codes and categories with which I felt comfortable, I remapped the final list under the headings of role, pedagogy, and accountability.*

Here is a further example of how I used thematic analysis in a study where I examined the development (and interviewed the writers) of the three versions (the draft, the revised draft, and the final) of the current social studies curriculum.⁵

> *The interviews were also analysed in this constant comparative manner. Interview transcripts were printed with wide margins to allow the coding of items of interest. Each transcript was coded several times—after it was initially produced, after a first set of themes was compiled for comparison and verification, after other transcripts were individually coded, and then in a major comparative exercise where categories were compiled, reclassified, omissions were noted, and broader patterns and themes established. As with the analysis of the documents, the "establishing linkages and relationships" stage included using data from other sources. Where the constant comparative thematic analysis did not seem to provide solutions, other document analysis techniques were called upon—semiotic, discourse, and visual analysis.*

Semiotic analysis

Semiotic analysis looks at the internal composition and relations of grammatical and syntactical elements, that is, what can be learned from the way particular words are selected and where they are placed in the text and in relation to each other.

From the social studies study, here is an example from an interview transcript where the participant did a little of her own semiotic analysis.⁶

> *Spending hours on every single word. It was something I have certainly learned from the whole process—how powerful words are. A word like "advance"—it's just so powerful, and to talk about "<u>the</u> influences on something" is quite different from just "influences on". It has had a significant impact on my thinking in all sorts of ways.*

Discourse analysis

Discourse analysis situates texts in their social, cultural, political, and historical contexts. Burr (1995, p. 48) explains, "A discourse refers to a set of meanings, metaphors, representations, images, stories, statements, and so on that in some way produce a particular version of events" and "deconstruction refers to attempts to take apart texts and see how they are constructed in such a way as to present particular images" (p. 164). Here is a further example from the study of the social studies curriculum.[7]

> *In the first draft, the post-colonial/liberal feminist discourse was more apparent, for example, in the use of "Aotearoa New Zealand" and "women, men and children". In the revised draft, the neo-conservative and neo-liberal discourses had more prominence. The final version took a more neutral stance, restoring some of the bicultural flavour of the first draft and removing some of the overt new right representations of the revised draft.*

Visual analysis

As Rose (2001, p. 6) explains, ". . . these images are never transparent windows on to the world. They interpret the world; then display it in very particular ways." The following is another example from the social studies research.[8]

> *The symbolic representation in the revised draft completely reconfigures the representation of social studies. . . . A closer reading of this representation focuses on the debates surrounding social studies and, in particular, the first draft and how they [the debates] found their way into the graphics that express the intentions of the content strands. Although the whakatauki (proverb), "What is the greatest thing in the world? It is people. It is people. It is people" is retained, the representations focus on institutions and artefacts rather than people. These artefacts tend to favour a new right (both neo-conservative and neo-liberal) view of the world.*

How do you display qualitative data?

In qualitative research, the aim is to provide rich description in order to illuminate particular ideas, views, and experiences. Your data might be participant quotes from interview transcripts, researcher field notes, excerpts from documents, participant diary entries or concept maps, or examples of visuals. Here are five suggested ways you might display your data.

1. Let the data speak for themselves

Although it is debatable whether data can ever "speak for themselves" as the researcher selects, edits, and places the text in a way that portrays a particular image, the text remains relatively true to the original. In this excerpt from the social studies development research, the participant's formal and professional voice (from a published paper) is put alongside her personal and emotive voice from the interview transcripts to highlight the "story behind the story".[9]

Story 1: the academic voice	Story 2: the personal voice
"After *Social Studies in the New Zealand Curriculum: Draft* was released in December, 1994, the Ministry contracted teams to deliver professional development, and initiated a period of consultation and feedback. The Ministry received 150 submissions about the Draft over a three month period in early 1995."	The revised draft I think it was a very fearful time. It was a very scary time. For instance, it was to marginalise the original writing team. There had been a lot of hurts in that process and I don't think have ever been resolved. I stuck my neck out and lobbied very hard against the revised draft. I think I made myself very unpopular with the Ministry. I criticised aspects of the revised draft in various forums.

2. Using selected examples to highlight your themes and categories (and/or tentative theory)

Karen, whose study we read about earlier, distilled three main themes from her study of itinerant music teachers—temporality, invisibility, and adaptability. She used her data to support the theme of invisibility, especially in relation to identity:[10]

> In the eyes of participants, "itinerant" and "teacher" are not terms of equal value. Although "itinerant" accurately describes the component of their employment that has an ITM moving from school to school, it does not describe their role. ITMs and HoDs Music commonly understood "itinerant" in disparaging terms.... ITMs described itinerancy as:
>
>> A gypsy. To me it has a feeling of being a bit loose, a bit tenuous.... It's not a very good description of the work we do. It has a casual connotation associated with it.
>
>> [An itinerant] is some poor soul who parks their car, loads everything up onto a wheeled trolley, trundles it in to the building, teaches some music, trundles out and sometimes nobody notices... It has that sense of no fixed abode.

3. Using a theoretical framework from the literature and supporting it with examples from your data

This is a further example from the social studies research, where excerpts from the interview transcripts support a theoretical model from the literature:[11]

Walker suggests that there are three key stages that curriculum planners go through—platform, deliberation, and design. The platform stage is where individuals bring their own values and beliefs, ideological positions, and preconceptions related to the task to the first meetings. They also come prepared to compromise on some issues and not on others. . . . What then were the conceptions, theories, aims, images, or procedures that members of the first draft writing team brought with them to this task? . . . In terms of Walker's comment about the strength of personal beliefs, Convenor 2's interview transcript provides this example:

> *On the first draft we spent some time debating whether culture and heritage should be there at all as a strand. I was determined it should be. I remember that, but others were not convinced. They thought that maybe it should be woven through. But it is a bit like women's history. Weave it through the programme—you never actually do it. I was quite determined that the culture and heritage component should stay there.*

4. Displaying your themes, categories, or findings diagrammatically, for example, as a concept map, matrix, or model

Karen displayed her themes from her study of itinerant music teachers as a diagram (Figure 9.12).[12]

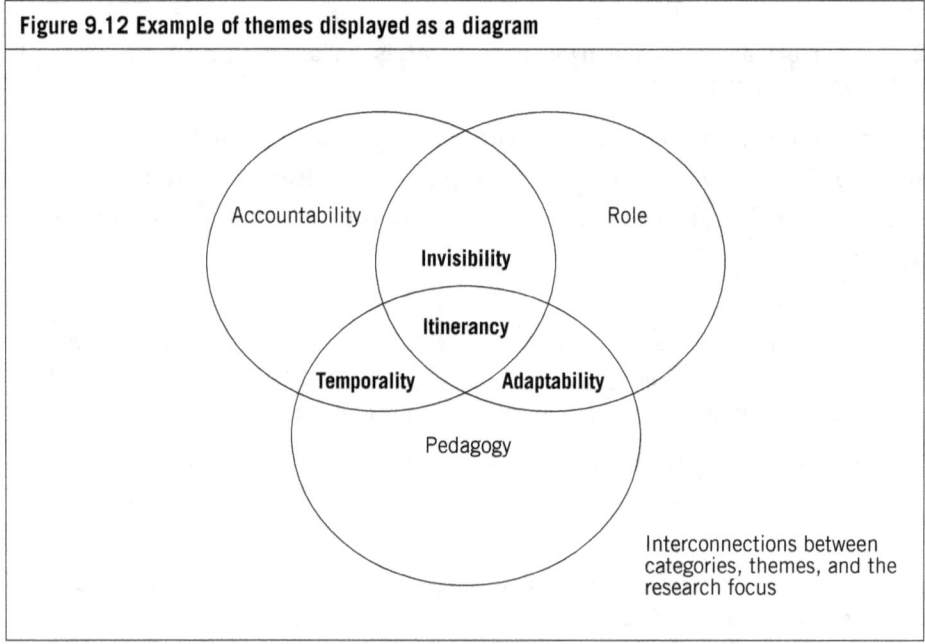

Figure 9.12 Example of themes displayed as a diagram

Interconnections between categories, themes, and the research focus

5. Constructing a representation of the phenomena in narrative, dramatic, poetic, or artistic form

Karen, cited above, also took her interview transcripts, observations, and documentary analyses and created a fictional "day in the life" of an itinerant music teacher. She based her description on real people and events and returned to the participants to verify with them that she had realistically portrayed their job. Here is an excerpt.[13]

> *8.23 am: I arrive at my first school. Someone has already taken the music car park. I find a space near the administration block. I carry my instruments on my back, get my wheeled bag of resources from the boot and grab my bag and thermos. I just have time to set up and pour a cup of coffee. The studio is freezing; the heating hasn't reached this far yet. I leave my jacket and scarf on. I should have brought in my heater, but I couldn't carry anything else. My two seniors arrive punctually. We get straight into it, as they have a performance assessment in two weeks' time. I accompany them on piano as they do a practice run-through of their pieces. They're getting there. No time for aural today. Twenty minutes goes really quickly. I zap out to the ITMs' pigeonhole and get my roll. There's a note from Bill, the HoD Music, asking me if I could look at a video assessment for him today. He would like another opinion on the performance.*

How do you interpret your findings?

This is the stage where I say to myself, "So what?" By this, I mean, so what is really important in my findings? What really matters? What is significant? What is of interest? I then consider *why* it is important, *how* I can best explain this, and *how* my data support this.

I recently helped a young colleague in the final stages of her doctoral thesis. It was a very comprehensive mixed methodology study. I ploughed through many statistical tables, each individually interpreted with levels of significance, and finally (but nicely) said to her, "So what?" I then followed this with questions like:

- What is it that you are trying to tell me?
- How does this prove or disprove your hypothesis?
- Which findings are significant in the everyday (not just statistical) sense?
- Why should someone read your thesis?
- What is the argument you are making, and how can you support this with your data?
- What is the new knowledge that you have created or new theory that you are putting forward?

I understood her difficulty at this point. You get so close to your material; it bears your blood, sweat, and tears, so to speak, but eventually you have to distil and interpret it for your audience. Here are some hints that might help you extract a sound and reasoned interpretation from data display overload.

1. Realise from the start that you cannot display every statistical table or participant quote.

2. Learn to reduce, distil, summarise, and synthesise as you go.
3. Interpret and summarise each table, graph, diagram, observation, description, category, and theme.
4. Group these summaries and divide them into sections.
5. Resummarise at the end of each section.
6. If your study is a large one, group your sections into chapters. Resummarise at the end of each chapter.
7. Use your section or chapter summaries to synthesise the main points of your findings. This will be useful for your abstract and the introductory and concluding parts of your report.
8. Check that your summary statements accurately reflect your findings and that the data support them.
9. Select appropriate examples of your data to display in the relevant sections.
10. Relate your findings to your original hypothesis or intentions. Explain any variance from your expectations. Explain any limitations.
11. Review your findings in relation to the literature. Do your findings correlate or resonate with current understandings? If so, why? If not, why not?
12. Explain the "so what"—the relevance, significance, and implications of your findings.
13. Finally, move over-detailed explanations, unused data displays, or other superfluous material to your appendices. (Later, evaluate their place in the appendices. You might end up removing them altogether, but putting them there in the meantime is a gentle first step in letting go of some of this material.)[14]

The following is Karen's summary statement from her itinerant music teacher study.[15]

I argue that itinerancy as encountered by ITMs is characterised by three main themes: temporality, invisibility, and adaptability. Time dominates itinerant work. Teaching is compressed into 20-minute blocks; travel times are minimised. An ITM's day is intensive, with scarcely a wasted minute. This influences the quality of their work and interactions with colleagues. Their present situation is affected by historical discourses of itinerancy; their future determined by current restrictions. To be itinerant, with multiple work sites and frequent travel, is to be largely invisible. This invisibility, as ITMs engage in their work, impacts on their identity, status, relationships, and place in schools and educational discourses. Adaptability and flexibility are essential ITM traits. ITMs are required to conform to the demands and expectations of diverse school systems, HoDs Music, and students, as well as their own employers, as they work within systemic constraints.

What is the place of tentative theorising?

In Chapter 3, I suggested that theories (in this case, micro-level theories) can appear at the beginning of a study as a proposition to prove or disprove, or they can appear at the end of the study as a new theory arising out of the data. Remember the discussion in Chapter 1 of the purposes of educational research. What was your purpose? Was it to explore, describe, explain, generalise, or predict? Your purpose helps you frame your conclusions and, if appropriate, your theory, in a way that relates to your intentions. If you have followed the advice in the previous section, you will have a summary statement of your key findings. You might feel this is sufficient, or you might wish to formulate your ideas into a micro-level theory (see Chapter 3 for the example of Maureen's theory). Remember that, at a minimum, a theory needs to contain a set of concepts and a statement about the relationship between those concepts. Here is a process for you to follow in order to establish a tentative theory:

1. List important concepts related to the study (from your original hypothesis, your emergent categories and themes, or your summary statement).
2. Draft some initial statements about the relationships (e.g., cause and effect) between some or all of these concepts in the light of your findings.
3. Review your statements in relation to the literature and other theories in the field.
4. Put your theory into a single, coherent statement.

This final example is the tentative theoretical model from the social studies research.[16]

> This synthesised model of "curriculum construction as a multi-dimensional process" arising from this study has both strengths and limitations. To summarise, it is based on the premise that any curriculum construction process is dependent on the interrelationship between the people involved, the process undertaken, and the intended product. Each of these key aspects is subject to factors which make the process more complex and contested. Internal and external factors, for example, influence the participants. Contextual factors and available curriculum models (whether articulated or not) influence the process, and prescribed contents and intended audiences influence the product.

Chapter summary

- Quantitative data analysis requires the selection of categories, coding of data, and presentation of findings.
- Quantitative measures can be nominal, ordinal, interval, or ratio.
- A raw data grid is the first step in organising data into categories.

- Data can be analysed using measures of central tendency, measures of dispersion, measures of relative position, and/or measures of relationship.
- Reduced data can be displayed as tables, graphs, and/or diagrams.
- Common graphs are scattergrams, bar, line, and pie graphs, and histograms.
- Raw qualitative data are mainly textual, either as original or created texts.
- Thematic analysis is the most common qualitative analysis strategy.
- Other qualitative analyses include semiotic, discourse, and visual.
- Qualitative data can be displayed by themselves, as support for theories or categories, as diagrams, or they can be reconstructed as representations of the key ideas.
- The interpretation of data must relate to the original intentions, resonate with the literature, summarise key findings, and be supported by the data.
- Micro-level theories can be formulated from the findings by writing a statement that describes the relationships between key concepts.

Notes

1. Quantitative computer packages: Excel (see http://www.microsoft.com); SPSS (see http://www.spss.com); http://www.statview.com)
2. Although this study is hypothetical, the data are real and taken from the source described.
3. Qualitative computer packages: NVivo or Xsight, see http://www.qsrinternational.com/software.htm
4. Carter, K. (2003). *Itinerant teachers of music: A state of flux*. Unpublished Master of Teaching and Learning research project, Christchurch College of Education, p. 22.
5. Mutch, C. (2004). *Context, complexity and contestation in curriculum construction: Developing social studies in the New Zealand Curriculum*. Unpublished doctoral thesis, Griffith University, Brisbane, p. 126.
6. Mutch (2004), p.152. See also, Ferguson, G. (2004). *You'll be a man if you play rugby: Sport and the construction of gender*. Palmerston North: Dunmore Press.
7. Mutch (2004), p. 154. See also, Lee, A., & Poynton, C. (2000). *Culture and text: Discourse and methodology in social research and cultural studies*. St Leonards, NSW: Allen and Unwin.
8. Mutch (2004), p. 159. See also, Moore, H. (2000). *Imagin-ing the nation: Illustration in the New Zealand School Journal 1945–55 and 1965–75*. Unpublished Master of Design thesis, Massey University.

9. Mutch (2004), p. 228.
10. Carter (2003), pp. 48–49.
11. Mutch (2004), pp. 168–169.
12. Carter (2003), p. 92.
13. Carter (2003), p. 26.
14. I am grateful to Missy Morton for this suggestion—it works!
15. Carter (2003), p. vii.
16. Mutch (2004), p. 272.

References

Best, J., & Kahn, J. (1998). *Research in education* (8th ed.). Boston: Allyn and Unwin.
- Detailed step-by-step explanations of statistics.

Bouma, G. (1996). *The research process*. Melbourne: Oxford University Press.
- Useful and detailed discussion of quantitative analysis.

Burr, V. (1995). *An introduction to social constructionism*. London: Routledge.

Kellehear, A. (1993). *The unobtrusive researcher*. St Leonards, NSW: Allen and Unwin.
- Useful qualitative analysis discussion.

LeCompte, M., & Preissle, J. (1993). *Ethnography and qualitative design in educational research* (2nd ed.). San Diego, CA: Academic Press.
- An approach to qualitative analysis.

Marshall, C., & Rossman, G. (1999). *Designing qualitative research*. Thousand Oaks, CA: Sage.

Rose, G. (2001). *Visual methodologies*. London: Sage.
- An excellent discussion of interpreting visuals as a research method.

Wilkinson, D. (2000). Analysing data. In D. Wilkinson (Ed.), *The researcher's toolkit: The complete guide to practitioner research*. London: RoutledgeFalmer.
- An easy guide to analysing data.

Other useful references and sources

Anderson, G. (1990). *Fundamentals of educational research* (1st ed.). London: Falmer.

Bell, J. (1997). *Doing your research project*. Buckingham: Open University Press.
- Simple data tables and graphs clearly explained.

Burns, R. (2000). *Introduction to research methods* (4th ed.). Melbourne: Longman.
- Useful explanations of statistical terms and analysis.

Campbell, A., McNamara, O., & Gilroy, P. (2004). *Practitioner research and professional development in education*. London: Sage.

Cohen, L., & Manion, L. (1994). *Research methods in education* (4th ed.). London: Routledge.

Davidson, C., & Tolich, M. (Eds.) (1999). *Social science research in New Zealand: Many paths to understanding*. Auckland: Longman.
- Examples of analysis of survey research, experimental research, unstructured interviewing, focus groups, action research, ethnography, discourse analysis, content analysis, and others.

Kvale, S. (1996). *InterViews: An introduction to qualitative research interviewing*. Thousand Oaks, CA: Sage.

Liberty, K., & Miller, J. (2003). *Research as a resource for evidence-based practice*. Palmerston North: Dunmore Press.

Lofland, J., & Lofland, L. (1995). *Analysing social settings: A guide to qualitative observation and analysis* (3rd ed.). San Diego, CA: Academic Press.

Neuman, W. (1997). *Social research methods: Qualitative and quantitative approaches* (3rd ed.). Boston: Allyn and Bacon.

CHAPTER 10

Writing up, reaching out, and moving on

How do you write a research report?

How do you tailor your report to reach different audiences?

How do you prepare for a conference presentation?

How do you get published?

How do you stay motivated?

Is research worth it?

Where to next?

How do you write a research report?

> Report writing is not, or should not be, a frantic activity carried out at the end of a project. It is a process of varied stages all of which need to be recorded at the time they are completed. (Bell, 1997, p. 152)

Your research is completed and the seemingly daunting task of writing up and reporting your findings is ahead of you. But it need not be daunting. Consider how much writing you have already done as you put together your proposal, ethical clearance application, and participant information sheet, and as you analysed your data. The hard part is not deciding what to put in but what to leave out! Before you start writing, there are some practical aspects to consider—what you need to get started, how you write best, what a report format looks like, and what the style expectations are.

Report writing: what do you need to get started?

The effort you put into your filing system should now be paying off. You should be able to locate the following:

- Background material (filed articles, literature review);
- Research details (research proposal, ethical clearance application);
- Research implementation materials (completed research instruments, e.g., questionnaire returns, interview transcripts, observation sheets);
- Research analysis (from raw data to data processed as graphs and tables or categories and themes);
- Reflective materials (field notes, research journal, analytic memos, tentative findings); and
- Bibliography (all material that was accessed, read, and/or cited, carefully recorded and filed).

If you've maintained a good filing system and written up each aspect as you proceeded, all you need now is time, space, and motivation.

Report writing: how do you write best?

We all approach the task of writing in different ways, but the literature on successful writing suggests the following:

- A conducive physical environment (free from distractions, adequate space, air, heat, and light, and quiet music if that helps);
- All materials prepared and on hand (this is where your filing system becomes so important);
- A logical plan or structure to follow (broken into achievable chunks);

- A timeline with realistic deadlines (you need to find out your own style, speed, and pace);
- An understanding of when and how you work best (perhaps you're a morning or night person; maybe you need long uninterrupted chunks of time or short focused bursts); and
- Motivation and rewards (set small goals and celebrate when you achieve these).

Bell (1997) suggests the following guidelines:
1. Set deadlines (make sure these are achievable and stick to them).
2. Write regularly (the same time and place each day if possible).
3. Create a rhythm of work (don't let yourself be needlessly interrupted).
4. Write up a section as soon as it is ready (set a minimum word-length goal for each writing session).
5. Stop at a point from which it is easy to resume writing (don't always stop at a difficult place because it can be hard getting back into your writing from there).
6. Leave space for revisions (be prepared to revise and rewrite; be prepared to move paragraphs around; only write on one side of each page).
7. Publicise your plans (share your goals with your friends and family so they don't distract you and will encourage you to keep going).

There are many useful books on writing research reports, and student support units provide tip sheets and seminars, so there is no excuse for not knowing what to do. The most important point to remember is that we never get it right first time; it always requires planning, preparation, drafting, revising, and checking. Gilbert Haisman (1997 pp. 48–49) has the following advice:

> Good writers see pre-writing, writing, editing and proofreading as four quite distinct tasks. *Pre-writing* is planning and research. Writing is a creative process requiring free-wheeling confidence and enthusiasm; it can be destroyed by worrying about errors and weaknesses. *Editing* removes those weaknesses so that the writing is clear, accurate and logical. *Proofreading* eliminates errors of detail, rather than overall meaning.

By now, because you should understand the parts of the research process and have already prepared a research proposal *and* have been filing materials under the relevant headings as you go, the typical outline of a report will come as no surprise.

Report writing: a typical format

Tentative title

Abstract

Introduction:
- Purpose
- Context
- Literature review
- Theoretical framework

Research Question
- Question, problem, or hypothesis
- Sub-questions
- Definitions

Methodology
- Overarching methodology
- Method
- Sources of data
- Sampling
- Ethical considerations
- Research tool
- Analytic tools

Findings
- Data presentation
- Data analysis
- Limitations

Discussion
- Relationship of findings to initial question(s)
- Relationship of findings to theory, literature, and/or practice

Conclusion
- Implications
- Recommendations
- Suggestions for further research
- Summary

Reference list

Appendices

Remember these headings are only a guide. You might reorder them, compress some sections together, leave some out, or add new headings. This all depends on the nature of your research and findings. A longer report might also need a contents page and an index of tables and diagrams. Check the guide or specifications from the research approval body. Read a variety of research reports to see how others assemble them.

- *Quantitative reports* tend to be more structured and adhere to a consistent format. They are written in a detached tone, and the researcher often refers to him/herself as "the researcher". The researcher goes to great pains to assure the reader of the study's validity and reliability. Findings are displayed as tables and graphs.
- *Qualitative reports* are more discursive and can be written in the first person. The researcher can refer to matters outside the research problem, for example, his/her own experience in conducting the research. Findings are generally discussed as themes, with relevant examples taken from interview transcripts, researcher field notes, and/or textual material.

Report writing: style guidelines

Regardless of the kind of report, Kathryn Rountree (1997) suggests that you should:

1. Be clear;
2. Be straightforward;
3. Be succinct;
4. Be engaging;
5. Be fairly formal;
6. Use fresh, vivid language;
7. Emphasise your main points;
8. Vary sentence and paragraph lengths;
9. Use active rather than passive constructions;
10. Pace writing carefully;
11. Use Māori correctly;
12. Avoid sexist language;
13. Avoid jargon;
14. Avoid slang and colloquialisms;
15. Avoid clichés;
16. Avoid inversions;
17. Avoid repetitions;
18. Avoid contractions;
19. Avoid spelling, punctuation, and grammatical errors; and
20. Check the conventions are acceptable for the context.

How do you tailor your report to reach different audiences?

You don't need to report all your study at once. Different aspects will interest different audiences. Some audiences will have specialist knowledge; others only a lay understanding. Table 10.1 suggests ways to present your report to different audiences.

Table 10.1 Suggestions on how to present a research report to different audiences

What?	Who?	How?
Local	• Immediate colleagues • Other interested groups (school staff meeting, parent group, principals' association, school trustees association)	• Verbal report • Sharing written report • A copy on personal/ institution's website • A newsletter summary • Magazine or newspaper item • A research seminar
National	• Others in your field or sector • Those in related fields	• Subject association newsletter • Professional association newsletter (e.g., NZEI *Rourou*) • Field-related or research journals, non-refereed and refereed (e.g., *set: Research Information for Teachers*, *Early Childhood Folio*, *New Zealand Journal of Education Studies*) • Local or national conference presentation
International	• Wider academic audiences interested in your topic or methodology	• International academic refereed journals • International research or subject area conferences

How do you prepare a conference presentation?

Once you have completed a sound piece of research, you have something worth telling your colleagues. Their interests may be in the topic and how it adds to their knowledge, the research questions and the answers you propose, the research approach and how it worked for you, or the implications of your research for their own practice. A conference presentation is a useful and informative way to do this.

Becoming a confident conference presenter

1. If you haven't presented research to an audience before, I suggest that you first attend a local conference and watch what is done. What makes a successful presentation? What would you avoid doing?

2. Next, prepare an oral presentation of your research findings for a smaller, less formal audience—a staff meeting, a parent meeting, a subject association meeting, a research seminar, or forum. Take on board the feedback about how you could strengthen your presentation.
3. Talk to your colleagues, research advisory committee, research supervisor, or mentor about suitable venues for presenting your research.
4. Search the web, relevant educational publications, and academic journals for information about forthcoming conferences. These are often advertised up to a year or more ahead.
5. Start out small (so that you can gain confidence) and in a place where the audience will attend because of interest in your topic and will provide supportive feedback.
6. Find out the process for applying to present a paper. Here are some examples:
   - Smaller local, regional, or national conferences ask for abstracts of papers to be submitted by a certain date. They'll notify you of your acceptance. Unless your topic is well out of the scope of interest of the anticipated audience or your abstract poorly written, you can almost be certain they'll accept your abstract. Some national conferences use a peer-review process. This means that at least two people on the conference committee independently read and assess your abstract. The NZARN (New Zealand Action Research Network) is an example of a smaller national conference that supports the work of beginning researchers and teacher-researchers.
   - Larger national or smaller international conferences also ask for abstracts to be submitted ahead of time and follow a similarly rigorous peer review process. These conferences might have categories for both completed research and research-in-progress papers. They might have a range of presentation formats, such as individual papers, panel and symposium presentations, and poster displays. They might offer opportunities for refereed and non-refereed papers. This might mean you need to send your completed paper well in advance for peer review. Your paper might also be later selected for publication in conference proceedings. The website for NZARE (New Zealand Association for Research in Education)[1] provides a good example of this process.
   - Larger international conferences follow a similar process to that employed by national conferences. Abstracts are often peer reviewed, and some conferences limit places, for example, AERA (American Educational Research Association), which has an acceptance rate of about 40 percent.

Don't let this put you off, however, as a well-written, coherent, and convincing proposal still stands a very good chance of acceptance.

7. The rule in writing a good abstract is "give them what they want". By this, I mean follow any guidelines or headings provided, keep within the word limit, and show how your paper relates to the conference theme or the goals of the organisation. If guidelines haven't been provided, try this format:
   - *Title:* give a clear indication of your topic and perhaps use a word or two from the conference theme, if relevant.
   - *Your name, position, and contact details:* some organisations might ask for these to be kept separate from the text to ensure the peer review is anonymous.
   - *Content:* research topic, purpose, methodology, theoretical framework, findings, and significance or implications and relevance to conference theme or anticipated audience.

8. Once your abstract has been accepted, make sure you follow the procedure for registering for the conference, organising payment, making travel arrangements, and finding accommodation. These matters are your responsibility, but most conference organising committees are only too willing to provide information.

9. Now you need to write the paper. Make sure you tailor your research to the presentation time limit and conference audience. A paper of 3,000 to 5,000 words is large enough for you to make a sound argument based on your findings but not so large that you wander off the topic or include too much detail. I find that I start with a set of headings and work from there, with approximate word limits per section (for an example, see Table 10.2).

10. Once your paper is written, give it to a trusted peer or critical friend for comment. Do not be upset or intimidated by any feedback. Discuss it calmly and weigh it up sensibly. (I do not always take the advice I am given, but I do consider it seriously first.) Now rewrite, reread, read sections out of order, read aloud, craft and polish. Don't forget to include a title page with your name, affiliation, contact details, and a statement such as "A paper presented to the ... [conference, date, place]." This becomes the formal reference if others wish to use your paper and refer to it.

11. Because you do not read from your paper at a conference (there is not enough time to do so, and you need to keep your audience attentive and listening), you must prepare a presentation. A set of overhead transparencies or a Powerpoint presentation are the most common formats. I prepare both (with the overheads as back-up in case the technology fails). Don't try to include everything. You can refer your audience to the paper if they need the detail.

Table 10.2 Sections of a conference paper	
Sections of a conference paper	Word length
• Introduction—why this topic is important; where it fits with the conference theme	(500)
• Background, context, setting—historical background, current educational context, cultural setting as relevant	(500)
• Literature and prior research—where this research fits	(500)
• Theoretical framework—where the research or the researcher sits theoretically, or framework used for design or analysis	(500)
• Research purpose, question—what exactly you set out to do	(250)
• Methodology—how did you gather your data; what were your data sources; any important methodological or ethical decisions made	(750)
• Findings—what did you find along with supporting data evidence	(1,000)
• Discussion, implications—relationship to original question and the literature; what this means for the topic or for practitioners	(750)
• Conclusion—what is the summary of the argument based on the findings	(250
Total	(5,000)

If you make five important points that your audience will remember, that is far more useful than 25 overheads in tiny font filled with overwhelming detail. You might only have 10–20 minutes, so adapt your presentation to suit. A 15-minute presentation might have the following look:

- Title, presenter, and conference details (1 frame, 1 minute)
- Mihi/personal introduction (included in the above)
- Presentation outline (1 frame, 30 seconds)
- Topic, question, key literature (2 frames, 2 minutes)
- Research design overview (2 frames, 3 minutes)
- Key findings (3 frames, 5 minutes)
- Discussion and implications (2 frames, 3 minutes)
- Closing frame (1 frame, 30 seconds)
- Total (12 frames, 15 minutes).

12. Practise your presentation (for content and timing) with colleagues.
13. Consider these presentation tips:
    - Keep your overheads or slides clear, uncluttered, and with a large font (e.g., 18 point or higher).
    - Overhead transparencies are best with a light background and dark type, whereas Powerpoint displays look best with light print on a dark background.
    - If using Powerpoint, avoid distracting audio-visuals.
    - Take 20 hard copies of your paper with you. Provide your email or website details if more copies are needed or if people wish to contact you.

- Arrive early to check out the room layout and equipment (or check in a prior session break).
- Speak slowly and clearly, especially at international conferences. Not everyone has English as their first language and those that do don't always find a New Zealand accent easy to follow.
- Talk to your overheads (otherwise people get lost trying to follow your logic), but don't just read them aloud.
- Keep your presentation moving along without rushing.
- Keep to the time limits.
- Don't take it personally if people leave (they may be in the wrong room) or go to sleep (they may have had a long flight).
- Smile and look interested in your topic—you only have a brief time, so make it a positive experience for you and your audience.
- Be prepared for questions or comments—these are an important part of the presentation. Answer as best you can without being defensive. If you don't know the answer, say something like, "That is an interesting question. I hadn't considered that idea, but I'd be happy to continue this discussion with you later."

14. Use the time after your presentation to continue discussions, follow up questions, and make contacts. Networking with people with similar interests is one reason people go to conferences.

How do you get published?

If your conference paper was a success and generated real interest, or if your study is quite substantial, you might consider getting it published. Return to Table 10.1 and the sections that suggest possible publications. Each publication has guidelines that focus on *content*, *style*, and the *submissions process*. Read these carefully. If unsure, write or email the editor directly with your questions so you don't waste your precious time now or that of the publication's editorial committee later.

- *Content guidelines* outline the areas of interest or fields of study of the publication's readers. Some publications focus on subject disciplines, some on a field of study, yet others on educational research in general or on particular methodologies. An editor's first question will be, "Will this be of interest to our readers?"

- *Style guidelines* are generally based on those accepted for the particular discipline or on a more general style, such as that set down by the American Psychological Association (APA). Style guidelines ensure that each article in a publication follows consistent writing conventions. If you want your article to be considered, then you need to follow these carefully. Some seem a little pedantic, but you just need to go along with them.
- *Submission guidelines* tell you to whom and how to forward your article. These might include a certain number of hard copies, and keeping your name and contact details separate from the text of the article.

If all goes well, the usual process is as follows. (Note, however, the time it takes usually varies from 3 to 18 months, and so a good bit of the process can involve a waiting game.)

1. You select a suitable publication, read their guidelines carefully, and rewrite your research to suit. Citing previous articles from their journal can be helpful.
2. You mail or email your article as requested.
3. You receive an acknowledgement that your article has arrived.
4. You receive information that the editor/editorial board has deemed it suitable for the publication and that they have sent it to people with proven expertise in the topic area.
5. You receive notification that the reviewers:
    a. Recommend publication as is (very rare);
    b. Recommend publication with amendments (most common);
    c. Recommend major amendments and resubmission (more common for very prestigious journals); or
    d. Reject your article (also rare—the most likely scenario is "c").
6. The editor provides the reviewers' feedback with suggestions on how to address their concerns and a deadline for your amended version.
7. You complete a contract with the publisher in which you agree to publication in return for a copy (or copies) of the journal.
8. Typeset proofs are sent to you for checking.
9. The article is published.
10. A copy is mailed to you (or made available electronically).

The following extract is a comprehensive statement about what editorial teams look for. It comes from a guide to getting published by Kenway, Gough, and Hughes (1998).

The publishable paper

Publishable papers have generic qualities that cross all fields of intellectual inquiry, even though what is considered to be an accepted writing style may vary widely between disciplines.

The papers most likely to get published will:
- Present new knowledge;
- Demonstrate a thorough knowledge of the particular field;
- Address the current issues which the field confronts;
- Ask and, at the least, attempt to answer provocative questions in a persuasive manner;
- Bring new insights to current debates and issues;
- Be well written and argued; and
- Know what appeals to particular journals and readers.

Each publishable paper has its own internal consistency and coherence. It will be:
- Theoretically adequate
  - The theoretical perspective is clear and focused;
  - The concepts used are clearly defined;
  - The findings relate to the research literature presented in the article; and
  - The conclusions are a logical consequence of the arguments presented in the paper.
- Methodologically adequate;
  - Sufficient information is given on how the research was undertaken;
  - Rationale for the use of the particular methodology is clear;
  - Data presented relate to the method; and
  - Title, abstract, literature review, and text are all relevant to the argument.
- Stylistically adequate;
  - Attention is given to referencing, grammar, and punctuation;
  - Language is inclusive and non-sexist;
  - Abbreviations and acronyms are defined; and
  - Any features local to the research site are explained for an international audience.

The challenge for you, as the author, is to develop a set of strategies that get you, with the least amount of delay, frustration, and duplication of effort, to the stage of having a publishable paper.

How do you stay motivated?

> To be a teacher means to observe students and study classroom interactions, to explore a variety of effective ways of teaching and learning, and to build conceptual frameworks that can guide one's work. This is a personal as well as a professional quest, a journey toward making sense out of and finding satisfaction in one's teaching. It is the work of teacher-researchers. (Fischer, 1996, p. 33)

My experience with practitioners is that once research gets hold of them, they're hooked. Sometimes, however, busy workloads, balancing work and family commitments, and/or other life events get in the way, and it is hard to keep motivated. This is especially true for people undertaking research for a qualification. Once they have that piece of paper, the motivation to continue tends to dissipate. Again, however, experience has shown me that, at some time in the future, the wish to get back into research resurfaces. So what tips are there for fitting research into your already busy life and keeping up your research?

Tips to stay motivated

- Relate your research to what is happening around you;
- Only pick topics that you feel passionate about;
- Don't do it alone—find ways to work collaboratively;
- Get involved in research or subject associations;
- Keep up with the research literature;
- Tell your colleagues, students, interested friends, and family about your projects, and enlist their help to keep you motivated;
- Attend conferences and research seminars;
- Find "like minds" and set up discussion groups;
- Look for ways to streamline your work and research and avoid duplication;
- Set goals and realistic timeframes; and
- Reward yourself frequently!

Action research

One of the ways to keep researching without having to add it to your workload is to research your own practice. Action research is a good place for beginning researchers to start, and it's a manageable way for busy practitioners to continue researching. This approach comes under many names—action research, practitioner research, action learning, reflective practice, and teacher research.

- Action research covers the range of methodologies that focus on investigating and improving the researcher's (or researchers') own practice(s) in their regular work settings.

Sometimes, this investigation is done by a team that works together on a larger institutional goal; at other times, the research is supported by an outside mentor. As Bell (1997, p. 7) suggests:

> The essentially practical, problem solving nature of action research makes this approach attractive to practitioner researchers who have identified a problem during the course of their work, see the merit of investigating it and, if possible, of improving practice.

Action research can use a range of methods and strategies depending on the research problem or question and the ease and relevance of gathering certain types of data. The research design is cyclical and ongoing: the completion of one cycle suggests the focus for the next. One of the simplest action research designs is that suggested by Ernie Stringer (1999)—"Look, think, act." Figure 10.1 shows how it can work.

Figure 10.1 Action research in action

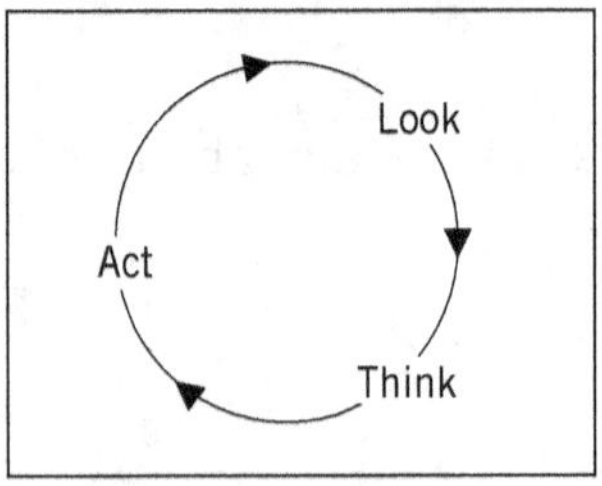

Look—what is happening in your workplace that could be investigated, evaluated, or improved?
↓
Think—how might you investigate this? What would be useful data sources and methods?
↓
Act—gather and analyse the data and consider what the implications of the findings are.

Look—in what ways can you use these findings to improve practice?
↓
Think—how might you gather data to evaluate whether these changes are working?
↓
Act—now what further changes or adaptations might you make?

Here are two examples of action research projects—one an individual, ongoing research interest, the other a team project with mentor support.

> Bridget is a student dean in a tertiary institution. Her action research project developed out of concern that the particular needs of distance students were not being met. Bridget helped students set up an informal online community. She then used a range of data-gathering strategies—analysing formal and informal documents (diary entries, minutes of meetings), formal and informal discussions with students, and quantitative data (site log-ins).

From this, she found that "the notion of community does not form naturally in an online environment", which led her to cycle two, in which she conducted a more comprehensive survey of distance students enrolled in web-based or web-supported courses. One of the results of the survey led her to cycle three—semi-structured interviews with lecturers working in online environments. Bridget commented that, "In using this methodology, I was able to work with students and staff to identify needs, and to implement changes that would address those needs."[2]

The middle syndicate of a primary school wanted to improve the literacy practices in their classrooms so they invited Liz, the local Resource Teacher of Literacy, to work with them. Liz discussed their concerns and then conducted observations in their classrooms. From here, they were able to put an action plan in place. Liz commented on action research as the most appropriate methodology because it was "situational, collaborative, participatory and self-evaluative". The action plan included Liz modelling new approaches for the teachers to try for themselves and helping them refine their current skills and improve their assessment practices. Both the teachers and the other staff in the school could see the shifts in teacher practice, and they were all enthusiastic about completing a further cycle the following year.[3]

Is research worth it?

I would like to give the answer to this question over to a practitioner-researcher. Remember Vikki in Chapter 2, and her research with children who had lost a parent? I asked Vikki if she would jot down a few comments about how she chose her topic, managed her research, and the impact it had on her. The following is the letter she sent to me, which I have left intact.[4] Although it is rather long, I think the points she raises are worth reinforcing and that it's important to hear the "voice" of a practitioner-researcher—to follow her highs and lows. Some of the points Vikki makes are:

- It helps to believe in the importance of your topic.
- All parts of the process take longer than anticipated.
- Initial ideas need refining to something more manageable.
- Talking to others, especially experienced researchers, is invaluable.
- Time management, careful planning, and self-discipline are key, but so is being flexible when necessary.
- Finding a life-work balance—building in rest, relaxation, and family time—is important. Research can become all encompassing if you let it!
- Debriefing with a professional is useful if your topic is emotionally charged.
- And, yes, it is worth it!

Carol

I have jotted down my ideas around what you have asked for. I hope they are helpful.

My topic—how did I decide upon it? This is explained quite clearly within the introduction of the thesis so rather than rewrite this all here, you will find that in there.[6] The choice of topic is so challenging. I had no idea how long it would take to refine my topic to something that was manageable. Discussing it with my supervisors, who of course had experience, was the best thing I did, as they helped me to see that my initial ideas were just too big!! I quickly came to realise that, even when I started, I needed to keep refining to ensure manageability. I believe you need to feel quite passionate about your question, as that will give you the motivation to complete the journey. My passion for the area I focused on is definitely what kept me going. It would be difficult not to carry that.

Fitting study around family and work: as you will know Carol, my family always comes first, but there were times throughout the research process when I think they wondered if they still had a mother/wife. In hindsight, I would prepare them far more than I did for the realities of what I was taking on. I had no idea myself how consuming this project was going to be on top of my full-time workload and family commitments. I was so thankful for the flexibility that my work allowed me, as not everyone has that. I pencilled in every Wednesday to be at university and "squashed" my full-time job into the other four days and nights—nearly every night. I was very hard on myself about this and the pull to be in two or three places at once was very strong. Maintaining the integrity of a full-time job and the integrity of the research was utterly draining on top of my family commitments. However, I totally believed in the process I was going through and knew that it would only be for a time. I had set myself a timeframe and I was determined to stick to it.

I quickly realised that it was absolutely up to me to plan, monitor and undertake the work involved in the thesis. No one is there with a big stick—it comes down to you. The supervisors can only do so much. You feel very supported by those around you, but this is ultimately you. Individual research is all you—it is your vision, your passion, your debate, your struggle. No one owns it like you—no one can own it like you. At times, it is consuming. The frustration when what you have written does not portray the whole picture—words do not seem enough. My time management had to be impeccable. At times, especially initially, there was no room in my days or weeks to breathe. I soon learnt to book in time to "breathe"—just as I booked in everything else. My swimming and walking became a vital part of my survival through the research. Time management is absolutely key—a good diary, planner, is a must. Being disciplined to stick to your plan is essential, with a little flexibility for the unknown. Allowing yourself to be human is also important within the commitment. Plan in family, work, research time, as well as time for yourself. It does not need to be huge but it is vital.

There was a continuous battle between believing wholeheartedly in the integrity of the research and balancing that with the demands of family, personal health and wellbeing and work. Having to make decisions about manageability when you really want to expand or go back over areas you would love to pursue further—much further. At times, shortcuts would appear. I made sure not to take any shortcuts within the research, as it would have depreciated its value and ultimately I would not have been happy with the outcome. I did, however, take shortcuts elsewhere. I hired a cleaner once a week for the house—it was heaven to know that each Wednesday I would go home to a clean home. I delegated more responsibility to the members of my family and learnt to step back and realise that a messy teenage bedroom is not really the end of the world. Work, of course, continued to expect 150% of me. I temporarily stepped back from some extra work commitments and learnt to say no to new ones on offer. I did maintain some extra work commitments that I felt were really worthwhile and those that I really enjoyed, but allowed myself, after discussion with my director, to step back from others.

The majority of my friends and family have not undertaken research of this type. They therefore did not have any awareness or understanding of what I was doing, especially in relation to the work involved. I certainly did not expect that from them. Work colleagues provided a tremendous amount of support, as they were aware of the undertaking and were pursuing similar journeys. I found the opportunity to talk with others in the same boat invaluable. The sensitivity of my topic meant that it did not make good conversation for most people and so I learnt not to talk about it too much. It may be the most important topic for you for the day but it is important not to bring it to every conversation that you are involved in. You need a mental break from it, as do those around you.

During the writing-up stage, I started to do more and more work from home. It allowed me the physical space and peace to complete this. I took two weeks away from work to write. I had to complete all domestic tasks first thing each morning, and then committed myself to write for the day. Once a day I would walk for 30 minutes to clear my head. However, in the writing stage, there were times when I was so "on a roll" that walking away from it was the last thing I could have done. When it is absolutely flowing, keep writing! There were nights when the keys of the keyboard would be tapping away very, very late. They were often the times when I did my best writing. Conversely, there were times that I had set aside to write when nothing would flow. After 60 minutes or so of trying, I would usually leave it and come back to it later. There are ongoing challenges with the research project, like never being sure if you have done enough and never being sure if you have read enough. Even when you think you are sure, you aren't. Should I just speak to one more person or find one more reading? Research is not exhaustive in that way and can be thoroughly frustrating for someone who likes things pretty organised like me. There are also psychological challenges—mental and emotional—of becoming involved with the lives and experiences of your participants. I arranged for an independent person who worked in children's grief to be my support. This was invaluable, as she was able to listen, laugh and cry with me when it was needed.

BALANCE is very important. You are spreading yourself rather thinly at times, and it is important to maintain balance and be a little selfish! The research is not forever—it does come to an end, although it is hard to see that at times. PERSEVERANCE is also important. There are times when you feel as if you are stuck. Looking at things from a different perspective or discussing it with a supervisor can restart you. Finding a new path is sometimes necessary and can be surprising. You cannot have a single-minded version of how it is going to go. Research is full of surprises—it keeps it exciting and dynamic and alive.

Was it worth it? ABSOLUTELY. I was tremendously proud of my work and so appreciative of the fact that I felt I had given my participants a voice. I actually felt that my findings would be useful for those working with children who had lost a parent. That was a strong goal of mine. Finishing the work was strange. Binding and handing it in to the university office for marking seemed so simple—where were the trumpets, the fanfare? What would I do with all that free time?? Ha, ha—no such thing! By the time the marking was completed, I was well in to the next year's work, with new challenges and next steps. The real sense of achievement grew slowly from there. Having had the subsequent chance to share my findings with groups of people has been fabulous. I feel as if I have really achieved something. I made the research happen, and I did it. It feels great!

Regards,
Vikki.

Where to next?

Just as Vikki reached the end of her journey, so I have now nearly reached the end of mine—that of sharing my thoughts about and experiences of educational research with you. However, for some of you, it is just the beginning of your research adventures; for others of you it may mean renewed confidence in continuing down this path. My experience has been that becoming involved in research opens up many opportunities you might have not otherwise considered.

One opportunity arises from viewing your practices differently. You might be spurred on to teach or conduct your work in new ways. Are there innovative methods you want to trial, new programmes you want to evaluate, different people you want to collaborate with, or even different places in which you might want to work? Now that your research has helped you understand teaching and learning in a different way, are there management opportunities you'd like to take? Has research enabled you to see the work of others differently? Are there new career possibilities based around your new skills or understandings?

Another opportunity revolves around furthering your research involvement. Research doesn't need to be a lonely exercise, in the way Vikki described; it can be a collaborative and interactive endeavour. You can begin small by working with colleagues and associates on areas of mutual interest or you can indicate your interest in being involved in larger projects offered by national providers or through your local educational institution. As you gain more experience, you will find there are rich rewards in mentoring others into the research community. Many of my most enjoyable research moments come from supervising research students or mentoring my colleagues.

Tied to furthering your interest in research is the prospect of furthering your qualifications, often leading to career changes or new opportunities within your field of work. Jan, whose study of farmers' learning was mentioned in Chapter 1, took a career turn after being a nurse and then a farmer and entered the Christchurch College of Education's Certificate in Adult Teaching programme, went through the Diploma in Adult Teaching and Learning, and then the Master of Teaching and Learning, and is now enrolled in a PhD. I await the results of her doctoral study on women in farming with great interest.

Further opportunities relate to presenting your research. When I started conducting research and attending research conferences, I little thought that I would be presenting in Colima, Mexico, or Hiroshima, Japan. I didn't realise that I would gain an international circle of friends and colleagues that I might only meet every year or two but with whom I share in-depth conversations about mutual research interests.

Finally, there are publication opportunities. Your inclusion in conference proceedings and your writing of journal articles will see your reputation grow, and you could be invited to submit chapters to books or articles to special editions of journals. Sometimes, there are calls for expressions of interest to write on a particular topic. If the call relates to an area of interest, respond with your proposal. You might just be successful. You might even have enough to fill a book of your own!

This seems a good place to leave you with my latest publication—this book. You will take your own understandings from the text and relate these to your own situations. You might even wish to contest some of my ideas and engage me in healthy academic debate.

Whatever your response, I trust it will give some of you the confidence to try small research projects for yourselves. For others of you, I hope it will be the first cycle in an ongoing practice, and yet for others, I hope it will spur you on to further study or involvement in larger projects. Whatever path you take, there will be more than one beneficiary. The overall purpose of educational research, as I stated in Chapter 1, is ". . . the improvement of teaching and learning systems and practices for the betterment of all concerned and society at large." In undertaking educational research, whether to improve your own practice, promote better teaching approaches, enhance educational opportunities for disadvantaged groups, or influence educational policy, it will be time well spent—personally satisfying, professionally challenging—and maybe even life changing.

Good luck.

Kia kaha!

E tū kahikatea
Hei whakapae ururoa
Awhi mai, awhi atu
Tātou tātou e

Stand tall kahikatea as shelter for the next generations
Embrace this way and that, all of us together

Chapter summary

- A research report is the culmination of the project and builds on all the writing that has gone before.
- Quantitative reports are more formal and structured.
- Qualitative reports can be in the first person and written in a more narrative style.
- All writing needs preparation, drafting, revision, and editing.
- Research findings can be tailored to suit different audiences, from those with specialist knowledge to those with a lay understanding.
- Conferences are useful for disseminating research findings, sharing new ideas, and networking with people with interests in common.
- Research can be published at several levels, from research summaries in professional newsletters to academic articles in refereed journals.
- It is important to follow publication guidelines.
- Action research is a good way to begin practitioner research or to stay motivated as a researcher.
- Involvement in research provides many rewards and many opportunities.

Notes

1. New Zealand Association for Research in Education website address: http://www.nzare.org.nz
2. O'Regan, B. (2004, May/June). *Distance study: On and off shore perspectives*. Paper presented at the Pacific Association of Teacher Educators' Conference, Apia, Samoa.
3. Oldridge, L. (2003). *Action research: Literacy practices: Preventing reading failure by ensuring effective practice*. Unpublished paper, Resource Teacher of Literacy Training Programme, Christchurch College of Education.
4. Personal communication, 21 September 2004.
5. Pink, V. (2003). *School re-entry after the death of a parent*. Unpublished Master of Education dissertation, University of Canterbury.

References

Bell, J. (1997). *Doing your research project: A guide for first time researchers in education and social science.* Buckingham: Open University Press.
- Has a useful checklist to go with writing a research report.

Fischer, J. (1996). Open to ideas: Developing a framework for your ideas. In G. Burnaford, J. Fischer, & D. Hobson (Eds.), *Teachers doing research: Practical possibilities* (pp. 33–50). Mahwah, NJ: Lawrence Erlbaum.
- Actual teacher-researcher projects.

Haisman, G. (1997). *SWOT: Study without tears.* Wellington: New Zealand Council for Educational Research.
- Useful advice for those new to studying and writing.

Kenway, J., Gough, N., & Hughes, M. (1998). *Publishing in refereed academic journals: A pocket guide.* Geelong, VA: Deakin Centre for Education and Change.
- A wise little guide on getting published.

Rountree, K. (1997). *Writing for success: A practical guide for New Zealand students.* Auckland: Longman Paul.
- Useful tips for academic writing.

Stringer, E. (1999). *Action research: A practitioner's guide.* Thousand Oaks, CA: Sage.
- A simple approach to action research.

Other useful references and sources

Cardno, C. (2003). *Action research: A developmental approach.* Wellington: New Zealand Council for Educational Research.
- A readable book written for the New Zealand context.

Clanchy, J., & Ballard, B. (1994). *Essay writing for students: A practical guide.* Melbourne: Longman Cheshire.

McNiff, J. (2000). *Action research in organisations.* London: Routledge.
- Useful when looking at action research in larger settings.

Mills, G. (2000). *Action research: A guide for the teacher researcher.* Upper Saddle River, NJ: Prentice Hall/Merrill. See also: http://www.sou.edu/education/ActionResearch/index.htm

Oliver, P. (1996). *Writing essays and reports: A guide for students.* London: Hodder and Stoughton.

Rountree, K., & Laing, T. (1996). *Writing by degrees: A practical guide to writing theses and research papers.* Auckland: Addison Wesley Longman.
- Useful for those writing up longer projects and theses.

Siebert, A., Gilpin, B., & Carr, M. (2000). *An adult student's guide to survival and success.* Portland, OR: Practical Psychology Press.

Wadsworth, Y. (1997). *Everyday evaluation on the run.* St Leonards, NSW: Allen and Unwin.
- A useful action research approach.

Wallace, A., Schirato, T., & Bright, P. (1999). *Beginning university: Thinking, researching and writing for success.* St Leonards, NSW: Allen and Unwin.

Webber, B,. Wagemaker, P., and Kane, R. (2006). *Getting published - Principles, process and pitfalls: A guide for researchers.* Wellington: NZCER Press.

Wellington, J. (2000). *Educational research: Contemporary issues and practical approaches.* London: Continuum.

CHAPTER 11

Current trends and future possibilities

How have changes in technology influenced research?

What are some recent developments in quantitative research?

What are some recent developments in qualitative research?

Is mixed methods research a 'third paradigm'?

How similar or different are research and evaluation?

Are there new developments in cultural and ethical frameworks?

How have textual, visual and arts-based approaches developed?

How can reflective approaches contribute to research?

What can be gained from collaborative research?

Where might research go in the future?

Introduction

I asked a range of people who had used the earlier edition of *Doing Educational Research*, as students or teachers of research methods, what they thought was missing, what I should have said more about, or what they thought were recent trends in educational research. I also read recent books or new editions of books on educational research and reviewed journals that focused on this area. To these ideas I added methodologies that I had been investigating in more depth. From the resulting long list I came up with the topics that follow.

Although I haven't included every good idea, and there is much more I could say about the ones I have chosen, I hope this brief summary sparks your interest to read further and consider how these topics or trends might have an impact on the research you are considering undertaking.

How have changes in technology influenced research?

The influence of changing technology was the most common topic people suggested to me. When reviewing the literature or talking to colleagues, I found that technology was talked about in three main ways:

- Technology as a research tool
- Technology as a data source
- Technology for dissemination.

> Technology as a research tool or data source allows researchers to access, store, manipulate, analyse, present and disseminate vast amounts of data in a variety of ways. It saves times, adds breadth and depth, strengthens the credibility of the research and makes the findings available to wider audience. The use of technology in and for educational research is, in itself, a topic of interest to researchers.

Technology as a research tool

The availability of tools to locate, store and manage data is something that has changed researchers' lives. I can hardly imagine how I managed to conduct my earliest research without a computer or access to the Internet. I used a tape recorder, wrote my notes out by hand and read the literature in hard copy on site in the library. The ease of conducting a literature review using electronic sources not only saves me time now but also gives me broader coverage. More recently I have been finding tools that support researchers to work collaboratively, such as Dropbox, Google Drive or SugarSync, and these are further enhancing the research experience.

The constantly changing nature of technology can be a double-edged sword, though. Yes, it makes things faster, smoother or more easily managed, but no sooner do you master a program, strategy, application or piece of equipment than it is updated and you are running to catch up. The use of technology also changes the nature of the research. In this section I want to introduce you to some positive enhancements (summarised in Table 11.1) and some cautions (Table 11.2) in relation to embracing technology as part of your research, knowing that as soon as I write these words they are immediately out of date. Never mind. A quick search on Google will put you back on track!

Table 11.1: How technology can positively enhance research	
Enhancements	
Widens the scope of research	With the availability of historical and archival material, contemporary and real-time accounts, statistical databases and media reports, and easy access to policy and other documents, your research can go deeper or wider, take a broader sweep or narrow down to specific detail. The scope of research is only limited by your time, resources and imagination.
Widens access to participants, sources and literature	A wider range of participants is more easily accessed and communicated with. You can tap into the many online networks in order to garner interest, source participants, expand participation and disseminate information. A greater number and wider variety of data sources are available electronically. Data can also be verified or triangulated through a variety of sources and media. Prior research and useful literature can be accessed quickly and reliably through online libraries and depositories. Bibliographic tools can store, manage and correctly reference your literature.
Provides quicker response and recording times	Using cellphones, texting, emails and attachments, social media, forums, websites, wikis, online data-gathering methods, data-sharing sites, digital voice recorders, voice recognition software and other technology can significantly reduce time in setting up, undertaking, managing and following up your research project.
Stores and backs up vast amounts of data easily	Internal and external hard drives, data storage devices (pen drives, data sticks and those with the strangest of names—like 'buffalo clips'), devices that 'talk' to each other, or storage in the 'cloud' mean there is now no excuse for not backing up your data and your work in progress. Not only backed up but stored, organised, categorised, tagged and able to be reduced or manipulated by a quantitative or qualitative data analysis programme.
Allows you to work in real time or asynchronously	Many technological advances free up the researcher from restrictions of time and place. No longer do you need to be there, on site, with the participant. Online surveys can be done at a time, place and speed that suits the participant, or you can conduct interviews face to face using Skype without needing to travel. Data can be gathered sporadically, systematically, individually, collaboratively or iteratively.

Saves time inputting and analysing data	Quantitative data can be input manually or automatically into spreadsheets, data management programs or analytical tools. Data can be easily imported and moved between databases. Different statistical analyses can be undertaken quickly and accurately. Qualitative data can be input into programs, where they can be stored, moved around, tagged, coded and analysed. Such programs can also store researcher field notes, imported text from electronic documents and bibliographical material.
Presents data in multiple, complex and innovative ways	Quantitative researchers can produce an amazing array of graphs and tables, ranging from simple black-and-white scatter plots to coloured, moving, three-dimensional displays. Qualitative researchers can use programs that display their themes in quirky shapes, or they can embed links to video clips or dramatic performances into their text. Technological advances have been especially helpful to those working in mixed method modes, where they are crossing traditional data creation and transformation boundaries.

> *Jennifer used a range of technological tools to help her undertake her research into attitudes towards teaching in low socioeconomic schools. She used communication technology to approach institutions, seek permission, recruit participants and set up face-to-face interviews; used multiple software programs to gather and analyse data; created an online forum for students to comment on important issues; and set up a questionnaire on Survey Monkey for students to complete before and after their teacher preparation programme. Finally, she used NVivo to sort, manage, code and analyse all the textual material—course documentation, interview transcripts, qualitative questionnaire responses and researcher field notes.*[1]

Having undertaken research that requires me to understand and use new technologies means that I have learnt some lessons along the way. As well as the obvious advice about knowing how to use the technologies, including their strengths and limitations, and having a back-up plan if needed, I outline some general cautions in Table 11.2.

> *I am currently undertaking a UNESCO-funded project that allows schools to share their experiences of the 2010/11 Canterbury earthquakes. The use of technology greatly enhanced the quantity and quality of the data I gathered: audio recordings, video recordings, still photographs, YouTube and cellphone clips, children's written stories and artwork, media reports, websites, personal records and artefacts. Some of the difficulties I faced were technological. They included gathering, storing and managing the large amount of data gathered from a variety of sources. Eventually, I resolved this by keeping each school's material on individual external hard drives and making it available to co-researchers through cloud sources.*[2]

Table 11.2: Cautions when undertaking research using new technologies

Cautions	
Data overload	With access to so much data it is more important than ever that you consider the parameters of your research project. Although you need to have a reasonable amount of data that can be reduced to credible findings, unless you have unlimited time and resources you need to manage the scope of your project. In quantitative research, numbers are more easily recorded and manipulated, but considering what will actually answer the research question helps to keep your research focused. Inputting qualitative research data can be time consuming, even with tools such as data recognition software, because the technology is not yet fool proof. Narrowing the setting or timeframe or reducing the sample size might ensure you get enough in-depth richness, but keep your workload manageable.
Data quality	When you have not been the actual creator or first-hand collector of the data, how can you be sure of its quality? Being sceptical about the material you find, unless it has some quality assurance (such as being published in a peer-reviewed journal), is important. Try checking the source, the website, the author's credentials, the level of detail, the recency, and how it resonates with other findings or similar statistical sources.
Version control	Because you have access to, and create, vast amounts of material, knowing which version you have downloaded, uploaded, altered or saved is very important. Train yourself to record URLs (uniform resource locators), retrieval dates and access pathways, and to label versions. These days new electronic material often has a unique DOI (digital object identifier).
Ethics	In what ways does researching online include or exclude certain groups? What right do you have to data you find online? Is it public or private? How do you know? How do the rules of informed consent, anonymity, confidentiality, privacy and right to withdraw operate in an online or electronic environment? There are ways around these ethical dilemmas, but they need to be thought through before the research is undertaken and carefully explained to the participants.
Retrieval	We all know stories of someone's embarrassing Facebook photo or YouTube clip going viral. Deleting makes little difference because these things become embedded in and linked to sites far from the original and can reappear in the strangest of places. What safeguards do you have in place for the material you share electronically? How does this apply to your research participants? How are they protected from unintended retrieval or alteration now or in the future? These, and other questions we haven't even thought of yet, are all challenges to working in a cyber environment.
Keeping up	Many people get excited by the latest 'apps'. Research projects can be undertaken over an extended period of time, so researchers can be distracted by trying to learn the latest program or converting to the latest application. How important is it that you keep up? Will it enhance your data collection or analysis? Can you still get credible findings with your current technology? All research findings are only a snapshot in time, so I find I reach a certain point where I need to say, for this project, this is all I need or have time for. I can then take a more considered approach to the latest technology when I'm not pressured by deadlines.

Technology as a data source

With the explosion of electronic communication and information technology, researchers now have access to a huge array of raw and processed data. Common technologies such as phones and computers have moved so rapidly in terms of function and data storage capacity that it is hard to keep up. Since 1989 the World Wide Web has changed how we find, use and transfer information. There has also been a huge increase in social media. Dabner (2012) informs us that in 2010, 83 percent of New Zealanders used the Internet regularly; of these 80 percent checked it daily, 33 percent used instant messaging (e.g., texting), 25 percent played multi-player games at least weekly, and 50 percent were members of social networking sites (e.g., Facebook, LinkedIn).

Dabner (2012, pp. 69–70, citing Armstrong and Franklin, 2008) also helpfully lists and explains common Web 2.0 technologies:

- blogs (cumulative books where authors publish entries and invite responses)
- wikis, which enable the collaborative creation of a series of web pages
- social bookmarking, which enables users to collate, tag, and share websites of interest
- media sharing spaces, which enable users to post and share photos, podcasts and video
- RSS [Rich Site Summary] feeds, which enable users to view information from a wide variety of sources quickly
- collaborative editing tools, which enable multiple users to share and edit documents
- micro-blogging sites, such as Twitter, which enable users to publish very short messages
- social networking sites, which enable the creation of online communities.

Not only do these functions provide new data; they are also of interest as research topics in themselves.

> *Nicki found herself in the midst of the 2010/11 Canterbury earthquakes. She documented quantitatively and qualitatively how the University of Canterbury used social media to provide support, information, communication channels, learning programmes and collaborative opportunities throughout the earthquake response and recovery period.*[3]

Merriam (2009) asks in what ways are these sources similar to conventional sources, such as documents, and in what ways are they different? Web pages, for example, could be considered as 'electronic paper', which can be analysed as text, and YouTube clips can be viewed using quantitative or qualitative observation techniques, but their creation, accuracy, placement, location, reliability and transience mean they bring with them an extra set of cautions and layers of complexity. Add to this the creation of virtual identities and Merriam (2009) comments:

> Under these conditions, the assumption that the world is composed of multiple, changing realities—part of the qualitative paradigm—becomes at once a trivially self-evident observation and a magnified complication. (p. 159)

Technology for dissemination

Not only has technology opened up access to a wider range of sources to us, it has also made it possible for us to disseminate our ideas easily and quickly to a wider audience. Informally, we can set up our own web page, write a blog (web log), insert links, upload a YouTube clip, start a discussion thread, text, tweet, or email links and attachments. I find blogs or vlogs (video logs) from eminent academics very useful. They are often their latest thoughts on complex topics. The downside is that I have had to learn how to reference electronic sources and to take care that I record the full URL (uniform resource locator) and the date I retrieved the material.

Technology has also made it easier to disseminate more substantial pieces of work. Large research reports and theses can be reduced to PDF (portable document file) format; journals are available as open or closed source, hardcopy or electronic; and books can come in hardcopy and e-formats. Electronic versions of print and other media can be downloaded to computers, e-readers and smartphones. Hardcopy books and journals can be produced more cheaply or printed on demand.

> *As part of the UNESCO-funded earthquake research, each school is entitled to a copy of their story in a format of their choice. Little did I know that each school would request a different format: an interactive website, a hardcopy book, a video documentary or a collaborative art work. Luckily, modern technology and experts with access to the right equipment and computer programs have been able to turn these wishes into reality.*[4]

With each technological update comes a new set of dilemmas. Lawyers now specialise in electronic intellectual property rights and copyright law. Libraries, publishers and institutions try to keep abreast of what can and can't be copied, shared, reproduced, cited, referenced and disseminated. For those of us constantly gathering research material, it is important to be vigilant and to be respectful of other people's ideas and rights to remuneration. If in doubt,

I ask a librarian; if they don't know, they always seem to be able to find out for me. Merriam (2009) concludes her discussion on research technology with these thoughts:

> This is new territory, with unfamiliar rules that change as quickly as they are identified. My best advice for researchers is to recognise that the results of their research are strongly influenced by the characteristics of the data revealed, concealed or altered because of the nature of the medium through which they are presented. Analyzing, describing and discussing the potential effects of these characteristics will be an important aspect of research conducted [in this field]. (p. 160)

What are some recent developments in quantitative research?

Although quantitative research is sometimes held up as 'the gold standard' in educational research overseas (for example, in the United States), in New Zealand, educators seem to undertake more qualitative research. There might be various explanations for this. For example, many educational researchers come to research from a practitioner background rather than through an academic pathway that includes training in statistical research methods. Also, much educational research focuses on what happens in schools and classrooms, where experimental or large-scale quantitative studies are not as easy to undertake. And culturally appropriate approaches used in Māori or Pacific settings prefer kanohi ki te kanohi (face-to-face) or fono (conversational) methods.

Whatever the reason, many New Zealand educational researchers shy away from quantitative methods. My approach is that you look for methods that will best help answer your research question. Quantitative research is very useful for quantifying the size of the problem, highlighting relationships and tracking the trends—very helpful for trying to influence policy, for example.

If your question requires gathering and analysing numerical data, this need not be a barrier if your knowledge of statistics is not as strong as it could be. There are many useful texts and websites that explain quantitative methods step by step,[5] and much of the work can be done using an Excel spreadsheet or a research tool such as Survey Monkey. If you are confident with quantitative research, there are many more exciting things that can be done with programs such as SPSS (Statistical Package for the Social Sciences) or StatView, or other data management, statistical analysis and data mining products.

Three trends that I would like to discuss in this section spring from trying to maximise the use, and usefulness, of quantitative data: the increased prevalence of meta-analyses and research syntheses; the use of small-scale quantitative interventions through design-based research; and crossing paradigm boundaries through the use of mixed methods approaches to educational research.

Meta-analysis of research findings

In New Zealand we have become familiar with meta-analyses through the work of John Hattie (see, for example, Hattie, 2009). *Meta-analyses* of quantitative studies help educators make sense of the vast amount of research on teaching and learning, especially where the results seem to be in conflict with each other. Rosenthal and DiMatteo (2001) claim that

> meta-analysis has come to occupy a major place in contemporary scientific research partly because ... it helps overcome much of the equivocation about research findings in the social sciences and medicine by providing a method for combining research results. (p. 63)

Meta-analysis combines the numerical results of a range of related studies and uses descriptive statistics to produce 'moderated' or 'mediated' results. The effects in each study are converted to a common measure—an effect size—which can be further analysed to highlight the aspects that have the most impact. An effect size of $d = 1.0$ indicates an increase of one standard deviation on the outcome. An effect size of 0.2 or less is considered low, 0.4 is medium and 0.6 or more is high.

John synthesised over 800 meta-analyses (over 50,000 studies) relating to influences on student achievement. His book, Visible Learning, *was the result of 15 years' research. He examined 138 different influences on student achievement and placed the results along a continuum of effect sizes, ranging from $d = -.34$ to $d = 1.44$. He was then able to identify and discuss what he considered were the factors or strategies that had the most impact. These included feedback, challenging goals, direct instruction, mastery learning and student self-verbalisation.*[5]

Rosenthal and DiMatteo (2001) discuss the important contribution of meta-analyses to research. In order to arrive at the combined results, the initial studies are carefully scrutinised and evaluated against meticulous criteria before being selected. This adds a layer of peer review to the original studies. Meta-analyses draw out the similarities and differences in methods and findings, and therefore provide a broader picture of the research enterprise than individual studies do. Rosenthal and DiMatteo also claim that by combining multiple studies, meta-analysis allows researchers to extract clear answers to important problems.

Research syntheses

As with meta-analyses, *research syntheses* can pull together a wide range of studies on a topic to highlight significant findings, discuss the outcomes of different methodologies and draw out key themes. We have become familiar with research syntheses through the Ministry of Education's Iterative Best Evidence Synthesis Programme (known as the BES), which has received world-wide acclaim from organisations such as the International Academy of Education. The first BES publications were produced in 2003, including *Quality Teaching for Diverse Students in Schooling: Best Evidence Synthesis* (Alton-Lee, 2003). Since then there have been a number of other syntheses focusing on topics such as family influences, early childhood, mathematics, social sciences, teacher professional development and school leadership.

> Research syntheses draw on the findings of a wide range of relevant high-quality studies, which can be both quantitative and qualitative, to highlight key themes, provide sets of principles and share relevant case studies of the principles in action.

Viviane and colleagues conducted a synthesis of 134 New Zealand and overseas research studies or reviews on effective leadership practices. In New Zealand, the mean effect size for student gain from a year's teaching is .35. The big finding of this BES is that when school leaders promote and/or participate in effective teacher professional learning, this has twice the impact on student outcomes across a school than any other leadership activity.[6]

Design-based research

The two approaches outlined so far rely on large-scale national or international data, but there are other recent approaches that are more suited to smaller, intensive research projects. One such approach is design-based research (DBR). My interest in design-based research is that it aims to bridge the gap between research and practice—a little bit like practitioner research but with stronger quantitative input. Anderson and Shattuck (2012) have this to say:

> DBR is a methodology designed by and for educators that seeks to increase the impact, transfer, and translation of education research into improved practice. In addition, it stresses the need for theory building and the development of design principles that guide, inform, and improve both practice and research in educational contexts. (p. 16)

Anderson and Shattuck (2012) reviewed the past decade of design-based research publications and concluded that the characteristics included:
- being situated in a real educational context
- focusing on the design and testing of a significant intervention
- using mixed methods
- involving multiple iterations
- involving a collaborative partnership between researchers and practitioners
- the evolution of design principles
- similarity to action research
- having a practical impact on practice.

> Design-based research starts in a real classroom or institutional context with a real problem that needs to be solved. Needs analysis, context assessment and an overview of relevant literature begin the project. A design process is used to suggest an appropriate innovation or intervention. Through a series of trials and iterations, the intervention is implemented and evaluated, with adaptations being made until useful results are obtained.

> *Jody and colleagues set up an MUVE (multi-user virtual environment) called River City with the aim of keeping teenaged girls motivated and interested in science. Their project used design-based research principles. They used multiple iterative cycles in their design. The first cycle gathered observational, survey and pre- and post-test data to inform theory and design. Although the first results were encouraging, student feedback led to design modifications. This continued through a further three cycles of data gathering, feedback, design modification and theoretical refinement.*[7]

Mixing methods: quantitising qualitative data and qualitising quantitative data

Another of the more recent trends in using quantitative analyses more creatively comes as researchers look to *mixed methods research* (I say more about this later). Mixed methodologists are experimenting with ways to quantitise qualitative data and qualitise quantitative data. How might this work?

This is not a completely new idea. For example, qualitative researchers have often counted themes or occurrences in text as part of their analysis. Then there is the *Delphi technique*, which derives categories from qualitative data (for example, through interviews) and then iteratively revises and tightens the resulting categories before using them for quantitative purposes, such as rating or ranking.

Some of the more recent studies I've seen have quantitised qualitative data by:
- giving weightings to qualitatively derived attributes and examining them statistically
- assigning a numeric to inductively derived categories and looking for correlations.

Examples of qualitising quantitative data include:
- examining or following up the outliers more closely to understand why they fall outside the norm or trend, or
- grouping quantitative attributes together and creating a descriptive profile of the group or cluster.

Christopher and colleagues used a complex research methodology—involving both qualitative and quantitative data from individual semi-structured and narrative interviews, group interviews, critical event timelines, questionnaires, document analysis, student assessment data and case studies—in a longitudinal study. The data were reformulated and combined, for example, when teachers' perceptions of their effectiveness were matched with statistical analyses of their students' achievement. The researchers explain their approach further:

> Case studies were developed for all 300 teachers, a process that involved qualitizing quantitative evidence, quantitizing qualitative evidence, and integrating the two (followed by a consequent synergistic interpretation). This interactive combination of data collection, on-going analysis, tentative hypothesis generation, and testing and interpretation of results ... provides greater mapping, analysis, interpretation, and holistic understandings of the research area than would be gained by relying on single paradigm or approach.[8]

I gave a seminar on mixed methods recently and asked the audience whether you could play with data sets in this way and still have valid and ethical results. It certainly caused some debate! This is an area in which to watch developments with interest.

What are some recent developments in qualitative research?

Qualitative research has always been about pushing the boundaries and embracing creative ways to produce, gather, analyse and report research findings. As Cohen, Manion and Morrison (2011) claim:

> The social and educational world is a messy place, full of contradictions, richness, complexity, connectedness, conjunction and disjunction. It is multi-layered and not easily susceptible to the atomization process inherent in much numerical research. It has to be studied in total rather than in fragment if true understanding is to be reached. (p. 219)

My interest in new and innovative qualitative methods could fill a book on its own, so I have limited myself in this section to respond to two of the questions that my colleagues or students suggested I address: how do you make qualitative research more rigorous, and how do you write up research that doesn't fit traditional research reports? In preparation for this book I also surveyed recent qualitative journals and noted popular topics. The most common included research quality, mixed methods, race/culture, reflexivity, the place of theory, alternative methodologies, ethics, auto-ethnography and narrative. Later in the chapter I briefly dip into a range of narrative, visual, arts-based and reflective approaches to address some of these interests and further expand your qualitative repertoire.

One of the common questions I have been asked by new researchers is how to respond to critiques that qualitative research doesn't meet the requirements for 'scientific research'. While many qualitative researchers feel that there is no need to engage in this debate because it only gives further credibility to the narrow definition of scientific research, we can all benefit from ensuring our research is rigorous regardless of the underpinning paradigm.

Merriam (2009) provides a detailed list (Table 11.3) of ways that you can enhance the rigour and defend the credibility of qualitative research. Using a mixture of these strategies and explaining them in your report can strengthen the acceptance of your findings.

Table 11.3: Strategies for promoting validity and reliability in qualitative research

Strategy	Description
1. Triangulation	Using multiple investigators, sources of data or data collection to confirm emerging findings.
2. Member checks	Taking data and tentative interpretations back to the people from whom they were derived and asking if they are plausible.
3. Adequate engagement in data collection	Adequate time spent collecting data such that data become 'saturated'; this may involve seeking discrepant or negative cases.
4. Researcher's position or reflexivity	Critical self-reflection by the researcher regarding assumptions, world-view biases, theoretical orientation and relationship to the study that may affect the investigation.

5. Peer review/ examination	Discussions with colleagues regarding the process of the study and the congruence of emerging findings with the raw and tentative interpretations.
6. Audit trail	A detailed account of the methods, procedures and decision points in carrying out the study.
7. Rich, thick descriptions	Providing enough description to contextualise the study, such that readers will be able to determine the extent to which their situations match the research context, and, hence, whether findings can be transferred.
8. Maximum variation	Purposefully seeking variation or diversity in sample selection to allow for a greater range of application of the findings by consumers of the research.

Source: Merriam, 2009, p. 229

A second question I am asked, especially by research students completing dissertations and theses, is how to present qualitative findings that don't fit traditional research report formats. One of the joys of qualitative research is that you come to learn as much about yourself as you do about your participants or your topic. You come to see a world of complexity with multiple perspectives and fluid end points. How will you represent this? If your project is being examined for a qualification, how can you fit within your institution's regulations?

> *Sally's thesis concerned autobiography, memory and identity. It was presented as two bound artists' journals (one was autobiographical, containing many complex images; the other was more theoretical, with illustrations), enclosed in a cardboard box painted to look like a steamer trunk. This was despite her university's regulations about formal bindings for the cover. She discusses her approach: "The creative part involved creative writing, creative non-fiction, poetry, graphics and design, and a/r/tography (where text and image become entwined to form a new entity). In addition I learnt three computer programs, elements of graphic design theory and book-binding."*[9]

It takes courage to go against convention, and I would not recommend doing this for a qualification without the support of your supervisor(s) and/or department. As Knowles and Promislow (2008) state:

> It would be comforting to imagine that this kind of developmental work is plain sailing. But often it is not. In large institutions—even where the arts in qualitative research is supported by a cluster of faculty—it is not uncommon for thesis and dissertation proposals involving the arts in research to be rejected or watered down, or for the new researcher to flounder around in efforts to find a supervisor and supervising committee to support the work. (p. 514)

While some candidates add photographs, drawings, poetry and personal narrative to their theses, these are often additional or complementary to the main text.

Further along the continuum are candidates who present their theses as a performance or exhibition. Where this happens, an 'exegesis' (critical essay, dissertation, annotation, report or documentation) usually accompanies the presentation (Kroll, 2004). Milech and Schilo (2004) suggest three types of exegesis models: context (provides the historical, theoretical or social context for the work), commentary (provides a detailed annotation or explanation of the work) and research-question (where the research question and the creative work constantly interact with each other). There is a slow but increasing acceptance of alternative formats, and some conferences and journals are encouraging presenters to push the boundaries.

> *In 2007 Pauline was the winner of the 2007 Arts Based Educational Research Outstanding Dissertation Award from the American Educational Research Association. Her thesis was written as a series of letters and poems between the protagonist, Julia, and her academic supervisor, as a critical personal narrative. She used the five elements (wood, fire, earth, metal and water) as chapter headings, and the thesis was illustrated with her artworks—mosaics, paintings, and black and white botanical line drawings. Pauline's dissertation has since been published as a book.*[10]

Is mixed methods research a 'third paradigm'?

Many writers are finding ways to blur the line between the quantitative and qualitative paradigms. One of the critiques of the first edition of *Doing Educational Research* was that I focused too much on the differences between the two. My justification was that I didn't think researchers could choose the appropriate methods to answer their research questions if they didn't understand what each approach *could* and *could not* do.

I still maintain that you need to understand the assumptions on which each approach is based and how they shape the types of questions investigated, and the way data are gathered, analysed and reported. I have, however, been investigating ways in which to break down the idea that they are polar opposites and to consider how the strengths of each paradigm could be used to the give more insightful interpretation of findings. Many other writers are doing the same.

Ragin and Amoroso (2011) see research approaches as falling along a continuum according to the number of cases a researcher is investigating. For them,

- **qualitative research** focuses on the commonalities that exist across a small number of cases
- **comparative research** focuses on the diversity that exists across a moderate number of cases
- **quantitative research** focuses on the correspondence between two or more attributes across a large number of cases.

Tashakkori and Teddlie (2003, p. 4) see it differently and suggest that there are currently three types of researcher:
- **quantitatively oriented** (those working within the post-positivist tradition and focused more on numerical analysis)
- **qualitatively oriented** (those working within the constructivist tradition and using narrative data)
- **mixed methodologists** (those working within other paradigms; e.g., pragmatism or transformative-emancipatory paradigms, and using a range of data).

In fact, Johnson, Onwuegbuzie & Turner (2007) would claim that mixed methods research is the 'third paradigm':

> Mixed methods research is an intellectual and practical synthesis based on qualitative and quantitative research; it is the third methodological or research paradigm ... It recognizes the importance of traditional quantitative and qualitative research but also offers a powerful third paradigm choice that often will provide the most informative, complete, balanced, and the most useful research results. (p. 129)

Many would say that mixed methods research is as old as inquiry itself, as early scientists used mixtures of qualitative observations and practical experiments to make sense of the world and derive scientific laws. In the 20th century we faced the 'paradigm wars' as interpretive (qualitative) researchers challenged the dominance of positivist (quantitative) approaches. Mixed method research recognises that both paradigms have their strengths.

> Mixed methods research uses a combination of quantitative and qualitative approaches. The mixing of quantitative and qualitative methods and data can happen in a variety of ways, with one or other paradigm dominant, the two complementing each other, or the two being mixed sequentially or iteratively. More recent approaches include transforming one type of data into the other.

Although some would say that because methods derive from different beliefs about the world and they cannot be mixed to achieve valid results (this is called *the incompatibility thesis*), others hold that methods arising from quantitative or qualitative traditions *can* be separated from their philosophical bases and mixed in various ways to suit the needs of the research (*the compatibility thesis*). Researchers who undertake mixed methods research use a range of justifications, which I have summarised in Table 11.4.

Table 11.4: Reasons for using mixed methods research approaches	
Justifications	**Examples**
Theoretical	Pragmatism is a theoretical approach used by mixed method researchers to justify choosing what works best regardless of a method's origins. Transformative-emancipatory researchers use mixed methods because they feel they provide more in-depth insights and varying perspectives. Some researchers take an atheoretical stance— they don't feel that theory should have any impact on their research design. Other researchers mix their theories with their approaches; for example, using positivist theory to support quantitative methods and interpretive theory to support qualitative methods.
Methodological	Some researchers claim mixed method research best answers the research question. Some claim mixed methods can answer more complex questions. Other researchers say mixed approaches are more rigorous and trustworthy. For example, they support: • triangulation • complementarity • clarifying contradictions, tensions or paradoxes • development • expansion.
Ethical	Some researchers claim a mixed approach is more ethical; for example, this approach: • provides views from multiple perspectives • allows for culturally appropriate methods • lessens paradigmatic dominance • is iterative and reflexive • makes the process more transparent.
Practical	Some researchers justify their use of mixed methods from a practical standpoint, because it: • makes better use of time and resources • makes best possible use of the data gathered • adds to rigour • adds to clarity • meets a broader range of interests.

There are many decisions to be made when implementing mixed method research. Will the whole study be mixed or only part? Will one paradigm (either quantitative or qualitative) be dominant or will they be complementary? Where will theory fit? Will the mixing be sequential: quantitative followed by qualitative, or the other way round? Will the analysis of the data drawn from each method be kept separate, or will they be mixed in some way?

In a recent article (Mutch, 2009) I argued that it was no longer appropriate to 'do a bit of this and a bit of that' without thinking through the implications of the decisions you were making when you chose to mix methods. I concluded that article by outlining a framework from Yanchar & Williams (2006) in which they use a 'soft incompatibility thesis'. What I like about this framework is the set of criteria for consideration—contextual sensitivity, creativity, conceptual awareness, coherence and critical reflection.

- **Contextual sensitivity** means the selection of any method, or the mixing of methods, would have to fit the relevant context.
- **Creativity** could be brought to bear so that theory construction, question formulation and method development do not necessarily need to be bound by paradigmatic rigidity.
- **Conceptual awareness** ensures that a consistent philosophical or theoretical approach underpins the research.
- **Coherence** does not necessarily mean adherence to a restrictive step-by-step process, but it does mean there is an internal consistency and logic to the decisions made.
- **Critical reflection** should underpin all aspects of the research, from the research problem, through question formulation and method selection, to analysis and interpretation. (Mutch, 2009, p. 24)

Tony and colleagues developed a 10-step framework called an Instrument Development and Construct Validation. Their 10 phases begin by conceptualising the construct they want to examine (for example, cultural competence). Early phases develop, pilot and revise the construct, its attributes and a relevant instrument (for example, an observation schedule). Middle phases conduct individual quantitative and qualitative analysis. Final phases conduct mixed crossover analyses to inform the evaluation and validation of the construct and the instrument. They then used the framework to create their School-Wide Cultural Competence Observation Checklist.[11]

How similar or different are research and evaluation?

Between writing the first edition of *Doing Educational Research* and my current position, I spent 3 years working in evaluation for the Education Review Office. Prior to this role I had strong views, as I outlined in another paper (Mutch, 2011, p. 2):

> In the research I undertook, the relationship between research and evaluation, however, appeared unproblematic. Research was the set and evaluation was the subset. After all—it used the same methods and tools as research and in much of the literature it was called 'evaluation research'—that is, 'research' was the noun and 'evaluation' was the adjective describing a type of research. Without thinking more deeply, I thought that evaluation fitted into research at either the methodology or methods level. When I conducted evaluations, I did so through a research frame. In *Doing Educational Research* (Mutch, 2005) I devoted over 200 pages to research methods and about four lines to evaluation.

Those three years opened up a new way of seeing the place of evaluation, and in the paper I have just cited I spent some time describing what this experience had taught me about the similarities and differences between research and evaluation. Figure 11.1 summarises my ideas.

I also argue in this paper that evaluation can now be considered a discipline it is own right. It has its own body of theory, practice, research and literature, along with professional organisations, journals, conferences, qualifications and sets of professional standards. It has recognisable purposes, questions, approaches and outcomes.

External and internal evaluation are common activities in most organisations, especially in New Zealand, where the Education Review Office (ERO) and the New Zealand Qualifications Authority (NZQA) conduct reviews at most levels of the education sector. My role in ERO was to develop a complementary evaluation framework, whereby the processes of internal evaluation (self-review) and external evaluation (e.g., an ERO review) were combined to produce a useful set of findings and a resultant action plan. Figure 11.1 was adapted from material developed for ERO and school professional learning seminars. It highlights important questions that can be used by anyone undertaking internal and/or external evaluations.

> *Sandra led a team of evaluators who conducted an external evaluation in over 200 New Zealand schools to find out about the quality of engagement between schools and the parents and whānau (families and extended families) of their students. These schools represented a mixture of school types and sizes, both urban and rural,*

and ranged across the decile (socieconomic) levels. The main data sources used were: school documentation and school-based interviews; written questionnaires (in both English and te reo Māori); facilitated discussion groups; and eight in-depth case studies of good practice.[12]

Figure 11.1: Description of similarities and differences between research and evaluation

Similarities	Differences
Contested histories • Both have long informal and formal histories, but in recent times have faced paradigmatic tension around legitimacy and ascendancy.	**Purpose** • Although research often aims to contribute to understanding a problem or situation, evaluation goes a step further and makes a judgement about aspects of the setting or situation.
Theoretical underpinnings • Both call on a range of theories along the positivist–interpretive continuum.	**Questions** • Research questions are framed to gather data to address the problem or describe the situation; evaluation questions are framed to aid decision making.
Rigorous methodologies • Both take issues of rigour seriously through paradigmatic-appropriate validation strategies.	**Samples and settings** • Researchers generally have more scope in selecting samples and settings, whereas evaluators are limited to the setting under investigation.
Ethical considerations • Both consider how to resolve the ethical issues raised by the investigation.	**Roles and relationships** • Both researchers and evaluators develop relationships with their participants, but the extra element of what is 'at stake' affects the evaluative relationship.
Contextual sensitivities • Both are concerned with the contextual sensitivities within the particular paradigmatic approach, especially the issue of cultural competence.	**Implementation** • Both research and evaluation gather, analyse and interpret data, but evaluation turns data into evidence to support a claim, judgement or decision.
Political conundrums • Both, especially in the field of education, acknowledge that whether conducting research and evaluation, there are political choices with political consequences.	**Results and outcomes** • Who owns, and what happens to, the results can differ between research and evaluation, and an evaluation can also aim for more utility during and after the evaluation process.

Source: Mutch, 2011, p. 5

Are there new developments in cultural and ethical frameworks?

As a Pākehā, I have become more aware of the way in which culturally sensitive approaches have become more mainstream in educational theory, practice and research. While I would agree that there is still some way to go, it is heartening to see that acting in culturally appropriate ways is included in formal codes

Figure 11.2: Questions to guide external and internal evaluations	
An external evaluation process	**An internal evaluation process**
What is so? *What's important?* *What data are / information is there?* *What do people think of and do with their data/information?* *What do we need to ask or discuss?* **Why is it so?** *Why are things like this?* *What do our investigations show us?* *Where does our evidence come from?* **So what?** *What is the significance of our findings?* *What matters are most important?* *What judgements can we make?* **Now what?** *What are the next steps?* *How achievable are they?* *How will we prioritise them?* *What assistance can be provided?* *(e.g., timing, intervention)*	• What do we need to know more about? • What are the questions we need to ask? • Why will we ask these questions? • What data or evidence will we need to collect? • Who do we need to involve in the process? • How do we collect these data and from whom? • What do we want to do with the information we find? • How do we make sense of the data we have collected? • What are our data telling us? • How have we made a difference? To what? To whom? How do we know? • What do we need to do to improve, change or move forward? • What do we need to do now?

Adapted from Mutch, 2007, p. 32

of ethics and research guidelines, as well as being more embedded in actual research practices.

The Aotearoa New Zealand Evaluation Association (2008) suggests that researchers and evaluators in in Aotearoa New Zealand display:

- an understanding of Te Tiriti o Waitangi [the Treaty of Waitangi] as New Zealand's founding principles and active application of those principles in evaluation practice
- acknowledgement and understanding of cultural uniqueness and the importance of cultural sensitivity and cultural inclusiveness
- knowledge of tikanga and how to work and behave in various Māori contexts
- ability to behave respectfully in unfamiliar cultural contexts.

I find the *Te Ara Tika Guidelines for Māori Research Ethics* (Putaiora Writing Group, 2010), published by the Health Research Council, provide a succinct but insightful way to think about researching in Māori contexts. I have reproduced an appendix to this document (which appears here as Table 11.5). It outlines the difference between 'research involving Māori', 'Māori-centred research' and 'kaupapa Māori research'. This is a helpful way to re-think what we do as researchers in Māori contexts, with and for whom. While the examples provided are from the health sector, we could easily substitute educational examples.

Table 11.5: Te Ara Tika guidelines for Māori research

Characteristics	Research involving Māori	Māori-centred research	Kaupapa Māori research
Description	Research where Māori are involved as participants or subjects, or possibly as junior members of a research team; research where Māori data are sought and analysed; research where Māori may be trained in contemporary research methods and mainstream analysis	Research where Māori are significant participants, and are typically senior members of research teams; research where a Māori analysis is undertaken and which produces Māori knowledge, albeit measured against mainstream standards for research	Research where Māori are significant participants and where the research team is typically all Māori; research where a Māori analysis is undertaken and which produces Māori knowledge; research which primarily meets expectations and quality standards set by Māori
Examples	Analysis of ethnic differentials in disease rates; genetic study of familial cancer	Longitudinal social science study of Māori households	Traditional study of cosmology; study of culturally specific determinants of health
Control	Mainstream	Mainstream	Māori
Māori participation	Minor	Major	Major, possibly exclusive
Methods/tools	Contemporary—mainstream	Contemporary—mainstream and Māori	Contemporary—mainstream and Māori
Analysis	Mainstream	Māori	Māori

Source: Putaiora Working Group, 2010, Appendix C, p. 23

The New Zealand Association for Research in Education recently completed a revision to its *Ethical Guidelines* (New Zealand Association for Research in Education, 2010) in response to changing researcher profiles and research environments. The guidelines explain (p. 1) that:

> For example, the advent of e-learning and social networking, systematic reviews and digital technologies all pose new ethical challenges for researchers, while

non-Western epistemologies and participatory research relations have become more accepted.

While sharing many features in common with overseas models, these guidelines are specific to the New Zealand context—acknowledging the Treaty of Waitangi, the United Nations Declaration on the Rights of Indigenous Peoples and the understanding of "Aotearoa New Zealand as (a) locally, a linguistically and culturally diverse state; (b) regionally, in the Pacific; and (c) globally, part of an increasingly networked society" (p. 3).

> *Sharyn (Kai Tahu, Muaūpoko, Rangitāne, Te Arawa) conducted research which showed that although there was a move to integrate Māori language, knowledge and culture into New Zealand curricula, Māori terms and concepts are often used inappropriately or superficially. She used the concept of hauora to make her case: "Attempts to provide a universal definition of hauora translated simplistically as 'health and physical well-being' have the potential to undermine the autonomy and authority of iwi and hapū in favour of an all-encompassing assimilative construct."*[13]

Culturally sensitive research approaches have also broadened in scope internationally. Some aim to raise awareness of the place of indigenous people, as in the *Guidelines for Ethical Research in Australian Indigenous Studies* (Australian Institute of Aboriginal and Torres Strait Islander Studies, 2011), which had this to say:

> It is essential that Indigenous people are full participants in research projects that concern them, share an understanding of the aims of and methods of the research, and share the results of this work. At every stage, research with and about Indigenous peoples must be founded on a process of meaningful engagement and reciprocity between the researcher and Indigenous people. It should also be recognised that there is no sharp distinction between researchers and Indigenous people. Indigenous people are also researchers, and all participants must be regarded as equal participants in a research engagement. (p. 4)

Others focus on those groups whose ethnicity or culture is marginalised in society. In writing about research on African Americans, Tillman (2002) reminds researchers that this group differs from European Americans in many ways—culture, history, language patterns, world views and political experiences. The advice for culturally credible research with African Americans could equally apply to minority or marginalised groups in other societies, including New Zealand. Such research needs to be aware of:

- culturally congruent research methods
- culturally specific knowledge
- cultural resistance to theoretical dominance
- culturally sensitive data interpretations
- culturally informed theory and practice. (p. 6)

Specific examples of resistance to theoretical dominance in the New Zealand context include the rise of kaupapa Māori and Pacific theories and methods. Amituanai-Toloa (2009), for example, lists a range of Pacific theories and approaches that reflect location, language, culture, history and the richness of metaphor. The list includes *talanoa* (conversation method), *kakala* (opening of the fragrances), *tivaevae* (quilt-making), *fa'afaletui* (weaving), *fonofale* (meeting house) and *potou* (pillar).

> *Nesta, Jeanne and Lorraine used the Tongan concept of tauhi vā (peaceful and harmonious relationships within the collective) to analyse and reinterpret the early childhood curriculum, Te Whāriki, for the Tongan community. They felt that embracing the notion of tauhi vā would help nurture a safe and productive learning environment for Tongan children and their families and relate to practices in homes, schools, churches and other community settings.*[14]

How have textual, visual and arts-based approaches developed?

Many researchers are making more use of textual, visual and artistic data sources and analysis in the context of their research. Prosser and Loxley (2008) suggest that such data could be:
- examined as found
- created by the researcher
- created by the respondent, or
- compiled as a representation.

Textual and narrative approaches

Text is a common data source. It can be gathered or created through a range of methods and analysed quantitatively or qualitatively (or both). In Chapter 9 I briefly introduced thematic, semiotic and discourse analysis. I have used *semiotic analysis* to look more deeply at how interview participants construct their stories and *discourse analysis* to uncover ideological assumptions. I am also moving into *conversational analysis* to articulate the emotional and cognitive strategies that participants might use to frame their stories.

When examining text, Wengraf (2001) suggests three levels of analysis: the surface analysis of text, the middle-level narrative structure and the deep structure of underlying themes. Through examination of the use of time, space and action, how the story teller positions him/herself and the listener, or how the story goes from its opening to its closing event, we can gain an insight into more than a simple thematic analysis might provide.

> *As part of my research into the development of the social studies curriculum, I took three interviews and examined them against Wengraf's (2001) critical linguistics semiotics model. I was able to analyse how each viewed the problem, the moment of transformation and the resolution. I could show how one participant framed her account as a set of small problem-solution sequences, another framed his story as a quest metaphor, and the third as a search for redemption.*[15]

When research participants, especially in more open-ended research, answer questions or discuss the topic being investigated, they frame their responses in certain ways. One of the most common ways is to tell it as a narrative. Narrative research has grown to be a field of study in itself. Polkinghorne (2007) describes it this way:

> Narrative research is the study of stories. Stories are ubiquitous, appearing as historical accounts, as fictional novels, as fairy tales, as autobiographies, and other genres. Stories are also told by people about themselves and about others as part of their everyday conversations. In addition to the stories that appear in people's ordinary conversations, narrative researchers study stories they solicit from others: oral stories obtained through interviews and written stories through requests. The study of stories and the 'storying' process is undertaken by various academic disciplines including literary criticism, history, philosophy, organizational theory, and social science. (p. 1)

Although discourse analysis was mentioned briefly earlier in the book, I want to return to this as an important tool for undertaking research into policy and politics. Table 11.6 indicates a range of possible research approaches to analysing policy, including discourse analysis.

Discourse analysis as a term can be a little confusing. Some researchers working in linguistics, for example, Gee (1995), use the term to mean "a connected stretch of language" (p. 142) that can be analysed grammatically. I want to focus more on discourse analysis as it arises out of the philosophical tradition of *post-structuralism* (for example, Foucault, 1981). In this way, it is a tool that gets beneath surface features and uncovers ideological meanings.

Table 11.6: Policy as a research context	
Policy research interests	**Suggested research methods**
Policy changes over time	Historical research Document analysis
Policy makers	Élite interviews Non-participant observations Discourse analysis
Policy stakeholders	Focus group interviews Questionnaires
The content of policy documents	Document analysis Discourse analysis
Policy evaluation	Impact analysis Case studies

Discourse analysis, in a political or policy context, aims to uncover hidden meanings in language. It enables researchers to investigate how power is used and misused. It requires a knowledge of the historical, social and political setting in which these discourses are used. A researcher also needs to know the assumptions that underpin the beliefs of the various ideological factions and the meanings they attach to significant words and concepts.

Growing up in socialist Czechoslovakia in the 1970s and 1980s, Marek was involved in daily encounters with politics and the production of political subjectivities. Through analysis of the government-supported children's magazine Little Bee, *he documented the attempted production of desired political childhood subjectivities. To analyse these stories, he used Václav Havel's political philosophy of power relations and the production of citizens within a specific political context, as well as adding autobiographical and personal narratives.*[16]

As well as developments in a range of textual analysis strategies for analysing more conventional forms of text, such as documents and interview transcripts, Denzin alerts us to the possibilities of what he calls "new writing practices" (2006, p. 420):

> These new writing practices include autoethnography, fiction-stories, poetry, performance texts, polyvocal texts, reader's theatre, responsive readings, aphorisms, comedy and satire, visual presentations, allegory, conversation, layered accounts, writing stories, and mixed genres. Creative nonfiction, performance writing, mysteries, memoirs, personal histories, and cultural criticism can be added to this list of narrative forms that can be used by the creative analytic ethnographer.

Esther wanted to explore the ethical role of herself as the researcher when she was undertaking research as a collaborative and participatory practice. Through a scripted fictional conversation with John Steinbeck, she drew on stories from her research practice using emerging ethnographic methodologies to illustrate the critical role of the researcher. At a recent conference, Esther shared her fictional conversation as a dramatic performance.[17]

Visual media as a data source

Prosser and Loxley (2008) suggest that creating, examining or responding to visual data opens up possibilities that other methods might overlook:

> Visual methods offer a range of alternative, diverse and creative possibilities that will expand and support the shifting orientation of social science research and ultimately advance knowledge. Simply put, visual methods can: provide an alternative to the hegemony of a word-and-number based academy; slow down observation and encourage deeper and more effective reflection on all things visual and visualisable; and with it enhance our understanding of sensory embodiment and communication, and hence reflect more fully the diversity of human experiences. (p. 4)

Cohen, Manion and Morrison (2011) list the variety of visual media an education researcher can draw on:

> film, video, photographs, television, advertisements, pictures, artefacts, objects of fine art, memorabilia, moving images, still images, media images, maps, representations, cartoons, everyday objects and deliberately non-commonplace. (p. 528)

I would add the range of visual images now available from, created by and altered through electronic media.

When examining visual media, there are many aspects to take into consideration as well as the item itself: how was it produced? who is it for? what is the social or historical context of its production? what is it composed of? where is it located? where and why is it placed in this position? and so on. Cohen, Manion and Morrison (2011) also remind us that

> Visual media are not neutral; they give messages, deliberately or not, and we interpret them in many different ways … They are constructions of social events and perspectives, of power and power relations, of social relations and social difference. More than that, we look at them in different ways, i.e., we bring our own values, biographies, culture and background to bear on images. (p. 528)

Kirsten explored how architecture was a visual representation of the political ideologies behind education in tertiary contexts. By comparing a 1970s university campus with a 2000s business school building, she discussed how the exterior and interior designs both overtly and covertly shaped the teaching and learning experience.[18]

Arts-based approaches

Although researchers in this field of inquiry distinguish research that is in and on the arts, arts-based and arts informed, I am including all the variations under the *arts-based research* umbrella. McNiff (2008) defines arts-based research in this way:

> Arts-based research can be defined as the systematic use of the artistic process, the actual making of artistic expression in all of the different forms of the arts, as a primary way of understanding and examining experience by both researchers and the people that they involve in their studies. (p. 29)

Arts-based research is growing in popularity. Its proponents suggest that it covers a broader range of personal, emotional and aesthetic engagement than more traditional forms of research. Arts-based research is often participatory and collaborative. It aims to encompass a range of alternative perspectives, lived realities and ways of knowing. It excites researchers because it opens up wider possibilities of gathering, creating, reflecting, analysing and responding to data in new ways. It pushes boundaries and challenges assumptions.

The artistic endeavour or performance could be the subject of the research—as either a product or process—or it could be placed anywhere in the research sequence. The art work or performance could be a catalyst that inspires the research question. It could be used along the way to gather data (as in photography), or to create data (as in drama), to interpret data (as in poetry), to display data (as in computer-generated graphics), or to respond to data (as in dance)—or in any combination of these or other arts disciplines, in any way and place in the research.

> Arts-based research is a qualitative approach in which the arts can inform, complement, gather, create, synthesise, interpret, represent or respond to the self, setting, participants, topic, data or findings.

> *Meredith's study was both through and about an arts-based approach. She worked with prisoners at Christchurch Men's, Women's and Rolleston Prisons. A voluntary selection of prisoners created art works and auctioned them off for charity. Meredith returned to interview the participants some months later and told the story of the process and how the participants were changed by it through the metaphor of 'calling forth the hero within'.*[19]

Denzin (2006) would claim that all qualitative research (and here he talks specifically about ethnography) is arts-based, personal and political:

> Ethnography is a not an innocent practice. Our research practices are performative, pedagogical, and political. Through our writing and our talk, we enact the worlds we study. These performances are messy and pedagogical. They instruct our readers about this world and how we see it. The pedagogical is always moral and political; by enacting a way of seeing and being, it challenges, contests, or endorses the official, hegemonic ways of seeing and representing the other. (p. 422)

What can reflective approaches contribute to research?

Many of my colleagues engage in various forms of reflective research—self-study, action research, practitioner research, reflective practitioner, auto-biography and auto-ethnography—to name a few. Each of these approaches has the researcher as a key participant. The variation is whether the focus is on the researcher and/or their story as the object of study, as in *auto-biography* or *auto-ethnography*; the researcher's practice, as in *action or practitioner research*; or a combination of the two, and proponents of *self-study* make this claim.

The idea of reflecting on one's practice as an educator is not new. John Dewey (1938) encouraged educators to actively engage in reflection on their teaching. The curriculum movements of the 1970s encouraged teachers to think more critically about their practice, and the 1980s saw an explosion of recommended strategies for doing this. My introduction to these ideas was as a teacher in the 1980s through action research (e.g., Kemmis and McTaggart, 1988). Later, as a teacher educator in the 1990s, I was introduced to Schōn's notions of the reflective practitioner (Schōn, 1983). It was also at this time I saw colleagues become interested in self-study through writers such as Loughran (1996) and Cole and Knowles (2000). Earlier in the book I introduced action research. In this brief section I will focus on two other approaches: self-study and auto-ethnography.

Self-study

> Self-study is conducted by educators who use themselves and records of their practice, such as journals or correspondence, as data sources for examining changes in practice alongside changes in the wider context of education. Self-study researchers often crystalise and present their findings as artistic representations.

In an article in *Educational Researcher*, Bullough and Pinnegar (2001) elaborate on what self-study is:

Self-study researchers stand at the intersection of biography and history. The questions self-study researchers ask arise from concern about and interest in the interaction of the self-as-teacher-educator, in context, over time, with others whose interests represent a shared commitment to the development and nurturance of the young and the impact of that interaction on self and other. (p.15)

The focus of the Bullough and Pinnegar article is on a set of guidelines for autobiographical self-study. I have listed these guidelines here because they provide a useful set of discussion points for other types of reflective or personal research. They suggest that autobiographical self-studies:
- should ring true and enable connection
- should promote insight and interpretation
- must engage with history
- are about the problems and issues that make one an educator
- include authentic voice
- have an obligation to improve the learning situation, not only for the self but for the other
- portray character development and include dramatic action
- attend carefully to context or person
- offer fresh perspectives on established truths (pp. 16–19).

My interest in such forms of study is in how they might illuminate bigger ideas—educational history, reform movements, learning environments or curriculum change—and in response to the Bullough and Pinnegar article Feldman (2003) had this to say:

> If the ultimate goal of self-study is to produce literary representations of research, then Bullough and Pinnegar's guidelines are sufficient ... But few of us want to end there. Instead we want our scholarly work to have direct effects on teachers, students and schools. Therefore it is political work and has implications for policymakers.

Feldman concludes by reminding self-study researchers to (a) provide clear and detailed descriptions of data collection and analysis; (b) provide clear and detailed descriptions of how the representation of the data was constructed; (c) extend triangulation beyond multiple data sources to include multiple representations; and (d) provide evidence of the ways in which their study made changes to educational practice.

> *In a recent book on teacher inquiry in New Zealand, Delia outlines how she used a range of analytical tools to explore her own and others' practice: teacher interviews, classroom observations, reflective learning conversations, a values and beliefs questionnaire, learning conversation analysis reviews, subjective/objective reviews, and the use of video for stimulated recall.*[20]

Auto-ethnography

Auto-ethnography is an approach I have come across more recently. Ellis, Adams and Bochner (2010, n.p.) describe it this way:

> Autoethnography is an approach to research and writing that seeks to describe and systematically analyze personal experience in order to understand cultural experience. This approach challenges canonical ways of doing research and representing others and treats research as a political, socially-just and socially-conscious act. A researcher uses tenets of autobiography and ethnography to do and write autoethnography. Thus, as a method, autoethnography is both process and product.

Auto-ethnography contains three key elements: a description or study (graphy) of the self (auto) in a lived cultural experience (ethno). It draws on the approaches used in autobiography and ethnography. Usually the experiences are recorded or recreated in retrospect to illustrate an important event or concept, but more recently researchers keep records (diaries, photographs, media clips), which they can assemble and analyse at a later date.

Common characteristics of auto-ethnographies are critical incidents or epiphanies—events or times when a significant moment in the researcher's life causes them to consider things differently, from a change in viewpoint to a life-changing decision. What makes these auto-ethnographies of interest to others is that they are more than an engaging story with rich emotional content; they are also placed within the social and cultural context of the time. Their purpose is more than personal therapy; the aim is to illuminate the relationship between the personal lived experience, with its accompanying emotional responses, and wider patterns of social life. These stories should resonate with 'insiders' and provide valuable insight to 'outsiders'. They should make historical and contemporary life come alive.

As a form of research they need to be carefully crafted, from the gathering, selection and analysis of data to the structure of the presentation or performance. Ellis, Adams and Bochner (2010, n.p.) elaborate:

> When researchers write autoethnographies, they seek to produce aesthetic and evocative thick descriptions of personal and interpersonal experience. They accomplish this by first discerning patterns of cultural experience evidenced by field notes, interviews, and/or artifacts, and then describing these patterns using facets of storytelling (e.g., character and plot development), showing and telling, and alterations of authorial voice. Thus, the autoethnographer not only tries to make personal experience meaningful and cultural experience engaging, but also,

by producing accessible texts, she or he may be able to reach wider and more diverse mass audiences that traditional research usually disregards, a move that can make personal and social change possible for more people.

I found myself personally involved in the 2010/11 Canterbury earthquakes and the 2010 Pike River Mine disaster. Even while dealing with immediate personal grief, I knew that one day I would have a story to share. I kept notes, made observations, took photographs, informally interviewed family and friends, collected newspaper cuttings and artefacts, and downloaded media reports. My first analysis and shared narrative was built around a Reuters photograph of my sister and me on hearing the news of the second Pike explosion. This became the basis of a public lecture and a media interview.[21]

What can be gained from collaborative research?

A response I received to the first edition of *Doing Educational Research* was that I gave the impression that research is an individual activity, whereas much educational research is conducted collaboratively. That is a valid comment and this edition gives me the opportunity to correct that impression.

Bukvova (2010) conducted a literature review of collaborative research. She opened her paper with the remark, "Collaborative research appears to be growing in popularity" (p. 1). However, finding a common definition of collaborative research proved elusive, as she explains:

> A research collaboration can take place between individuals from the same institutions as well as among individuals from different institutions, even from a different country. (p. 2)

> Collaboration brings together researchers and other collaborators who bring different disciplines, skills, strengths, perspectives and resources to investigating a topic of common interest.

Bukvova (2010) compiled a list of potential benefits of collaborative research:
- access to expertise
- access to resources
- access to funding
- exchange of ideas
- pooling of expertise
- keeping one's own activities focused
- learning new skills
- higher productivity

- higher-quality results
- prestige
- political factors
- personal factors
- fun and pleasure.

Research in educational settings is often collaborative and inter-institutional because it involves academics and practitioners working together. Each brings different skills and insights, understanding of the topic or setting, and a variety of perspectives to the research focus and process. Often these aspects are complementary and lead to reciprocal learning as well as stronger findings.

As part of the Centres of Innovation project, Kay and Helen, teachers at Rangiora's Bush Street Kidsfirst Kindergarten, were supported by university researchers Ali and Elaine to research their own practice. They investigated storytelling, especially the role of the central character. They state: "The research processes we have undertaken are grounded, not in individual interpretations of what is going on, but in our collective learning as our ideas emerge in the hurly burly of our daily lives." [22]

Bukvova's literature review also reminds us that collaboration can change the way the research is conducted: "The decision to perform research with partners instead of individually influences the research process as well as its outcomes" (p. 1). She highlights some issues to be aware of:

- **responsibility**—how does the team ensure that lines of responsibility and researcher roles are clear and understood by all?
- **accountability**—how does the team manage working across institutions and/or organisational systems and deal with the increased number of accountabilities and reporting lines that might be involved?
- **costs of co-ordination**—is the collaboration still worthwhile despite the extra costs that might be incurred, especially if working internationally?
- **attribution**—how does the team ensure that everyone who participates gets the credit that is due for their efforts and/or contribution?

I am part of a collaboration with researchers from other countries. Our interest is in advocating for children as co-researchers in research that is about them. We have called our project the Citizen Child Collaboration and, as well as conducting research in our own countries, we present and publish our work jointly. When we initially set up the collaboration we discussed our possible contributions, how we might work together, how to share the responsibility, where to seek funding, how to order the authors' names and other collegial matters—and, yes, we would say that our collaboration strengthens our research findings despite the costs and complexity of working across countries.[23]

Where might research go in the future?

Gazing into a crystal ball is always a risky activity. Some things have changed radically. History notes 1989 as the year of events such as the fall of the Berlin Wall, the Exxon Valdez oil spill, the Hillsborough Stadium collapse and the Tiananmen Square protest. It was also the year Tim Berners-Lee started working on the World Wide Web. Since then technology has got smaller and faster but with hugely increased capacity. It has both expanded and contracted our world.

Yet some things have not changed so much. In a recent report on the future of schooling (Bolstad et al., 2012, p. 31), one respondent felt that not much had changed in her school:

> Our department curriculum is out of the dark ages, with fact-based learning, and ridiculous topic tests for juniors. The junior curriculum does not support lifelong learning apart from learning facts. The content is prescribed. Students are often not engaged. They have little opportunity to gain skills.

I will take a punt and suggest that, in the future, research in and into education will be influenced by three factors:
- changes in technology
- developments in methodology
- education in a globalised world.

Changes in technology

In their recent report, Johnson, Levine, Smith and Stone (2010) identify the following trends as key drivers of technology in education for the period 2010 to 2015.
- The abundance of resources and relationships made easily accessible via the Internet will increasingly challenge us to revisit our roles as educators.
- People will expect to be able to work, learn and study whenever and wherever they want to.
- The technologies we use will become increasingly cloud-based, and our notions of IT support will become decentralised.
- The work of students will increasingly be seen as collaborative by nature, and there will be more collaboration between departments and institutions.

- There will be improvements in mobile computing and open content.
- There will be widespread adoption of electronic books and augmented reality.

Wheeler (2010) suggests we are moving from Web 1.0 (where the web connects information), to social software connecting people (Web 2.0), to the semantic web connecting knowledge with intelligence (Web 3.0) and on to the meta-web. The technologies that will enable this include:
- distributed cloud computing
- extended smart mobile technology
- collaborative, intelligent filtering
- 3D visualisation and interaction.

These changes in technology will change how research is done, who conducts it and what is researched. They will raise ethical questions about access in a digital world, ownership of data and information, actual and virtual representations of reality, and the safety of the researcher and the researched. They will raise methodological questions about what data are, how they are collected and stored, when and if a research project begins and ends, how to deal with multiple versions and contributors, and how to make sense of findings that are always fluid, continually updated and constantly revised.

Developments in methodology

Many developments in methodology will be related to changes in technology, but others will be driven by our drive for results that are accurate, informative, engaging, relevant and useful. Quantitative methodologies will be able to expand the scope of our understanding of a research problem and at the same time produce fine-grained statistical analyses that highlight relationships and trends that may have formerly gone unnoticed. This will allow a research consumer or policy developer to be able explore the big picture, make cross-country and institutional comparisons, or drill down to specific results.

This will excite some, but it also throws up questions of the ability of the average person to understand the purposes and procedures behind the findings and to recognise their contextual and statistical limitations. It also links to ethical questions of ownership and the use (or misuse) of data.

Qualitative methodologies will also develop in ways that expand our understanding of a topic or issue, and our ability to view it through multiple lenses and representations. Technology will enable mixed media and virtual representations to extend our current repertoire of presentation formats. Data and conclusions will be constantly updated, juxtaposed, created and recreated. There will be more emphasis on an affective dimension—an emotional response or cognitive resonance that connects the reader/viewer/performer with the phenomenon of interest. While all this goes on, qualitative researchers will continue to search for ways that further validate and give credibility to their methods and findings.

And will mixed method research become the third paradigm or even the methodology of choice? Mixed method research has contributed to philosophical, theoretical, methodological and ethical debates within the research community. It will continue to do so and in this way will contribute to a clearer articulation and justification of the choices researchers make. It will develop alongside technological and methodological advancements and challenge our notions of data collection, creation and transformation. All methodologies will be subject to scrutiny of their relevance and usefulness: in what ways do they contribute to new knowledge, re-evaluate old knowledge, or offer solutions and insights into the things that matter in our fast-moving and ever-changing world?

Education in a globalised world

As education changes in response to *globalisation* (by looking outwards to how it is done elsewhere) and *'glocalisation'* (by looking inwards to protect local characteristics and uniqueness), so the interests of educational researchers will change. Researchers will continue to seek solutions to ongoing educational problems and disparities while highlighting creativity and innovation. Bolstad et al. (2012) outline the contemporary issues as they see them:

> Alongside economic, social, political and technological changes, many serious challenges characterise the 21st century world. Some authors describe these as 'wicked problems'. They are 'highly complex, uncertain, and value-laden', spanning multiple domains: social, economic, political, environmental, legal and moral. It is argued that learners—*and* teachers, school leaders and families/communities—need support to actively develop the capabilities they need to productively engage in 21st century wicked problem solving. (p. 2)

Bolstad et al. suggest six emerging themes or principles that are linked with contemporary views of learning for the 21st century. They anticipate that these themes will change the face of teaching and learning and, as such, provide important areas of research:
- personalising learning
- new views of equity, diversity and inclusivity
- a curriculum that uses knowledge to develop learning capacity

- 'changing the script'—rethinking learners' and teachers' roles
- a culture of continuous learning for teachers and educational leaders
- new kinds of partnerships and relationships—schools no longer siloed from the community (pp. 9–10).

Facer (2009) suggests that rather than try to develop a single blueprint for dealing with change, we should instead develop a resilient education system based on diversity to deal with the different challenges of an uncertain future, but, he cautions:

> Such diversity will emerge only if educators, researchers and communities are empowered to develop localised or novel responses to socio-technical change – including developing new approaches to curriculum, to assessment, to workforce and institutions. (p. 243)

Conclusion

In summary, I believe that the fundamentals of educational research will not change. The wish to find credible answers to the problems that beset education, to go in depth and get a sense of what the experience is like for those in a range of educational settings, or to learn from good practice exemplars will still be important. What will change will be the more sophisticated and creative approaches we undertake—quantitatively, qualitatively and through mixed methods.

These methods will be supported by new technologies and new understanding of what constitutes data, evidence and knowledge. Research will be an important part of educators' toolkits, from examining their own practice and evaluating what works in their setting, to working collaboratively across classes, institutions and countries. Educational research will become more, not less, significant, but it is important that those who conduct it, disseminate it, use it and respond to it do so knowledgeably, accurately, ethically and responsibly.

Chapter summary

- Technology has changed what constitute research data, how they are gathered, analysed and disseminated, and has itself become a topic of research.
- Recent developments in both quantitative and qualitative research aim to push the boundaries of possibilities and usefulness for each approach and to address critiques of their limitations.
- Proponents of mixed methods research claim it is a third paradigm that draws from the strengths of quantitative and qualitative research and makes better use of available data to produce stronger, more credible findings.

- Although evaluation is a newer discipline, it has developed a distinct set of purposes and procedures that make it different from research, especially with regard to judgement formation.
- Cultural approaches have become more mainstream to the point where research and ethical guidelines expect cultural competence and sensitivity to be addressed as a matter of course.
- Textual, visual and arts-based approaches challenge traditional notions of data gathering, processing and presentation through artistic, narrative and performance approaches.
- Reflective approaches are particularly common in applied fields such as education, where theory, research and practice interact and have an impact on each other in ways that contribute to problem solving and enhance practice.
- Collaborative research offers a way to make the best use of expertise and resources to produce findings that might have wider applicability.
- Over time, the fundamentals of research have remained constant but the search for new, innovative and rigorous approaches that make the best use of data and findings will continue as long as there are problems to be solved, issues to be investigated and solutions to be evaluated.

Notes

1. Tatebe, J. (2012, December). *Waiting for time in the limelight: Discussing disadvantage and poverty in initial teacher education programmes.* Paper presented at the Australian Association for Research in Education conference, Sydney, Australia.
2. Mutch, C. (2012, November). *Christchurch schools tell their stories.* A talk presented to the 'Learning from Disasters' seminar hosted by Aotearoa New Zealand Evaluation Association and the Citizen Child Collaboration, Christchurch.
3. Dabner, N. (2012). 'Breaking ground' in the use of social media: A case study of a university earthquake response to inform educational design with Facebook. *Internet and Higher Education, 15,* 69–78. doi:10.1016/j.iheduc.2011.06.001
4. Mutch, C. (forthcoming). 'Sailing through a river of emotions': Capturing children's earthquake stories. *Disaster Prevention and Management.*
5. Hattie, J. (2009). *Visible learning: A synthesis of over 800 meta-analyses relating to achievement.* London, UK: Routledge.

6. Robinson, V., Hohepa, M. & Lloyd, C. (2009). *School leadership and student outcomes: Identifying what works and why: Best evidence synthesis.* Wellington: Ministry of Education.
7. Nelson, B., Ketelhut, D. J., Clarke, J., Bowman, C., and Dede, C. (2005). Design-based research strategies for developing a scientific inquiry curriculum in a multi-user virtual environment. *Educational Technology, 45*(1), 21–27.
8. Day, C., Sammons, P., & Gu, Q. (2008). Combining qualitative and quantitative methodologies in research on teachers' lives, work, and effectiveness: From integration to synergy. *Educational Researcher, 37*(6), 330–342.
9. Berridge, S. (n.d.). *Arts-based research and the creative PhD.* [A digital representation of her thesis is available as part of the Australian Digital Thesis program: http://erl.canberra.edu.au/public/adt-AUC20070510.151236/index.html]
10. Sameshima, P. (2007). *Seeing red/a pedagogy of parallax: An epistolary Bildingsroman on artful scholarly enquiry.* Youngstown, OH: Cambria Press.
11. Onwuegbuzie, T., Bustamante, R., & Nelson, J. (2010). Mixed research as a tool for developing quantitative instruments. *Journal of Mixed Methods Research, 4*(1), 56–78. doi: 10.1177/1558689809355805
12. Mutch, C. & Collins, S.. (2012). Partners in learning: Schools' engagement with parents, families and communities in New Zealand. *School Community Journal, 22*(1), 167–187.
13. Heaton, S. (2011). The co-opting of 'hauora' into curricula. *Curriculum Matters, 7,* 99–117.
14. Devine, N., Pau'uvale Teisina, J., & Pau'uvale, L. (2012). *Tauhi vā,* Spinoza, and Deleuze in education. *Pacific-Asian Education, 24*(2), 57–68.
15. Mutch, C. (2006). The art and craft of rigorous analysis and (re)presentation. *Qualitative Research Journal, 6*(1), 51–68.
16. Tesar, M. (2012). Socialist memoirs: The production of political childhood subjectivities. *Globalisation, Societies and Education* [special issue on socialism], *11*(1).
17. Fitzpatrick, E. (Forthcoming). What deathless power: A conversation with Steinbeck to problematise the role of the ethnographic researcher in education. *New Zealand Journal of Research in Performing Arts and Education: Nga Mahi a Rehia.*
18. Locke, K. (December, 2012). *The bodily space of New Zealand education.* Paper presented at the Australian Association for Research in Education conference, Sydney, Australia.

19. Standing, M. (2008). *An investigation of the benefits of creating art in a prison setting: A study in calling forth the hero within*. Unpublished master's dissertation. Whitecliffe College of Arts and Design, Auckland.
20. Baskerville, D. (2011). Organisation and design of analytical tools to identify effective teacher educator practice. In J. Higgins, R. Parsons, & L. Bonne, *Processes of Inquiry:*
21. *Inservice teacher educators research their practice* (pp. 11–28). Rotterdam, The Netherlands: Sense Publishers.
22. Mutch, C. (2012, August). *Media responses—from information to interaction*. Public lecture presented as part of the University of Auckland's Winter Lecture series, Hazards, Disasters, Risks and Responses: Auckland, are you ready?, Maidment Theatre, Auckland. Mediawatch interview available from: http://www.radionz.co.nz/audio/remote-player?id=2530096
23. Henson, K., Smith, H. & Mayo, E. (2009). *Central character story: Weaving families and their stories into children's learning in early childhood education*. Rangiora: Kidsfirst Kindergartens Bush Street.
24. Gibbs, L., Mutch, C., O'Connor, P., & MacDougall, C. (2013). Research with, by, for, and about children: Lessons from disaster contexts. *Global Studies of Childhood*, 3(2).

References

Alton-Lee, A. (2003). *Quality teaching for diverse students in schooling: Best evidence synthesis*. Wellington: Ministry of Education.

Anderson, T., & Shattuck, J. (2012). Design-based research: A decade of progress in education research? *Educational Researcher*, 41(1), 16–25. doi: 10.3102/0013189X11428813

Aotearoa New Zealand Evaluation Association. (2008). *Evaluation Competencies Project*. Retrieved from http://www.anzea.org.nz/index.php?option=com_content&view=article&id=91&Itemid=99

Amituanai-Toloa, M. (2009). What is a Pasifika research methodology?: The 'tupua' in the winds of change. *Pacific-Asian Education*, 21(2), 45–54.

Australian Institute of Aboriginal and Torres Strait Islander Studies. (2011). *Guidelines for Ethical Research in Australian Indigenous Studies* (2nd ed.). Retrieved from http://www.aiatsis.gov.au/research/docs/ethics.pdf

Bolstad, R., & Gilbert, J., with McDowall, S., Bull, A., Boyd, S., & Hipkins, R. (2012). *Supporting future-oriented learning and teaching: A New Zealand perspective*. Wellington: Ministry of Education.

Bukvova, H. (2010). Studying research collaboration: A literature review. *Sprouts: Working Papers on Information Systems,* 10(3). Retrieved from http://sprouts.aisnet.org/10-3

Bullough, V., & Pinnegar, S. (2001). Guidelines for quality in autobiographical forms of self-study research. *Educational Researcher,* 30(3), 13–21.

Cohen, L., Manion, L., & Morrison, K. (2011). *Research methods in education* (7th ed.). London, UK: Routledge.

Cole, A. L., & Knowles, J. G. (2000). *Researching teaching: Exploring teacher development through reflective inquiry.* Boston, MA: Allyn and Bacon.

Dabner N. (2012). 'Breaking ground' in the use of social media: A case study of a university earthquake response to inform educational design with Facebook. *Internet and Higher Education,* 15, 69–78. doi:10.1016/j.iheduc.2011.06.001

Denzin, N. (2006). Analytic auto-ethnography or déjà vu all over again. *Journal of Contemporary Ethnography,* 35(4), 419–428.

Dewey, J. (1938). *Experience and education.* New York, NY: Kappa Delta Pi.

Ellis, C., Adams, T., & Bochner, A. (2010). Auotoethnography: An overview. *Forum Qualitative Sozialforschung / Forum: Qualitative Social Research,* 12(1), Article 10. Retrieved from http://www.qualitativeresearch.net/index.php/fqs/article/view/1589/3095

Facer, K. (2009). *Educational, social and technological futures: a report from the Beyond Current Horizons Programme. For UK Department for Children, Schools and Families.* Bristol: Futurelab. Retrieved from: http://www.beyondcurrenthorizons.org.uk

Feldman, A. (2003). Validity and quality in self-study. *Educational Researcher* 32(April), 26–28. doi:10.3102/0013189X032003026.

Foucault, M. (1981). The order of discourse. In R. Young (Ed.), *Untying the text* (pp. 51–78). London, UK: Routledge and Keegan Paul.

Gee, J. (1995). *Social linguistics and literacy: Ideologies of discourses.* London, UK: Falmer.

Hattie, J. (2009). *Visible learning: A synthesis of over 800 meta-analyses relating to achievement.* London, UK: Routledge.

Johnson, B., Onwuegbuzie, A., & and Turner, L. (2007). Toward a definition of mixed methods research. *Journal of Mixed Methods Research,* 1(2), 112–133. doi: 10.1177/1558689806298224.

Johnson, L., Levine, A., Smith, R., & Stone, S. (2010). *The Horizon report.* Austin, TX: The New Media Consortium.

Kemmis, S., & McTaggart, R. (1988). *The action research planner* (3rd ed.). Geelong, VIC: Deakin University Press.

Knowles, J. G., & Promislow, S. (2008). Using an arts methodology to create a thesis or dissertation. In J. G. Knowles & A. L. Cole (Eds.), *Handbook of the arts in qualitative research: Perspectives, methodologies, examples and issues* (pp. 511–525). Thousand Oaks, CA: Sage.

Kroll, J. (2004). The exegesis and the gentler reader/writer. *TEXT, 3* (special issue). Retrieved http://www.textjournal.com.au/speciss/issue3/kroll.htm

Loughran, J. (1996). *Developing reflective practice: Learning about teaching and learning through modelling.* London, UK: Falmer.

McNiff, S. (2008). Arts-based research. In G. L. Knowles & A. L. Cole (Eds.), *Handbook of the arts in qualitative research: Perspectives, methodologies, examples, and issues* (pp. 29–40). Thousand Oaks, CA: Sage.

Merriam, S. (2009). *Qualitative research: A guide to design and implementation* (2nd ed.). San Francisco, CA: Jossey Bass.

Milech, B., & Schilo, A. (2004). 'Exit Jesus': Relating the exegesis and creative/production components of a research thesis. *TEXT, 3* (special issue). Retrieved from http://www.textjournal.com.au/speciss/issue3/milechschilo.htm

Mutch, C. (2007). *A starter pack for ERO professional learning: Self review.* Unpublished internal document, Educational Review Office, Wellington.

Mutch, C. (2009). Mixed method research: Methodological eclecticism or muddled thinking? *Journal of Educational Leadership, Policy and Practice, 24*(2) 18–30.

Mutch, C. (2011, November). *Research and evaluation: One and the same or not?* Paper presented to the New Zealand Association for Research in Education, Tauranga.

New Zealand Association for Research in Education. (2010). *Ethical guidelines.* Retrieved from http://www.nzare.org.nz/research-ethics.html

Polkinghorne, D. (2007). Validity issues in narrative research. *Qualitative Inquiry, 13*(2), 1–16.

Prosser, J., & Loxley, A. (2008). *Introducing visual methods.* National Centre for Research Methods & Economic and Social Research Council. Retrieved from http://eprints.ncrm.ac.uk/420

Putaiora Working Group. (2010). *TeAra Tika guidelines for Māori research ethics: A framework for researchers and ethics committee members.* Wellington: Health Research Council.

Ragin, C., & Amoroso, L. (2011). *Constructing social research: The unity and diversity of method* (2nd ed.). Thousand Oaks, CA: Sage.

Rosenthal, R., & DiMatteo, M. R. (2001). Meta-analysis: Recent developments in quantitative methods for literature reviews. *Annual Review of Psychology, 52,* 59–82.

Schōn, D. (1983). *The reflective practitioner: How professionals think in action.* London: Temple Smith.

Tashakkori, A., & Teddlie, C. (2003). *Handbook of mixed methods in social and behavioral research.* Thousand Oaks, CA: Sage.

Tillman, L. C. (2002). Culturally-sensitive research approaches: An African-American perspective. *Educational Researcher, 31*(9), 3–12.

Wengraf, T. (2001). *Qualitative research interviewing.* London, UK: Sage.

Wheeler, S. (2010). *Web 3.0: The way forward?* Retrieved from http://steve-wheeler.blogspot.com/2010/07/web-30-way-forward.html

Yanchar, S., & Williams, D. (2006). Reconsidering the compatibility thesis and eclecticism: Five proposed guidelines for method use. *Educational Researcher, 35*(9), 3–12.

Index

abstracts, research proposals 134
action research 108, 187–89
American Psychological Association (APA) style 96, 98, 185
analytic field notes 145
annotated bibliography 96
anonymity 78, 79, 81, 84
appendices, research proposals 134
applied research 23
archival data sources 52
artefact analysis 107
artefacts, as data sources 52
artistic presentation of qualitative data 168
arts-based approaches to research 223–24
attributes 43
audio-visual data sources 52
audit trail 209
auto-ethnography 226–28

bar (or column) graphs 159–60, 162
behaviourism 62–63, 65
bell curve 156
Best Evidence Synthesis Programme (BES) 206

bias 50
bibliographies 99
    annotated 96
biculturalism 66
book reviews 96
box plots ("box and whisker") graphs 161–62
brainstorming 120
Bronfenbrenner, Urie 60
budgets 136–37
    format 138
    key tasks and associated costs 137

case studies 65, 107, 108, 221
children and young people
    conducting research with 147–48
    ethical issues in approaching 83, 148
closed questions 114
coding data 154–55, 164
coercion 77, 78
collaborative research
    benefits 228–29
    working tools 198, 200, 202
collaborative student work 230

comparative research 211
compatibility thesis 213
conference presentations, preparing 180–84
confidentiality 70, 78, 81, 84
   see also privacy
constructionism 62–63, 65
content analysis 107, 122
   process 123
convenience sampling 52
correlation 157
correlational research 43
credibility 110
critical approach 65–66
critical pedagogy 65
critical theory 64, 65
cross-cultural settings 85, 86
cultural aspects of research 66–71, 85, 86, 121
   new developments in frameworks 217–20

data analysis
   qualitative data 163–66, 200
   quantitative data 152–57, 200
data gathering
   adequate engagement in 209
   content analysis 123
   difference from research 20–21
   ethics 76, 77
   online 199, 200, 201
   quasi-experiments 113
   and research design 47
   three Es 110–11
   tips for gathering 144
data management 145–46
   literature reviews 93–95
   and technology 198–201
data presentation
   qualitative data 166–69, 200
   quantitative data 157–63, 200
data quality 201
data sources 47, 49
   children and young people 148
   electronic 52, 198, 199, 201, 202–4
   human subjects 49–52
   non-human sources 52
Delphi technique 207
descriptive field notes 144–45

descriptive research 22
   qualitative 46
   quantitative 43, 46, 49–50
descriptive statistics 152
design-based research (DBR) 206–7
discourse analysis 66, 107, 166, 220, 221, 222
dissemination of research findings
   cross-cultural aspects 86
   ethical issues 77, 79, 86
   and technology 203–4
document analysis 107, 122, 164, 221
documents, as data sources 52
dot plots (scattergrams) 158–59
dramatic presentation of qualitative data 168

educational research
   common methodologies 106–9
   common methods, strategies and tools 110–25
   description and characteristics 23–24
   examples 29–30
   relationship to everyday work 28–30
electronic information sources 92–93
Endnote 93, 98
enquiring 111
equipment 142–43
ethical approval, preparing for 80
   ethical clearance form 80
   supporting materials 80–81
ethics 37–38
   and changes in technology 231
   importance in research 76–77
   key concepts 77–79
   mixed methods research 213
   new developments in frameworks 217–20
   online research 201
   research in own workplace 84–85
   research in Pacific context 70
   research with children and young people 83, 148
ethnographies 65, 107, 108
ethnography 224–25
   auto-ethnography 226–28
evaluation
   differences from research 215–17

programme evaluation 108
  questions to guide external and internal evaluations 216
examining 111
Excel 146, 154, 156, 204
exchange theory 65
experiencing 110
experimental research 43, 104
experiments 65, 107
explanatory research 22
exploratory research 22

feminism 60, 64–65
field notes 144–45
  examples 145
focus group interviews 121, 221
formal theories 60
functionalism 59, 62, 65

generalisable research 22
globalisation 232–33
glocalisation 232
graphs 158–63

hermeneutics 65
histograms 160, 161
historical research 108, 221
horizontal bar charts 160
humans
  as information sources for literature reviews 91
  as research data sources 49–52
hypothesis 45, 112

implementing research 142, 215
  factors to consider 144
incompatibility thesis 212
indigenous peoples 219–20
inferential statistics 152
informed consent 37, 78
insider research 70–71, 84–85
Internet
  data quality 201
  as a data source 52, 198, 199, 200, 202–4
  and dissemination of research findings 203
  and roles of educators 230
  Web 2.0 technologies 202

interpretation of research findings 169–70
interpretivist approach 65, 142
interval measurements 153
interventions 107, 111, 112
interview guide 120
interview schedule 120
interviews 107, 111, 119
  children 147
  as device for measuring variables 117
  focus group 121
  and Māori concepts 121
  online 199
  process for preparing questions 119–20
  qualitative research 120–21
  quantitative research 120
  semi-structured 107, 119, 121
  structured 119
  telephone 107, 108
  unstructured 119
Iterative Best Evidence Synthesis Programme (BES) 206

journal articles, guidelines for evaluating 28
journal keeping 146–47

kaupapa Māori research 68, 217, 218, 220
knowledge of topic, field and discipline 35–36
keeping up to date 36

libraries 91–92, 204
Likert scales 115
line graphs 161
literature reviews *see also* referencing conventions
  eight-step approach to writing 97
  evaluating relevance of material 94–95
  how to decide what material to read 91
  reasons for conducting 90
  recording and filing systems 93–95
  sources of information 90–93, 198, 199
  writing up 95–96, 97

Māori context, research in 67–69, 121, 204, 217–20
Marxism 59, 64
mean 156

measures of central tendency 155, 156, 157
measures of dispersion 155, 156
measures of relationship 157
measures of relative position 155, 156
median 156
member checking 110
meta-analysis of research findings 205
methodologies
   common methodologies in educational research 106–9
   definition 104
   future developments 231–32
   links to method and theory 104, 105
   Māori research 68, 69, 121, 204
   mixed methodology 125–26
   Pacific research 70, 204
methods
   in educational research 107, 110–25
   links to methodology and theory 104, 105
mixed methodology 125–26
mixed methods (quantitative and qualitative) research 207–8, 211–14, 232
   reasons for using 213
mode 156
morals 76
   see also ethics
motivation for research 187–89
multiculturalism 66
MUVE (multi-user virtual environment) 207

narrative
   approaches to research 220–22
   presentation of qualitative data 168–69
nominal measurements 153
non-participant observation 107, 118, 221
non-probability sampling 50–52
NVivo 146, 164, 200

objectivism 62
objectivity 50
observations 107, 108, 117
   qualitative research 117, 118–19
   quantitative research 117–18
open questions 114
oral histories 107
ordinal measurements 153

Pacific context, research in 69–70, 204, 220
"paradigm wars" 25, 212
participant observation 107, 118
participants in research
   approaching: ethical aspects 81–84
   approaching: practical aspects 81
   children and young people 83
   ethical issues 78, 79, 81
   informed consent 37, 78
   Māori 67–69
   online access and communication 199
   Pacific 69–70
   safety 78
   voluntary participation 78, 81
participatory action research 66
peer review 136, 181, 182, 205, 209
percentile ranks 156, 157
permissions required in research 78
phenomenology 65
pie graphs 162–63
plagiarism 95
poetic presentation of qualitative data 168
policy research 41–42, 108, 221
positivist approach 62, 64, 65, 142
post-colonial theory 65
post-structuralism 222
power 76, 78
predictive research 22
privacy 78, 201
   see also confidentiality
probability sampling 50
process 37
programme evaluation 108
publishing 184–85, 193
   qualities of publishable papers 186
pure research 23
purposive samples 50

qualitative research 25, 62, 204, 224–25
   data analysis 163–66, 200
   data presentation 166–69, 200
   definitions 20, 24
   descriptive 46
   differences from quantitative research 26
   future developments 231–32
   interviews 120–21
   non-traditional presentation of findings 210–11

observations 117, 118–19
quantisising qualitative data 207–8, 211–14
recent developments 208–11
report writing 179, 210–11
research design 47, 49, 105, 106, 109–10, 112
research questions 45–46, 51
researcher's personal stance 64
software packages 146
strategies for promoting validity and reliability 209–10
quantitative research 25
see also quasi-experiments; questionnaires; surveys
data analysis 152–57, 200
data presentation 157–63, 200
definition 24
descriptive 43, 46, 49–50
differences from qualitative research 26
future developments 231
interviews 120
observations 117–18
positivist tradition 62
qualitising quantitative data 207–8, 211–14
recent developments 204–8
report writing 179
research design 47, 48, 105, 106, 109, 112–13
research questions 42–45, 51
researcher's personal stance 64
software packages 146
quasi-experiments 107, 111–12
key stages of design 112–13
queer theory 65
questionnaires 107, 108, 111, 114–16
advice for setting out successful questionnaires 116–17
categories 115, 153
closed questions 114
grid or matrix 115
list of questions 115, 153
open questions 114
qualitative questions 116
quantitative questions 114–115
quantity questions 115, 153
ranking 115, 154
scales 115, 153–54

quota sampling 51
quotations, acknowledging in literature reviews 98–99

random sampling 50
range 156
ranking questions 115, 154
ratios 153
raw data grid 154–55
reference lists 99
referencing conventions 96
  acknowledging quotations 98–99
  American Psychological Association (APA) system 96, 98
  clarity 99
  in-text referencing 98, 99
reflective approaches to research 146, 214, 225–28
  field notes 145
reflexivity 146, 209
reliability 109, 209–10
report writing 176
  getting started 176
  qualitative reports 179, 210–11
  quantitative reports 179
  report format 27, 178
  style guidelines 179, 185
  tailoring to reach different audiences 180
  task of writing 176–77
reports of research findings
  content analysis 123
  critical approach to reading 26–28
  guidelines for evaluating 28
  tailoring to reach different audiences 180
  thematic analysis 124
research
  see also descriptive research; educational research; mixed methods (quantitative and qualitative) research; qualitative research; quantitative research
  action 108, 187–89
  comparative 211
  definitions and summary 20
  design-based 206–7
  difference from data gathering 20–21
  difference from evaluation 214–17

future directions 230–33
history 21–22
main approaches 24–26
opportunities resulting from 192–93
preparation and implementation 142, 143, 144, 148
reasons for conducting 22–23
relationship to everyday work 28–30
research design 47
  cross-cultural aspects 86
  ethical issues 79
  qualitative research 47, 49, 109–10, 112
  quantitative research 47, 48, 109, 112–13
  and research questions 104–6
research matrix 133
research proposals
  see also budgets
  approval mechanisms 132
  experienced researchers 136
  format 133–35
  novice researchers 135–36
  purpose 132–33
  timing and process 134–35
research questions 42, 51
  link to research design 104–6
  qualitative research 45–46, 51, 105, 106
  quantitative research 42–45, 51, 105, 106
research syntheses 206
research topic
  choosing 39–42
  knowledge of 35–36, 41
researchers 34
  bias and objectivity 50
  collaborative work 198, 200, 202, 228–29
  decisions 38–39
  defining personal theoretical stance 64–66
  enhancing knowledge and keeping up to date 36
  experienced 136
  insider research 70–71, 84–85
  knowledge of craft of research 36–37
  knowledge of topic, field and discipline 35–36, 41
  "location of self" 64
  mixed methodologists 212
  novice 135–36
  "personal biography" 64, 66
  personal experience of a practitioner-researcher 189–92
  qualitatively oriented 212
  quantitatively oriented 212
  research in own workplace 84–85
  "researcher-as-instrument" 108
  safety 78
  working with people from different cultures 66–71, 85
risk management 38

sampling 113
  see also non-probability sampling; probability sampling
  variation and diversity 210
scales 115, 153–54
scattergrams (dot plots) 158–59
self-study 225–26
semiotic analysis 165–66, 220
single-subject (single-case) design 107, 111, 112
snowball sampling 52
social constructionism 65
social media 202, 231
social research, definition 20
social theory, key aspects 58
spreadsheets 146, 154, 156, 200, 204
SPSS (Statistical Package for the Social Sciences) 146, 154, 156, 204
standard deviation 156, 157
standard scores 156, 157
stanines 156, 157
statistics
  data sources 52, 111
  descriptive 152
  inferential 152
Statview 144, 146, 204
strategies
  description 108
  in educational research 107, 110–25
stratified random sample 50
subjectivism 62
substantive theories 60–61
surveys 65, 107, 114
  online 199, 200, 204
symbolic interactionism 60, 65
systems theory 65

T scores 156, 157
tables 157–58

Te Ara Tika Guidelines for Māori Research Ethics 217–18
technology
  changes 230–31
  as a data source 202–4
  keeping up to date 201
  as a research tool 198–201
telephone interviews 107, 108
textual and narrative approaches to research 220–22
thematic analysis 122, 164–65
  process 124–25, 164
theoretical samples 51
theory
  defining personal theoretical stance 64–66
  description 58
  different types 58–59
  links to methodology and method 104, 105
  macro-level theories 59–60, 63, 105
  micro-level theories 61, 63, 105, 171
  mid-range theories 60–61, 62–63, 105
  relationship to research 63
  social, key aspects 58
  tentative theorising 171
  variation in explaining same phenomena 61–63
  working with people with different theoretical frameworks 66–71
tools
  description 108
  in educational research 110–25
topic of research *see* research topic
Treaty of Waitangi 66, 217, 218–19
triangulation 110, 209
trustworthiness of research 109

unit of analysis 42–43

validity 109, 209–10
variables 43, 117
variance 156
version control 201
visual analysis 107, 166
visual data sources 52, 223
voluntary participation in research 78
Vygotsky, Lev 60

Web 2.0 technologies 202, 231
Web 3.0 technologies 231
world view, working with people who have different views 66–71
writing, new practices 222

z scores 156, 157

www.ingramcontent.com/pod-product-compliance
Lightning Source LLC
Chambersburg PA
CBHW051148290426
44108CB00019B/2648